The Heroine's Text

The Heroine's Text

Readings in the French and English Novel, 1722–1782

NANCY K. MILLER

1980
COLUMBIA UNIVERSITY PRESS
New York

Library of Congress Cataloging in Publication Data

Miller, Nancy K   1941–
   The heroine's text.

   Bibliography: p.
   Includes index.
      1. French fiction—18th century—History and
criticism.   2. Heroines in literature.   3. English
fiction—18th century—History and criticism.
4. Feminism and literature.   I. Title.
PQ648.M56   809.3′352042   79-28473
ISBN 0-231-04910-2

Columbia University Press
New York   Guildford, Surrey

For My Parents

Contents

Preface

> I asked him if it were not hard that one deviation from chastity
> should so absolutely ruin a young woman.
> JOHNSON: 'Why, no, Sir; it is the great principle which she is
> taught. When she has given up that principle, she has given up
> every notion of female honour and virtue, which are all included
> in chastity.'
> —Boswell, *Life of Johnson*

In one way or another, the novel has always been associated with women. The eighteenth-century novel, it seems reasonable to say, indeed it has been said, would never have happened without a certain collective "obsessing" about an idea called "woman," and without a female reading public.[1] This book proposes to read the fictions of a feminine destiny, to plot the heroine's text in eight French and English novels of that period known as the Enlightenment. Although the dates—1722 to 1782—are only brackets, meant not to announce an evolutionary thesis, but to identify the chronological limits of this study, the readings are in fact arranged according to two thematic structures, which themselves correspond, roughly speaking, to two discernible historical moments in the eighteenth century. Part I, "The Euphoric Text," includes the earlier novels, *Moll Flanders* (1722), *La Vie de Marianne* (1731), and *Pamela* (1740), as well as the mid-century *Fanny Hill* (1748–49). Part II, "The Dysphoric Text," treats *Manon Lescaut* (1731), and *Clarissa* (1747–48), along with the later novels, *La Nouvelle Héloïse* (1761) and *Les Liaisons dangereuses* (1782). Despite this approximate symmetry, my project nevertheless remains in the margins of any diachronic argument; for while it is clear that changes in the form of the novel can be dated, it is less easy to demonstrate a parallel evolution in the representation of its heroines.

I chose these particular novels for two simple and arbitrary reasons.

They are all well-known eighteenth-century novels, many of them still read and readable; and more important, perhaps, except for *Les Liaisons dangereuses*, they all *name*, in and by their titles, the heroine's text as the truth of their fiction. By then conjoining a woman's name to a "history," "adventures," or the exemplary shape of a life— *Pamela: or Virtue Rewarded*—these titles predicate the primacy of female experience and thus *pose* as feminocentric writing. This common choice of focus, this solicitation of a readership *through* the feminine on the part of major novelists on both sides of the Channel, led me to bring together in a single weave French and English narratives; without, however, placing any special emphasis on local differences of national tradition as they might affect the relations of gender and genre; and without, for that matter, distinguishing the epistolary novel from the memoir, the major modes of the genre in this sixty-year span. These novels interest me primarily as a locus of cultural commonplaces about woman's identity and woman's place, and as an occasion to read the ideological subscript of *literary* femininity in the eighteenth century.

By the heroine's text, then, I mean in the first instance nothing more than the inscription of a female destiny, the fictionalization of what is taken to be the feminine at a specific cultural moment (at the moment, among other things, of the birth, or the rise, of the modern novel). Although the heroine's text is not contained within a single novel, what is taken to be the determining event in the private history of a female self, what is at stake in feminine experience, can be read schematically in the proverb: "Il n'y a que le premier pas qui coûte." Thus Rousseau's Julie, wiser after the fact of her erotic encounter, rewrites: "Ah! le premier pas, qui coûte le plus, était celui qu'il ne fallait pas faire." For if the first step is the hardest, she goes on to explain, it also leads easily and automatically to the others, and fatally to the abyss. The danger of the dangerous relation is dependent upon the logic of the faux pas: in the politics of seduction, once generally proves to be enough. Thus the rule of female experience is the drama of a single misstep: "in confirmation of the maxim," Cleland's Fanny intones, "that when women get out of compass, there are no lengths of licentiousness that they are not capable of running." The eighteenth-century feminocentric novel maximizes these maxims because the heroine's text is the text of an ideology that codes femininity in paradigms of sexual vulnerability.

But if the scenarios of illicit relations which are the context of this fragile fate depend on a social contract that reads "woman" as vulnerability, they all do not, of course, tell exactly the same story. There are at least two female-centered plots, which I have labeled the "euphoric" and the "dysphoric" text.[2] This distinction is primarily a heuristic device meant to serve as a frame of reference within which individual narratives can be delineated in their specificities. It is based on the assumption that endings, however conventional, overdetermine narrative logic, and in this sense might be thought of as a taxonomy of *telos*. Thus, the novels in the euphoric text end with the heroine's integration into society; all four novels under this rubric are structured by a trajectory of ascent. The heroine—orphaned except for Pamela—moves in her negotiation with the world of men and money from "nothing" to "all" in a feminine variant of *Bildung*. In the dysphoric text, the novels end instead with the heroine's death in the flower of her youth—except for Mme de Merteuil, the "negative" heroine who is banished to a living death—and the move is from "all" in this world to "nothing." (The positive heroine, of course, translates nothing back into all with the help of a Christian lexicon.) The heroine's text is plotted within this ideologically delimited space of an either/or closure, within the conventional rhetoric of the sociolect. What remains to be seen is the *play* between these poles; the idiolects of heroine-ism.[3]

Although the metacategories imply a reading by retroaction, in the essays themselves I trace the fictions in their linear continuity, and deliberately follow the sentences of the heroine's plot as it unfolds. This step-by-step reading derives both from my lingering attachment to the early structuralist preoccupation with narrative sequence—the grammar of the *consecutive*—and from the persistent sense of sexual *consequence* I feel to be at work in these novels which follow either the logic of seduction, or the logic of a female curriculum vitae—or both. While the individual chapters are bounded by the limits of a given novel, they are no less bound together by the supervising grid of a feminist narratology. They were written to be read with and against each other, and this interplay is at the heart of my undertaking. The thematic juxtaposition of the novels is intended to produce a sense of *déjà lu*, an effect of intertextual repetition that comes from rereading "for" gender, for the cultural ideology that underwrites certain narrative strategies.

Acknowledgements

This study originally took shape under the direction of Michael Riffaterre. I would like to thank him here both for his intellectual guid-
ance and for his generous support of a dissertation topic so remote
from his own preoccupations; to thank him, in short, for acknowledging me. I would like to thank too, in this chronology of indebted-
ness: Otis Fellows for his kind attention and scholarly emendations,
and Leo Braudy for his challenging comments during those early
stages; Jean Sareil, Michel Beaujour, and particularly Aram Vartanian, who took the time to read and criticize the thesis after the fact.
I am equally grateful to Rachel Brownstein and John Richetti, who
read this book in its penultimate form and offered always pertinent
comment and criticism. And there are other kinds of debts: to my
friend Jane Opper for her astute editorial counsel; to the students in
"The Heroine's Text," the graduate seminar I taught with Carolyn
Heilbrun (spring 1979) and especially to Carolyn herself, for an extraordinary moment of intellectual exchange. Last, but throughout,
Naomi Schor, my colleague, confidante, and example, who believed
in me and sustained me.

I would like to express my gratitude to Catherine Stimpson and
Domna Stanton for bringing about the publication of shortened ver-
sions of chapters 7 and 8 in *Signs* (Spring 1976), and to the University of Chicago Press for their permission to reprint that material
here. A summer grant from the Council for Research in the
Humanities at Columbia in 1975 permitted me to prepare that portion of the manuscript which appeared in *Signs*. A Mellon Teaching
Fellowship in the Humanities (1976–78) aided me indirectly by supporting my research and giving me the time to rewrite.

Part One
The Euphoric Text

Chapter One

A HARLOT'S PROGRESS: I

Moll Flanders

> *Paradoxalement, ces femmes qui exploitent à l'extrême leur fémi-
> nité se créent une situation presque équivalente à celle d'un
> homme; à partir de ce sexe qui les livre aux mâles comme objets,
> elles se retrouvent sujets.*
> —Simone de Beauvoir, *Le Deuxième Sexe*

The title page of *Moll Flanders* summarizes a life and underwrites its
authenticity by a disclaimer of fictionality:

THE FORTUNES AND MISFORTUNES
OF THE FAMOUS MOLL FLANDERS, &c.

Who was Born in NEWGATE, and during a Life of continu'd Variety for Three-
score Years, besides her Childhood, was Twelve Year a *Whore*, five times a *Wife*
(whereof once to her own Brother) Twelve Year a *Thief*, Eight Year a Transported
Felon in *Virginia*, at last grew *Rich*, liv'd *Honest*, and died a *Penitent*, *Written from
her own* MEMORANDUMS . . .[1]

Unlike "Novels and Romances," this "private History," as it is labeled in the preface, is pronounced a "Genuine" account: an account
of social ascent and spiritual transformation. The twin trajectory,
moreover, is attached to a woman's name; and despite the necessarily
fictitious status of that name, the ascription of the feminine stands as
a crucial *fact* of life: whore, wife, and although it is curiously not
previewed, mother. The passage from rags to riches, and sin to repentance, then, while an exemplary and potentially instructive narrative of individual determination and grace, is no less a graph plotted
by gender. Indeed, to read *Moll Flanders* as the novel of a certain

form of eighteenth-century economic man is, I think, to misread; and to confuse autonomy with androgyny. However illuminating a social history Moll's destiny may be, it is also a literary inscription of a woman's life. The question therefore is not—as has been argued—whether or not Moll's personality and character are feminine (or masculine)[2] but how conventional notions about women and female psychology—the eighteenth-century female codes—affect the plot and the thematic structuration of the novel.

In the chronology of a fictionalized life as it can be read in the eighteenth-century novel, the transition from childhood to adulthood constitutes the generative moment of narration. It is the "interesting" moment in the unfolding of a life.[3] In this sense *Moll Flanders* can be said to begin when Moll starts to look "a little Womanish." Since the self of the eighteenth-century novel is a social self,[4] the narrative's timing coincides with the protagonist's entrance into the world as a adult. (References to childhood usually are limited to establishing status, class, and family dynamics as they define the character's *social* relation to the world.) To enter the world, of course, is to become subject to the laws of the dynamics of innocence and experience; to become engaged in a process of initiation and education; to learn the ways of the world. That exposure to the ways of the world should be inseparable from sexual encounters in the eighteenth-century fictional universe need not be argued here.[5] But that these erotic encounters have different valences, different intensities according to the sex of the protagonists is perhaps less generally recognized. And yet the textual socialization of a female self is eroticized in a particularly insistent way. One cannot, for example, imagine an eighteenth-century heroine's plot that is not crucially dependent upon the uses and abuses of her chastity; nor is that statement gender-reversible—except, of course, in parody, like *Joseph Andrews*. When the protagonist is female, entrance into the world is always a psychosexual event coded according to certain recurrent and easily identifiable narrative patterns.[6] In *Moll Flanders*, *La Vie de Marianne*, *Pamela*, and *Fanny Hill*—all feminocentric novels of social initiation—the fundamental structuring sequence is set in motion by a confrontation between feminine virtue and illicit masculine desire. The story of attempted seduction lends itself to variations in tone and register

(*Pamela*, say, as opposed to *Fanny Hill*), but whatever the variations, the thematic structure is immediately recognizable; or at least it was to the reader of eighteenth-century novels. The heroine herself is a less sophisticated decoder. To her the text is new, not *déjà lu*, and she lacks practice in interpretation. She also lacks a parental gloss, especially when, as so often is the case in novels of initiation, she is an orphan. Moll, Marianne, and Fanny all make their entrances into the world bereft of natural family. The advantage of this disadvantage for the novel as memoir, as the record of the construction of a self in time, is obvious: the orphan's destiny, by definition, is about the vicissitudes of identity, hence about the insertion of the individual into the sociolect. The female orphan offers the eighteenth-century novelist still more built-in narrational fringe benefits because social insecurity is compounded by sexual vulnerability: the orphan-heroine constitutes a predictive series of blanks to be filled in.

Moll's history begins with her abandonment by her mother. Illegitimate and orphaned, Moll is raised in a home along with other poor little girls. They are "brought up as Mannerly and as Genteely as if [they] had been at the Dancing School" (10). Moll learns to read as well as to sew and spin, and when asked what she would like to do when she grows up, Moll answers that she wants to be a gentlewoman: "All I understood by being a Gentlewoman was to be able to Work for myself, and get enough to keep me without that terrible Bug-bear *going to Service*, whereas they meant to live Great, Rich, and High, and I know not what" (13). The local gentlewomen take an amused interest in Moll's future plans and single her out for their benevolent attention. As one of them says: "the Child may come to be a Gentlewoman for ought any body knows, she has a Gentlewoman's Hand" (13). In response to her naive ambition,[7] Moll becomes affectionately known as the "little gentlewoman" and is indulged in as such: "I WAS now about ten Years old, and began to look a little Womanish, for I was mighty Grave and Humble; very Mannerly, and as I had often heard the Ladies say I was Pretty, and would be a very handsome Woman, so you may be sure, that hearing them say so, made me not a little Proud" (14). By age twelve, through the patronage of older, motherly women and within the confines of her protected situation, Moll is able to fend for herself financially: "So

that now I was a Gentlewoman indeed, as I understood that Word"
(15). One of the ladies becomes so taken with Moll that she determines to have Moll spend some time in her own home among her
daughters, against the advice of the nurse who fears that Moll would
develop ambitions inappropriate to her station in life:

I was almost fourteen Years old, was tall of my Age, and look'd a little Womanish;
but I had such a Tast of Genteel living at the Ladies House that I was not so easie in
my old Quarters as I us'd to be, and I thought it was fine to be a Gentlewoman indeed, for I had quite other Notions of a Gentlewoman now than I had before; and as
I thought, I say, that it was fine to be a Gentlewoman, so I lov'd to be among
Gentlewomen, and therefore I long'd to be there again (16).

Moll, however, gets her wish, for when the nurse dies (like
Marianne, Moll is twice orphaned) and she is about to be cast "into
the wide World" (16), Moll is taken into the family with whom she
had stayed, to be treated as one of the daughters. She is given lessons
in French, dancing, and music—in other words "all the Advantages
of Education that I could have had if I had been as much a Gentlewoman as they were, with whom I liv'd" (18).

A fast learner, Moll soon rivals her betters and indeed discovers the
difference between what nature furnishes and what fortune provides:
"In some things, I had the Advantage of my Ladies, tho' they were my
Superiors. . . . First, I was apparently Handsomer than any of them.
Secondly, I was better shap'd, and Thirdly, I Sung better, by which I
mean, I had a better Voice; in all which you will I hope allow me to
say, I do not speak my own Conceit of myself, but the Opinion of all
that knew the Family" (18–19). With retroactive humility, however,
Moll tempers the autopanegyric by a commentary of self-denigration:
"I HAD with all these the common Vanity of my Sex (*viz.*) That being really taken for very Handsome, or if you please for a great Beauty,
I very well knew it, and had as good an Opinion of myself as any body
else could have of me" (19). (As will Marianne, Moll defines herself
as (de)limited by and subject to the frailties generally attributed to
femininity, as though it were an eternal and pre-encoded text.) Moll
then concludes this installment of her history with a moral summa-
tion: "I had the Character too of a very sober, modest, and vertuous
young Woman, and such I had always been; neither had I yet any
occasion to think of anything else, or to know what a Temptation to

Wickedness meant" (19); and in retrospect, acknowledges the fragility of such partial knowledge: "That which I was too vain of, was my Ruin, or rather my vanity was the Cause of it" (19). Having defined vanity as a failing of her sex, she presents her own "ruin" as having a high degree of inevitability. When she adds that the "lady in the House where I was, had two Sons" (19), the reader immediately recognizes the scenario: Moll's protectors are to become her seducers.

Since every genre constitutes its own overdetermined and self-contained frame of reference, it becomes possible to read proleptically: given certain textual triggers the reader can anticipate specific sequences of events. Whether one thinks of genre as a code that conditions expectations[8] or as a descriptive grammar,[9] the experienced reader (of eighteenth-century novels, and particularly popular fiction) will know that a virtuous and innocent heroine inevitably will be called upon to confront a seducer. And tempted she will, of course, either surrender or resist. Whatever the variations of register (comic, ironic, or tragic), the sequence itself is invariable. Such readily identifiable patterns have been called "narrative cliché."[10] At this juncture in *Moll Flanders*, the cliché at work is one that has been named "illicit love punished."[11] In its simplest form, it unfolds along a five-phase diachrony: seduction, fleeting happiness, threat, betrayal, retribution. Although this mini-narrative will play itself out (under the sign of a *will* to legitimacy) with each of Moll's partners, the pattern is articulated most explicitly in this first and specifically sentimental avatar.

Following the rules of our "grammar" of seduction, then, Moll's virtue is immediately put to the test. Where Marianne and Pamela resist, Moll capitulates. It is the Elder Brother in Moll's surrogate family who initiates the campaign. As will Mr. B., the Elder Brother combines insidious flattery with the offer of money, manipulating the sociosexual dynamics of *male master/female servant* relations with persistence and energy. Looking back, Moll can classify his behavior as typical, a well-known pattern, with coded linguistic constraints:

He began with the unhappy Snare to all Women, (*viz.*) taking Notice upon all Occasions how pretty I was, as he call'd it; how agreeable, how well Carriaged, and the like; and this he contriv'd so subtilly, as if he had known as well, how to catch a Woman in his Net as a Partridge when he went a Setting. . . . AFTER he had thus baited his Hook, and found easily enough the Method how to lay it in my Way, he play'd an opener Game" (19–20).

But on the moment, Moll does not perceive the pursuit as metaphor. Compliments establish the premise of communication, and the game continues with mild verbal taunts: "Don't your Cheeks burn, Mrs. *Betty?* I made a Curtsy and blush'd, but said nothing" (20). These also will be the terms of Pamela's reaction to Mr. B.: respecting class difference through silence and curtsying, but revealing (with a blush) the success of the thrust.

In the next phase, the verbal attack gives way to the physical, when the brother discovers Moll alone in a sewing room and clasps her in his arms:

I struggl'd to get away, and yet did it but faintly neither, and he held me fast, and still Kiss'd me, till he was almost out of Breath, and then sitting down, says *dear Betty* I am in Love with you.

HIS Words I must confess fir'd my Blood; all my Spirits flew about my Heart, and put me into Disorder enough, which he might easily have seen in my Face: He repeated it afterwards several times, that he was in Love with me, and my Heart spoke as plain as a Voice, that I lik'd it; nay, when ever he said, I am in Love with you, my Blushes plainly reply'd, *Wou'd you were* Sir (22).

For Moll, as for Pamela with Mr. B., the initial response to sexual confrontation is a *confusion* manifested in physical terms: blushes which like gazes express what is prohibited in words. Moll fears, as will Marivaux's Marianne, that she is transparent, and can be read like an open book. The brother presses his advantage, delivering his kisses on the bed. He leaves Moll not only with the assurance that he meant her no ill, but presses five guineas into her hand. The move proves to be effective, for the combination of sexual and financial advances causes Moll to lose her head and her footing: "I WAS more confounded with the Money than I was before with the Love; and began to be so elevated, that I scarse knew the Ground I stood on" (23–24).

At this point, Moll intervenes to comment on the importance of this phase of the proceedings. She at once justifies her subsequent behavior (ignorance of the laws of seduction) and reinscribes her text in the ideology of the *exemplum*, citing the pitfalls of female vanity:

I am the more particular in this part, that if my Story comes to be read by any innocent young Body, they may learn from it to Guard themselves against the Mis-
chiefs which attend an early Knowledge of their own Beauty; if a young Woman
once thinks herself Handsome, she never doubts the Truth of any Man, that tells her
he is in Love with her; for if she believes herself Charming enough to Captivate him,
tis natural to expect the Effects of it" (24).

With the wisdom of hindsight, Moll outlines—using the shorthand
of the maxim—the fable of seduction and betrayal in which she is to
play the victim's part. Thus, when the brother continues his kisses
and promises (making downpayments on their eventual marriage),
the "fine Words, and the Gold" (25) prevail: "THUS I gave up
myself to a readiness of being ruined without the least concern, and
am a fair *Memento* to all young Women whose Vanity prevails over
their Vertue" (25).

Moll insists upon her emblematic status: "Never poor vain Creature was so wrapt up with every part of the Story, as I was, not Considering what was before me, and how near my Ruin was at the
Door; indeed I think, I rather wish'd for that Ruin, than studied to
avoid it" (26). Indeed, although the brother has refrained from insisting upon "that which they call the last Favour" (25), Moll is aware
that she would offer no resistance and yearns for the inevitable *dénouement*. When at last the brother sets up the definitive meeting,
gives her a silk purse of a hundred guineas, promises to give her the
same every year until he marries her, and commits himself to providing for her should she become pregnant, Moll literally embraces her
fate: "MY Colour came, and went, at the Sight of the Purse, and
with the fire of his Proposal together; so that I could not say a Word,
and he easily perceiv'd it; so putting the Purse into my Bosom, I
made no more Resistance to him, but let him do just what he pleas'd;
and as often as he pleas'd; and thus I finish'd my own Destruction at
once, for from this Day, being forsaken of my Vertue, and my Modesty, I had nothing of Value left to recommend me, either to God's
Blessing, or Man's Assistance" (28–29).

Moll survives this first breach in her virtue, only to be put to the
test a second time. The younger brother, Robin, begins to find Moll
attractive: "And he finding me alone in the Garden one Evening,
begins a Story of the same Kind to me, made good honest Professions

of being in Love with me; and in short, proposes fairly and Honourably to Marry me, and that before he made any other Offer to me at all" (29). Moll can now clearly recognize the structure, but Robin presents a troubling variant (he proposes marriage before seduction), and again she is "confounded." When Robin begins to press his suit in the family, Moll regrets her past "easiness" "not from any Reflection of Conscience, but from a View of the Happiness I might have enjoy'd, and had now made impossible" (31). Moll begins to realize that she struck a bad bargain, for she considers herself married to the older brother and thus not free to marry Robin. When she sees that she cannot persuade the older brother to resolve the problem, she begs him to kill her. The hyperbole of her reaction and the dramatic change of register serve to counteract the impression of venality her previous enthusiasm might have conveyed to the reader; and the tactics of pathos reflect the victim's posture.

Indeed Moll is aggrieved by her lover's rejection: "THE bare loss of him as a Gallant was not so much my Affliction, as the loss of his Person, whom indeed I Lov'd to Distraction; and the loss of all the Expectations I had, and which I always had built my Hopes upon, of having him one Day for my Husband: These things oppress'd my Mind so much, that in short, I fell very ill, the agonies of my Mind, in a word, threw me into a high Feaver, and long it was, that none in the Family expected my Life" (41–42). Moll seeks to analyze her misery: the justification for her fault (the promise of marriage) has collapsed and she is thus deprived both of present pleasure and future gratification. She responds like a sentimental heroine: felled by the inexplicable fever that knows no remedy, the disease only nature can cure. When Moll recovers from her love sickness, the marriage with Robin is arranged. "MODESTY" forbids Moll from revealing "the Secrets of the Marriage Bed" (58) except to tell the reader that her husband never discovered her troublesome past. The marriage itself is recounted in a paragraph, by the end of which Moll is widowed, with some money and two small children—"taken happily off of my Hands, by my Husband's Father and Mother" (59). Moll thus portrays herself as a woman like other women: controlled by her emotions, misled by vanity, well-intentioned but easily led astray. The innocent orphan is a victim of circumstance, whose credulity is

abused by an unscrupulous male: seduced and abandoned. As sentimental heroine, Moll demonstrates her *physical* delicacy by falling
desperately ill and her *moral* sensitivity by self-castigation. The inscription of Moll's femininity in this phase of the narrative is limited
to a sequence of illicit love which will be repeated with variations
throughout the novel until legitimization is achieved.

Moll begins the account of her new career—"to be well Married, or
not at all" (60)—with a statement of principle and an analysis of the
dynamics of the market place: "I kept true to this Notion, that a
Woman should never be kept for a Mistress, that had Money to keep
her self" (61).[12] This desire for independence is a more sophisticated
reiteration of her childhood wish to be a "gentlewoman," by which
she meant to depend on no one. But since Moll does not have
enough money to keep herself, it is a husband that she needs. Unfortunately she discovers (citing her sister-in-law) that only money can
get her the kind of husband she wants: "Beauty, Wit, Manners,
Sence, good Humour, good Behaviour, Education, Vertue, Piety, or
any other Qualification, whether of Body or Mind, had no power to
recommend: That Money only made a Woman agreeable" (67). And
the market, as she puts it, primarily benefits men: "I found the
Women had lost the Privilege of saying NO, that it was a Favour now
for a Woman to have THE QUESTION ask'd. . . . The Men had
such Choice every where, that the Case of the Women was very
unhappy" (67–68). Inspired by the story of a female acquaintance
who cleverly acquired a reliable and prosperous husband, Moll
spends several pages explaining appropriate behavior for women in
the face of the general unreliability of men. She takes as her premise
that women a priori are vulnerable at the hands of men. Moll regrets
that women do not value their own safety, and "impatient of their
present State. . . . make Matrimony like Death, to be *a Leap in the
Dark*" (75).

She decries this self-destructive tendency in women as something
to struggle against, for it is the "Thing, in which of all parts of Life, I
think at this Time we suffer most in: 'Tis nothing but lack of
Courage, the fear of not being Marry'd at all, and of that frightful
State of Life, call'd *an old Maid*. . . . This I say, is the Woman's
snare" (75–76). Moll thus joins the sex she has been describing from

the outside, and obliquely justifies the great price she herself puts on marriage, for she herself often fails to heed her own warning and gets trapped in her efforts not to be caught. This discrepancy between an ideal female behavior and her own is less ironic in effect than deictic; it signals the power of the female code to inflect the life story of any woman. Just as "authorial" commentary returns consistently to generalize about the feminine condition, narrative event consistently demonstrates Moll's particular experience of it: Moll either denigrates herself by admitting she has fallen into femaleness (self-definition as a whore, for example), or elevates herself, asserting (innate) superiority over other women. In justifying the vagaries of her own life, she practices a theory of the female text. [13]

Moll's second and third marriages are no more successful than her first, but with unflagging resilience, Moll begins yet again: "I HAD now a new Scene of Life upon my Hands, and a dreadful Appearance it had; I was come away with a kind of final Farewel . . . and being now, *as it were*, a Woman of Fortune tho' I was a Woman without a Fortune, I expected something, or other might happen in my way, that might mend my Circumstances as had been my Case before" (105–06). The future is open, if bleak, and Moll takes stock, punning on her condition. She can, however, place the grid of her past upon the future and trust that history will repeat itself. Her lack of funds is, as usual, the crucial handicap: "As I had no settl'd Income, so spending upon the main Stock was but a certain kind of *bleeding to Death* . . ." (106). The hyperbole of her diction prepares the logic of the degradation [14] to come, and underwrites her subsequent actions as *vital* necessity.

Moll's landlady at Bath, one of several older women who help Moll in her schemes, [15] arranges a connection between Moll and an older wealthy gentleman. The working hypothesis of this relationship is the gentleman's affectionate respect for Moll and her virtue. After Moll nurses him devotedly through a serious illness, they live together as man and wife. With this nuance: the gentleman refuses to make love to her, since as Moll relates with some amazement, "he lov'd me he cou'd not injure me" (115). Moll feels that it is a noble experiment, but she inexplicably transforms the covenant. Her postmortem echoes that of her first seduction: "THUS the Government of our Virtue was broken, and I exchang'd the Place of Friend, for that unmusical harsh-sounding Title of WHORE" (116). Again Moll, not the seducer, insists upon the damning epithet. In recounting her initial "fall," Moll described herself as wishing for and rushing toward her ruin, almost usurping the prerogatives of the seducer. In this sequence, Moll in fact assumes that role, voluntarily breaking a contract designed to protect her. And just as pregnancy was the overriding anxiety in the first involvement, Moll must again worry about that eventuality. The gentleman from Bath, like the Elder Brother, engages himself to provide for the child: "These mutual assurances harden'd us in the thing; and after this we repeated the Crime as often as we pleas'd, till at length, as I had fear'd, so it came to pass, and I was indeed with Child" (117). Illicit sex generates the seeds of its own disaster. Or as she reflects later on: "Indeed I have often observ'd since, and leave it as a caution to the Readers of this Story; that we ought to be cautious of gratifying our Inclinations in loose and lewd Freedoms, least we find our Resolutions of Virtue fail us in the juncture when their Assistance should be most necessary" (119). Her story is to be taken as a cautionary tale and the reader is constantly brought up against the constraints of the genre.

When her benefactor abandons her, she finds herself (at 42) at still another beginning: "I found by experience, that to be Friendless is the worst Condition, next to being in want, that a Woman can be reduc'd to: *I say a Woman*, because 'tis evident Men can be their own Advisers . . . but if a Woman has no Friend to Communicate her Affairs to . . . 'tis ten to one but she is undone . . ." (128). Moll again defines her particular situation in terms of a generalized feminine condition, and again defines that condition by opposition to masculine self-sufficiency. In Moll's system, the simple fact of being a woman is to operate at a disadvantage. The vulnerability of a friendless woman, moreover, is more than economic. A woman on her own is fair game in the skirmish between the sexes: "When a Woman is thus left desolate and void of Council, she is just like a Bag of Money, or a Jewel dropt on the Highway, which is a Prey to the next Comer" (128). Moll accepts as a foregone conclusion the applicability of such a maxim: "THIS was evidently my Case, for I was now a loose, unguided Creature" (128). Eventually, however, through a new woman friend, Moll acquires her fourth husband. Although she is by now highly experienced and can reverse the dynamics of seduction ("I PLAY'D with this Lover, as an Angler does with a Trout"), and confident ("I found I had him fast on the Hook, so I jested with his new Proposal; and put him off" [140]), Moll outwits herself once more: Jemmy is as poor as she is. As she said of her second husband: "I was catch'd in the very Snare, which *as I might say*, I laid for my self" (60). And, although this marriage takes place under the sign of romance and true love, the couple mutually resolves to seek separate fortunes until they achieve a modicum of material success. Moll leaves Jemmy "with the utmost reluctance on my side," (159) but she still has to find a way to live. As one might expect, her misfortune is soon compounded by the discovery of yet another pregnancy.

If Moll at times appears casual about abandoning her children, "endeavouring to Miscarry" (161) is abhorrent to her; and, as she protests after the birth of her baby: "Let me be what I would, I was not come up to that pitch of Hardness, common to the Profession; I mean, to be unnatural, and regardless of the Safety of my Child" (176). Thus, while Moll willingly describes herself as a whore, she maintains a measure of distance from the role, insisting that she is still endowed with the essential attribute of positive femininity: maternal instinct.[16] Nonetheless, when Moll comes, at last, to her fifth husband, her banker friend, she has an attack of guilt: "What an abominable Creature am I! . . . He is going to Marry one that has lain with two Brothers, and has had three Children by her own Brother! one that was born in *Newgate*, whose Mother was a Whore, and is now a transported Thief; one that has lain with thirteen Men, and has had a Child since he saw me!" (182). The coda of the litany provides the measure of her perfidy: she has managed to produce a child in the interval between their meetings.

Despite Moll's initial misgivings about her morals, this marriage is persistently described as a refuge from vice, freedom from necessity, a happy virtuous life: "Now I seem'd landed in a safe Harbour, after the Stormy Voyage of Life past was at an end; and I began to be thankful for my Deliverance" (188). The clichés of redemption reinscribe the text as quest: every phase of degradation is followed by a hiatus, a period of stock taking, and elaborating good resolutions for the future in view of potential amelioration. Indeed, Moll, in looking back at her past life, adds at this point: "I flatter'd my self that I had sincerely repented" (188). But the element of doubt present in "seem'd" and reiterated in "flatter'd my self" undercuts Moll's optimism. Indeed, Moll's reprieve proves to be just that. Moll's husband dies, and she is again a widow with two small children. This materially replicates the situation in which she found herself after the death of her first husband. The new variable here is age: "I HAD had two Children by him and no more, for to tell the Truth, it began to be time for me to leave bearing Children, for I was now Eight and Forty, and I suppose if he had liv'd I should have had no more" (189). With characteristic euphemism, Moll acknowledges that she is past her prime, past "the flourishing time with me when I might expect to be courted for a Mistress" (189). Moll, then, menopausal,[17] is due for a change of career, but reduced to misery, "perfectly Friendless and Helpless" (190), she is, in all ways, at a loss.

At this juncture, Moll, "prompted by I know not what Spirit, and as it were, doing I did not know what, or why" (191), commits her first theft: "THIS was the Bait; and the Devil who I said laid the Snare, as readily prompted me, as if he had spoke, for I remember and shall never forget it, 'twas like a Voice spoken to me over my Shoulder" (191). The vocabulary used to describe the theft in no way differs from that used to describe the relations between men and women in the seduction sequences. Entrapment, irresistibility and remorse all recapitulate the paradigm of illicit love. The devil is cast as the ultimate seducer; and from this point on Moll describes herself quite literally as a woman possessed: "I had an evil Counsellor within" (193). Poverty, as she says, has *hardened* her heart so that her greatest fear is now realized; she has become what she despises: a criminal. In this period of her life, Moll makes an attempt to live by honest means: her needle. She even enjoys it but the "diligent Devil" (199) commands her to seek her fortune in other ways. Moll claims that had she been able to support herself with her needlework before turning to thieving, she would have "never fallen into this wicked Trade" (202). But once embarked, there is no turning back. The attempt, however short-lived, reminds us that Moll is a character of good *intentions*, and reinforces the reader's sense of her powerlessness to act against the forces of her destiny.[18] She returns to her governess and surrogate mother who, having once served her as a midwife, now takes Moll in and teaches her to be a pickpocket. With a partner behind her, Moll becomes "ingulph'd in Labyrinths of Trouble too great to get out at all" (203). As often before, she finds herself in a double bind: "As Poverty brought me into the Mire, so Avarice kept me in, till there was no going back" (203). Moll, then, is on the irrestible course that takes her to Newgate, the prison she was born in, and that ends her career as a woman of crime.

At one of the bleaker moments of her history, Moll retrospectively speculates about the discrepancy between her good intentions and their unfortunate realization:

> I knew what I aim'd at, and what I wanted, but knew nothing how to pursue the End by direct means; I wanted to be plac'd in a settled State of Living, and had I happen'd to meet with a sober good Husband, I should have been as faithful and true a Wife to him as Virtue it self could have form'd: If I had been otherwise, the Vice came in always at the Door of Necessity, not at the Door of Inclination (128–29).

This passage demonstrates the system of rationalization underlying the representation of what one might call the reluctant whore. According to the conventional logic that underwrites the motivation of the fallen woman, the original impulse is always grounded in the honest desires of positive feminity: husband and home. If so laudable a desire is subsequently thwarted, it is the fault of destiny. Victim of circumstance, what is a woman to do? Although the passivity implicit in such an attitude is belied by Moll's energetic activity, the conflict is resolved on another level of narration. The appeal to pathos, the claim to sympathy due the plaything of fortune, serves to prepare the reader for the leap of faith required to "believe in" Moll's repentance and redemption. Since Moll is to be saved, the reader must be reminded (if not persuaded) of her good will.

Moll perceives Newgate as the beginning of the end: "The Place where my Mother suffered so deeply, where I was brought into the World, and from whence I expected no Redemption, but by an infamous Death: To conclude, the Place that had so long expected me, and which with so much Art and Success I had so long avoided" (273). But fatality is then transcoded into the Christian lexicon: Newgate is "an Emblem of Hell itself, and a kind of Entrance into it"

(274). Moll's confrontation with misery and mortality stimulates a desire for repentance, but the event that precipitates her sense of remorse is the unexpected encounter with her Lancashire husband whom she feels she has ruined. It is thinking about *his* misery that transforms her:[19] "I bewail'd his Misfortunes, and the ruin he was now come to, at such a Rate, that I relish'd nothing now, as I did before . . . in a word, I was perfectly chang'd and became another Body" (281). The change is also reinforced by a reversal in Moll's system of protection. Although Moll's governess attempts to intervene on her behalf—"My Governess acted a true Mother to me, she pittied me, she cryed with me, and for me; but she cou'd not help me" (282) —mothering proves to be ineffectual against the efficiency of the institution; and despite her efforts, Moll is sentenced. Nonetheless, through the governess, Moll receives a minister. Faced with the fact that no help can come from this world, she turns to the other. The transformation that must occur, in order to insure the sincerity of repentance, is a reversal of values: what was valued in the past now must be rejected. The minister brings Moll to this stage by finding the key to her *true* self: "THIS honest friendly way of treating me, *unlock'd* all the *Sluces* of my *Passions:* He *broke into my very Soul* by it; and I *unravell'd* all the Wickedness of my Life to him" (288; italics mine). Moll's account of spiritual penetration, like her account of the devil's temptation, is coded by sexual metaphor; and the moment of conversion itself echoes the text of her first kiss: "He reviv'd my Heart . . . and so swift did Thoughts circulate, and so high did the impressions they had made upon me run, that I thought I cou'd freely have gone out that Minute to Execution" (289). Moll's spiritual climax— in perfect symmetry to her seduction—is presented as a superlative *undoing,* and thus overcomes her last resistance to a *return* to virtue.

Moll digresses briefly from the account of her moral progress to assure the reader that it is the heart of the story—"the best part of my Life, the most Advantageous to myself, and the most instructive to others"—and criticizes those who "had rather the History were a compleat Tragedy, as it was very likely to have been" (291). As narrator, she insists upon the integration of her salvation into the trajectory of her life, thus preparing the happy ending as announced. Having been granted a reprieve on the basis of the minister's intervention,

Moll then seeks to convert her husband since her own salvation is incomplete without his: "I USED the utmost of my endeavor to perswade him, and joyn'd that known Womans Rhetorick to it, I mean that of Tears" (302). He indeed succumbs to such feminine pressure and they soon find themselves together in America. Reinstating Jemmy as the official partner within the couple brings the dynamics of sexual circulation to a halt. But Moll's problems are not yet over: without revealing the truth of her past to her husband, she must find a way to discover the provisions her real mother has made for her in order to secure *social* integration.

When Moll finally meets her son (from the third and incestuous marriage to her brother) she is so charmed by him and his way of life that she has a moment of regret that she is not alone to fully enjoy her good fortune: "And thus I was as if I had been in a new World, and began secretly now to wish that I had not brought my *Lancashire* Husband from *England* at all. HOWEVER, that wish was not hearty neither, for I lov'd my *Lancashire* Husband entirely, as indeed I had ever done from the beginning; and he merited from me as much as it was possible for a Man to do, but that by the way" (335). Moll's afterthought suggests that her happiness comes from having found, not so much a prosperous life with her husband, but from having reintegrated her maternity:[20]

My Sons tender Carriage, and kind Offers fetch'd Tears from me, almost all the while he talk'd with me; indeed, I could scarce Discourse with him, but in the intervals of my Passion . . . this was . . . *the pleasantest Day that ever past over my Head in my Life, and which gave me the truest Satisfaction* (337; italics mine).

As in her conversation with the minister, kind words trigger passionate and moral enthusiasm. Thus the end of the orphan's quest culminates in familial harmony, which in turn assures worldly success: with the help of her son, Moll is able to set up her own plantation profitably and to live like a *gentlewoman*—her original desire—with servants of her own. The final obstacle to her happiness is then removed—the proof of the guilt of her previous career—the survivor of her unfortunate past: "When the old Wretch, my Brother (Husband) was dead, I then freely gave my Husband an Account of all that Affair" (342). The past having been successfully neutralized, all the terms of closure are in place. Moll reappears in England and the narrative necessarily comes to an end. The old life continues to exist only in counterpoint to the new, the "Fable" evinced by the "Moral" of the preface, as Moll plans her old age as an act of repentance. Unlike M. (Moll) Hackabout, Hogarth's less fortunate but equally celebrated harlot, whose destiny takes her to Newgate, and from Newgate to venereal disease, followed by an untimely death, Moll Flanders, *in fine* "at last grew *Rich*, liv'd *Honest*, and died a *Penitent*." This "myth of female endurance"[21] ends with a victory: comedic integration of the wayward whore within the received structures of social life. In the end, Moll has it all: well heeled and well married, the "little gentlewoman" no longer needs her needle.

This singular achievement, this individual overcoming of circumstance, I suggested at the beginning of this chapter, is a graph plotted by gender. A backward glance at the overall pattern of events should make the interplay between narrative logic and the fact(s) of Moll's femaleness clear. I have argued for a clearly telic structure and for a clear sense of an ending, or closure. Ian Watt, on the contrary, writes that "even when a resolution of the plot would seem to be both easy and logical, Defoe apparently prefers and certainly achieves the inconsequential and the incomplete." He sees *Moll Flanders* closing "in some confusion with the heroine and later her husband coming back to England."[22] But confusion vanishes if Moll's story is read as a quest for (female) autonomy. The ending is then both complete and *consequential*: Moll's fantasy, her little girl's "wish for self-sufficiency"[23] is fulfilled. Necessarily, the details of this fulfillment are less important (even implausible) than the victorious fact of symbolic transformation. The episodes of Moll's life, in a retroactive reading, do more than follow each other consecutively: they add up. I take the sequence with the Elder Brother to be the point of departure against which the meaning of the concluding section must be measured. Watt, arguing for the "episodic nature" of the novel, maintains that while the "seduction by the Elder Brother, forms a satisfactory and indeed symbolic prelude to the novel as a whole . . . it has no later connection with the plot."[24] At the same time, however, he recognizes that the third marriage "has links with the beginning of Moll's life and with the final scenes in Virginia."[25] I would suggest that the

Elder Brother/first marriage sequence is connected both to the third marriage (the second marriage to the gentleman-tradesman is as "amphibious" as the party himself) and to the resolution of the plot (if one charts plot line in terms of repetition and difference). In the first sequence Moll functions as an *object* of desire. She is acted upon in an economy over which she has no control. Within the sequence constituted by the third marriage, Moll establishes herself as subject: she chooses that husband specifically to further her own interests. What links the two is the logic of reversal: by her third marriage, Moll has become the determining agent of her destiny. This grammatical transformation from object to subject, however, only takes on full meaning in the larger context of Moll's quest; for it is not enough to *choose* a husband; that choice must be productive of integration and legitimacy in the world.

In closing, this rapid recapitulation of Moll's social history: Moll is abandoned by her natural mother and is given a surrogate family. This family proves to be the locus of her seduction and first marriage. Subsequently widowed, then abandoned by husband number 2, Moll remarries (number 3) and reconstitutes a family. When her mother-in-law turns out to be her real mother, the family is temporarily dissolved. Moll, however, produces children from this family, and it is the *son* (as financial advisor and executor of Moll's estate from her mother), who helps her construct the ultimate family with her fourth and favorite husband when they—like her mother before her—are transported to the colonies. Only when this fantasmatic genealogy is established does Moll cease being an orphan and attain the legitimacy she sought at the beginning. Although her name is neither her mother's, her father's, nor her husband's, it is no longer the generic Mrs. Betty. She has named herself,[26] and by living her *nom de plume* as a woman and *sui generis,* she becomes an eponymous heroine.

Chapter Two

THE VIRTUOUS ORPHAN

La Vie de Marianne

> *In no other century was woman such a dominating figure, the*
> *very essence of the rococo being a feminine delicacy.*
> —Mario Praz, *The Romantic Agony*

By its title, *La Vie de Marianne ou les aventures de Madame la Comtesse de* ***, Marivaux's novel announces a life story. But the trajectory which takes Marianne from infancy to the age of fifty proves to be more a narrative *frame* than a mimetic model. Unlike the adventures of Moll Flanders which embrace chronology from childhood to old age, Marianne's story in fact stops and starts at adolescence.[1] Curiously, however, although as readers we never learn the secret of her birth, nor the particulars of her marriage, and despite the literally unfinished status of the novel, we are left with the impression of a realized destiny; of a life, and not a fragment. This impression of biographical fulfillment is largely due to the mimetic power of the genre and the title as intertext (other lives) and as summary: the accomplished transformation from "then" to "now" is inwritten by the *"ou."* It is also due, of course, to the authority of the narrator. Looking back, Marianne has a mastery of the world that recontains the *non-finito* as closure; for whether one chooses to read Marianne's life as a "roman d'éducation"[2] or not, the *voice* of experience inscribes arrival. Her arrival, however, unlike Moll's and unlike Pamela's, is in no way that of a *parvenue*: Marianne merely accedes to the place she always thought was hers. Nevertheless, the novel is structured by the challenge an outsider poses to the social hierarchy. In that sense her text must be read as a vertical itinerary, and Marianne herself as an eighteenth-century and female incarnation of the hero of nineteenth-century novels Lionel Trilling has called the "Young Man from the Provinces."[3]

Like *Moll Flanders*, *La Vie de Marianne* begins with an account of origins, and orphanhood. The misfortune of Marianne's position is compounded by the ambiguous circumstances surrounding the accident that deprived her of her natural parents: "Par tout cela ma naissance devint impénétrable, et je n'appartins plus qu'à la charité de tout le monde."[4] There would seem to be no way of proving whether she is of noble birth or not, and that sealed mystery conditions her apprehension of the world. Despite her ascribed inferior social status, as narrator of her own history, Marianne, like Moll, from the beginning insists upon an innate superiority: "Je vous avouerai aussi que j'avais des grâces et de petites façons qui n'étaient point d'un enfant ordinaire; j'avais de la douceur et de la gaieté, le geste fin, l'esprit vif, avec un visage qui promettait une belle physionomie; et ce qu'il promettait, il l'a tenu" (15). The reluctant self-praise of conspiratorial confession ("je vous avouerai que") registers the distance between the countess and the misplaced orphan she once was. Marianne's guardians, a priest and his sister, respond to her coming of age (fifteen) as natural parents would: they try to assure her future by finding "quelque honnête homme" (15) to marry her. The sister takes Marianne to Paris, the better to seek her fortune, but within the space of a few days Marianne is orphaned for the second time. She is now more orphan than ever: "Enfin me voilà seule, et sans autre guide qu'une expérience de quinze ans et demi, plus ou moins" (23). Twice abandoned, with neither family nor friends, she must confront the world on its terms: money and men.

Despite her lamentations, or rather through them, Marianne manages to acquire another protector. This "religieux," reluctant to be burdened with such a charge, tries to find a replacement: "un homme de considération, charitable et pieux" (27)—a secular father figure. To encourage his sympathy, the curate presents this charity case in the light most likely to touch: "Et pour l'exciter encore davantage, il lui marquait mon sexe, mon âge et ma figure, et tout ce qui pouvait en arriver, ou par ma faiblesse, ou par la corruption des autres" (26). The man of the cloth thus evokes the worldly object of desire. Marianne's qualities, moreover, are enhanced by her availability; and the curate does not fail to draw the conclusions implicit in the terms of his analysis. M. de Climal, the prospective protector, inspecting his charge-to-be, articulates the terms of the equation in which Marianne defines herself: "On est même porté à croire qu'elle a de la naissance; en vérité son malheur est bien grand" (27). He offers her a place as a domestic with his sister-in-law (a tactic Mr. B. will try) but Marianne cannot accept that solution: "Cette proposition me fit rougir. Hélas! monsieur, lui dis-je, quoique je n'aie rien, et que je ne sache à qui je suis, il me semble que j'aimerais mieux mourir que d'être chez quelqu'un en qualité de domestique; et si j'avais mon père et ma mère, il y a toute apparence que j'en aurais moi-même, au lieu d'en servir à personne" (28). In the face of Marianne's proud hyperbole, Climal then proposes exactly what her guardian had planned: respectable work, "un état" (28).

In the course of the humiliating trip to her new destination, Marianne begins to decipher the code in which Climal is addressing her: "Je trouvais sa conversation singulière; il me semblait que mon homme se mitigeait, qu'il était plus flatteur que zélé, plus généreux que charitable; il me paraissait tout changé" (30), and senses the implications of his rhetoric. She lets the scenario play itself out as she learns to negotiate with ambiguity: "Je le laissais faire en rougissant de mon obéissance; et je rougissais sans savoir pourquoi, seulement par un instinct qui me mettait en peine de ce que cela pouvait signifier" (31).

At Climal's first visit to Marianne in her new home, he begins (like Mr. B. with Pamela) by taking her hand, declaring himself to be her friend and desirous of her friendship:

"A propos, j'oubliais à vous donner de l'argent. Et en disant cela, il me mit quelques louis d'or dans la main. Je les refusai d'abord, et lui dis qu'il me restait quelque argent de la défunte; mais, malgré cela, il me força de le prendre. Je les pris donc avec honte, car cela m'humiliait; mais je n'avais pas de fierté à écouter là-dessus avec un homme qui s'était chargé de moi, pauvre orpheline, et qui paraissait vouloir me tenir lieu de père" (35).

Again, Marianne's first impulse is to refuse but she finally accepts when she can nullify any grounds for humiliation on the basis of the familial overtones to the new relationship: *pauvre orpheline/père*. Indeed, Marianne shows her acceptance by an appropriate gesture of filial gratitude: "Je fis une révérence assez sérieuse en recevant ce qu'il me donnait" (35). But this kind of daughterly respect is not what Climal has in mind: "Eh! me dit-il, ma chère Marianne, laissons-là les révérences, et montrez-moi que vous êtes contente" (35). When Climal proceeds to outfit Marianne, she loses all doubts as to the motives underlying his friendship for her, although she postpones admitting this to herself as long as possible: "Ce fut le beau linge qu'il voulut que je prisse qui me mit au fait de ses sentiments; . . . car la charité n'est pas galante dans ses présents" (39). Marianne recognizes that a charity rather different from that of her surrogate mother is at work, but feels that her situation justifies her actions: "D'un autre côté, je n'avais plus de retraite, et M. de Climal m'en donnait une; je manquais de hardes, et il m'en achetait, et c'était de belles hardes que j'avais déjà essayées dans mon imagination, et j'avais trouvé qu'elles m'allaient à merveille" (40). Her own rhetoric of accumulation persuades her to capitulate; but she resolves not to act on her understanding until all ambiguity is erased. Her deferred resistance is based upon the notion that she is virtuous in her attitude, that is, honest with *herself:* "Si, malgré cet amour que je connaissais, j'avais reçu ses présents, c'était par un petit raisonnement que mes besoins et ma vanité m'avaient dicté, et qui n'avait rien pris sur la pureté de mes intentions" (45). But it is more than pure vanity that "dictates" Marianne's part in this exciting new game: "Il me prenait des *palpitations* en songeant combien j'allais être jolie" (50; italics mine).

The first installment of Marianne's life ends on this moment of anticipation, and the reader is warned that Marianne's first appearance in the world is "l'origine de toutes mes autres aventures" (52). Indeed, the clothing Climal gives Marianne serves to launch her in the world: her first appearance as his protégée is scheduled for church: the only *proper* place for her to be displayed. Upon finding a crowd at the church, Marianne decides to find a position where she can see and be seen: "Je tâchai, en me glissant tout doucement, de gagner le haut de l'église, où j'apercevais de beau monde qui était à son aise" (58). This spontaneous decision can be taken as a metonym for her ascent through the narrative: and prefigures her upward mobility.[5]

From this vantage point she can evaluate the responsiveness of her prospective audience, which she feels quite equipped to do by virtue of "l'esprit que la vanité de plaire nous donne, et qu'on appelle, autrement dit, la coquetterie" (59). This is a gift Marianne attributes to all women and one which she prizes along with her instinct. She instantly recognizes that women are rivals and men potential admirers.

When Marianne realizes that she has become the center of attention, she performs an artful striptease: "De temps en temps, pour les tenir en haleine, je les régalai d'une petite découverte sur mes charmes; je leur en apprenais quelque chose de nouveau, sans me mettre pourtant en grande dépense" (62). A true performer, what she reads in the eyes of an audience stimulates her. The men are a living mirror for her performance, and like a star she controls by dosage. Poor Marianne becomes a source of abundance, but not abandon, for she measures her offerings. Withholding as much as she gives, Marianne demonstrates the technique of the coquette: "Ensuite, c'était à ma coiffe à qui j'avais recours; elle allait à merveille, mais je voulais bien qu'elle allât mal, en faveur d'une main nue qui se montrait en y retouchant, et qui amenait nécessairement avec elle un bras rond, qu'on voyait pour le moins à demi, dans l'attitude où je le tenais alors" (62). In the system of the coquette, every gesture contains its own denial: thus, for example, when Marianne reveals her hand (and arm) the provocative content of such exposure is nullified by the necessity of adjustment. And the compensation for correcting (hence admitting) an imperfection, however minor, is the revelation of nudity, since the hand is only seductive by synecdoche. Excitement moves from the part to the whole: "pour fixer de certaines gens, il est bien aussi sûr de les tenter que de leur plaire" (63).

Marianne's tactics are successful in both securing the attention of others and selecting an object of attention for herself: "Parmi les jeunes gens dont j'attirais les regards, il y en eut un que je distinguai moi-même, et sur qui mes yeux tombaient plus volontiers que sur les autres. J'aimais à le voir, sans me douter du plaisir que j'y trouvais; j'étais coquette pour les autres, et je ne l'étais pas pour lui; j'oubliais à lui plaire, et ne songeais qu'à le regarder" (63). "He" causes her to forget herself, to become vulnerable to the unconscious fascination of love at first sight. Despite the earlier show of confidence and control while the object of Climal's attentions (and those of the crowd at church), Marianne, face to face with Valville, manifests symptoms of confusion and excitement associated with falling in love for the first time: "De mon côté, je parlai aux autres, et ne lui dis rien non plus; je n'osais même le regarder, ce qui faisait que j'en mourais d'envie: aussi le regardais-je, toujours en n'osant, et je ne sais ce que mes yeux lui dirent; mais les siens me firent une réponse si tendre qu'il fallait que les miens l'eussent méritée. Cela me fit rougir, et me remua le coeur à un point qu'à peine m'aperçus-je de ce que je devenais" (65). The dialogue of meaningful looks is a necessary preliminary to the verbal exchange. In accordance with the canons of masculine and feminine behavior (which presuppose naiveté on the part of the woman and experience on the part of the man), the man's gaze is a declaration, a communication that disconcerts; the woman's timorous ("je n'osais même le regarder") but compelled ("aussi le regardais-je, toujours en n'osant"). To the extent that eyes serve as mirrors to love's progress, Marianne perceives her own vulnerability in the eyes of her beholder. It is this involuntary revelation of self-involvement that causes disruption, and the inevitable blush.

Marianne then attempts to give an account of her new state:

Je n'ai de ma vie été si agitée. Je ne saurais vous définir ce que je sentais.

C'était un mélange de trouble, de plaisir et de peur; oui, de peur, car une fille qui en est là-dessus à son apprentissage ne sait point où tout cela mène: ce sont des mouvements inconnus qui l'enveloppent, qui disposent d'elle, qu'elle ne possède point, qui la possèdent; et la nouveauté de cet état l'alarme. Il est vrai qu'elle y trouve du plaisir, mais c'est un plaisir fait comme un danger, sa pudeur même en est effrayée; il y a là quelque chose qui la menace, qui l'étourdit, et qui prend déjà sur elle.

On se demanderait volontiers dans ces instants-là: que vais-je devenir? Car, en vérité, l'amour ne nous trompe point: dès qu'il se montre, il nous dit ce qu'il est, et de quoi il sera question; l'âme, avec lui, sent la présence d'un maître qui la flatte, mais avec une autorité déclarée qui ne la consulte pas, et qui lui laisse hardiment les soupçons de son esclavage futur.

Voilà ce qui m'a semblé de l'état où j'étais, et je pense aussi que c'est l'histoire de toutes les jeunes personnes de mon âge en pareil cas (66).

The commentary at the end of the passage invites the reader to generalize and to interpret Marianne's reactions against the text of first love per se.[6] The opening sentence establishes the key elements of the *topos*: unicity, confusion, and indescriptibility. Despite her disclaimer, however, Marianne *analyzes* the confusion: it is a mixture of pleasure and fear. Fear, though, not pleasure, proves to be the distinctive trait of love. (Indeed, the entire first paragraph is an expansion derived from the word fear.) Even the definition of pleasure ("fait comme un danger") is subject to its contamination. As if foreseeing the reader's objections ("oui, de peur") to such a formulation, Marianne supplies a justification: on the one hand, the anxieties of any unexperienced girl are a function of ignorance ("ne sait point où tout cela mène," "mouvements inconnus," "nouveauté"); on the other, these new feelings are overwhelming ("l'enveloppent," "disposent d'elle," "la possèdent"). The novice's lack of control ("qu'elle ne possède pas") thus subverts pleasure since a crucial feminine value ("pudeur") is threatened. In the next paragraph it becomes clear that these nameless, inexplicable feelings are in fact decipherable in terms of another text: the scenario of love's possession. If love is arbitrary and authoritarian ("maître," "autorité déclarée," "qui ne . . . consulte pas"), then love's victim is necessarily a slave. The prediction of future enslavement, however, on which the passage ends, with love personified as a masculine master, not only fulfills conventional verbal logic, but retroactively specifies what is *feminine* in the earlier exposition of fear. In this perspective, the verbs "menace," "étourdit," and "prend déjà sur elle" (following the reference to "pudeur") must be read as sexual coding, and "quelque chose," as a euphemism for desire. In other words, when the representation of first love is superimposed on the grid of positive feminity (virginal innocence) it becomes a scenario of *fear*: confusion derives less from newness as such than from the *signs* of incipient sexuality. To recognize those signs is to conjure up the system to which they belong. In the face of that recognition ("Car, en vérité, l'amour ne nous trompe point"), the heroine can proceed only with a sense of the irremediable.

When Marianne finds herself alone with Valville, she thus has no trouble decoding. Valville's glances convey a *specific* message: "Il n'en jetait pas un sur moi qui ne signifiât: *Je vous aime;* et moi, je ne savais que faire des miens, parce qu'ils lui en auraient dit autant" (67). The look of love is another language, and reciprocity the tacit condition of exchange: "ce muet entretien de nos coeurs" (67). But since, according to the rules of love's progress, the tête-à-tête is a stolen moment, the dialogue is soon interrupted—here by the arrival of the doctor. This is one of the key episodes in the novel, for it legitimizes the "accidental" encounter between Marianne and Valville and sets in motion the courtship sequence. Marianne is asked to show the doctor her foot:[7] "A cette proposition, je rougis d'abord par un sentiment de pudeur; et puis, en rougissant pourtant, je songeai que j'avais le plus joli petit pied du monde; que Valville allait le voir; que ce ne serait point ma faute, puisque la nécessité voulait que je le montrasse devant lui" (67). Marianne's response is registered in a series of reasoned steps demonstrating a system of values in which virtue and vanity coexist in a flexible hierarchy. The result is her equation: necessity + exposure = innocence. Just as she did in church, Marianne finds a way to short-circuit modesty by establishing an alibi. Her behavior has been justified and she summarizes the case for the reader: "C'était ma chute qui avait tort" (67). The dialectics of virtue and vanity overdetermine the action in this crucial scene. For example, the doctor recommends that she stay and rest. Marianne would like to, but would then have to *appear* to give word to her "people." The choice at this juncture is whether to admit to being "une fille de boutique" and thus to forfeit her rights to Valville's respect,[8] or to take a chance on a more ambiguous course of action: "J'aimais mieux lui paraître équivoque que ridicule, et le laisser douter de mes moeurs que de le faire rire de tous ses respects" (71). Temporarily paralyzed by the double bind, Marianne, after a struggle, finally finds the solution—tears: "Je pleurai donc, et il n'y avait peut-être pas de meilleur expédient pour me tirer d'affaire, que de pleurer et de laisser tout là. Notre âme sait bien ce qu'elle fait, ou du moins son instinct le sait bien pour elle" (80). Tears, which Moll called "Womans Rhetorick," are a well-documented tactic for the innocent heroine. An effective means of nonverbal communication, they deliver a message while temporarily suspending dialogue. Tears also have the advantage of reversing the balance of power. Thus where Valville had been angrily pressing Marianne to explain herself, to accede to his wishes, Marianne's tears transform the relationship: Valville rises to the nobility of his own birth to comfort her.

This reversal allows Marianne to present herself in a sympathetic light: "C'est que cet abattement et ces pleurs me donnèrent, aux yeux de ce jeune homme, je ne sais quel air de dignité romanesque qui lui en imposa, qui corrigea d'avance la médiocrité de mon état" (80). Once Marianne has demonstrated her vulnerability, Valville, responding to the scenario, can assume the role of protector: "Est-ce qu'on peut voir vos larmes sans souhaiter de vous secourir?" (81). Having injured and rescued Marianne a first time in the accident, Valville again offers reparation. In the light of this noblesse oblige, Marianne can admit to lodging with Mme Dutour as the *victim* of "les plus grands malheurs du monde" (83). While reaping the fruits of such a painful confession (Valville is on his knees, humbled and loving, kissing Marianne's hand), the lovers are again interrupted, this time by M. de Climal, Valville's uncle. Such a triangle necessarily puts Climal at a disadvantage. And when he comes to see Marianne, directly after the last episode, her eyes are opened: "En un mot, ce n'était plus le même homme à mes yeux: les tendresses du neveu, jeune, aimable et galant, m'avaient appris à voir l'oncle tel qu'il était . . . son âge . . . ses rides . . . toute la laideur de son caractère" (108). Climal now appears as that inevitably ridiculous figure, *senex amans*. Sensing that he is losing in the struggle, Climal, in a reiteration of his original pronouncement, seeks to regain stature by reminding Marianne of her inferior position: "Vous êtes une orpheline, et une orpheline inconnue à tout le monde" (111). Expanding redundantly upon the logic of his premise, he defines Marianne as a type subject to the maxims of the system: "Vous qui êtes la plus aimable personne de votre sexe . . . par conséquent seriez aussi la plus déshonorée. Car, dans un pareil cas, c'est ce qu'il y a de plus beau qui est le plus méprisé" (114–115). Climal then poses the solution to her problem: he will protect her, as his mistress. When Marianne resorts to tears, Climal tries another tack: pleading on his knees. Valville then appears to revive the triangle and the symmetrical recurrence is lost on none of the players. Valville does not wait for an explanation; Marianne's hysterical reaction angers Climal, who decides to leave. Marianne is apparently again reduced to poverty and solitude. But Valville's scorn goads her into action.

Having had such success in playing with appearances, Marianne is loath to find herself defeated by them.[9] Mme Dutour would commit her to shabbiness; but Marianne sees her destiny in grander terms. She feels confident that her plan will succeed: "Premièrement, j'avais mon infortune qui était unique; avec cette infortune, j'avais de la vertu, et elles allaient si bien ensemble! Et puis j'étais jeune, et puis j'étais belle; que voulez-vous de plus?" (131). Marianne, like Moll, has a clear idea of her potential value on the marketplace. She understands how her particular attributes can be successfully parlayed. Thus she sets out to conquer Paris only to find herself in vulnerable isolation: "De cette forêt, j'aurais pu m'en tirer; mais comment sortir du désert où je me trouvais? Tout l'univers en était un pour moi, puisque je n'y tenais par aucun lien à personne" (134). This moment provides a poignant counterpoint to Marianne's earlier description of Paris when she first arrived from the country, full of hope and anticipation about her prospects in the big city: "Je ne saurais vous dire ce que je sentis en voyant cette grande ville, et son fracas, et son peuple et ses rues. C'était pour moi l'empire de la lune . . ." (17). Here the description of the crowd and the bustling city ends on the word "personne." Marianne, as Climal had predicted, is connected to no one. With no one to turn to, the "virtuous orphan"[10] retraces her steps. In a repeat performance, Marianne, (re)abandoned, confronts Paris. Helpless, she seeks help; the source of help is the same. Marianne finds the curate reluctant to protect her as he was the first time. Although she succeeds in making him at least mistrust Climal, the curate offers no consolation. Finally, wearing the same dress she wore for her first appearance in the world, Marianne enters the church of a convent to collect herself. She again attracts attention, but this time it is women who respond to her charms as she relates her story to her prospective benefactress and a prioress: "Là finit mon petit discours ou ma petite harangue, dans laquelle je ne mis point d'autre art que ma douleur, et qui fit son effet sur la dame en question" (153). Just as her "strip-tease" in church revealed just enough of her person to stimulate general interest, here Marianne's rhetorical manipulation of her history motivates compassion without unfolding the whole story. Thus, when the prioress discovers that she had been misled by Marianne's affluent appearance (in the clothes Climal had supplied), "la dame en question" is sufficiently moved to offer to pay for Marianne's expenses. Marianne can then enter the convent, which affords protection from the world, with a protectress who belongs to the world. The withdrawal, however, is to be temporary, for as Marianne announces: "Finissons . . . par un événement qui a été la cause de mon entrée dans le monde" (160). Indeed, to Marianne's great satisfaction, Valville shows up at the convent disguised, and bearing a love letter. It soon emerges that Marianne's "mother" is also Valville's mother and that a new family configuration is developing. Marianne fears that this triangle will cause her to be abandoned but Mme de Miran commits herself to Marianne: "Qu'il ne vous arrive donc plus, tant que je vivrai, de dire que vous êtes orpheline" (181). Marianne's membership in the family, through Valville or through his mother, is thus assured: Marianne is to be redefined for she is no longer unprotected. Mme de Miran accepts her son's passion for Marianne and the possibility of their marriage, regardless of the obstacles that arise: "On vient à bout de tout avec un peu de patience et d'adresse, surtout quand on a une mère comme moi pour confidente" (207).

The question that remains to be resolved, however, is whether Valville's family will tolerate the marriage despite her adoption; for although Marianne, like Pamela, considers herself to be innocuous and innocent, both are perceived as a threat to the established order: Lady *Towers* thus refers to Pamela as a "little rogue," the curate calls Marianne "la dangereuse petite créature" (141), and Mme de Miran herself: "Quelle dangereuse petite fille tu es Marianne" (200). Mme de Miran's determination to integrate Marianne into society is unexpectedly favored by a death in the family. M. de Climal falls ill suddenly and from his death bed provides Marianne with an income for life, as reparation for his bad intentions: "Je ne l'ai secourue, en effet, que pour tâcher de la séduire; je crus que son infortune lui ôterait le courage de rester vertueuse, et j'offris de lui assurer quoi vivre, à condition qu'elle devînt méprisable" (249). The terms of their previous relations are thus recapitulated in a simple equation: to succor is to seduce. His legacy transforms the old algebra: misfortune is converted to (good) fortune by his deathbed confession; Marianne's virtue is publicly validated and her success materially assured. But social difference is not so easily erased. Looking the part is not enough.

Marianne's being, her orphan-ness is still at fault. She is still without a *name*. Marianne is brought to trial before a court minister by an outraged female relative who is scandalized at the prospect of the marriage between Valville and Marianne. The question upon which the marriage turns is one of nomenclature: whether Marianne is entitled to be called *Mademoiselle*. The defense is undertaken by Mme de Miran for whom Marianne "est demoiselle autant qu'aucune fille, de quelque rang qu'elle soit, puisse l'être" by virtue of her *natural* qualities: "Il faut que cela soit dans le sang" (329). In the face of so noble a position, once Marianne realizes that she will not be obliged to marry the unsuitable suitor the other members of the family have chosen for her, she voluntarily decides to sacrifice the marriage with Valville ("Je le fais aujourd'hui par pure reconnaissance pour elle et pour son fils" [336]), and to enter a convent for the rest of her life, seeing no one but her mother. In response to her heroic gesture, the minister returns the daughter to the authority of the mother, granting Marianne the mark of recognition she had lacked: "La noblesse de vos parents est incertaine, mais celle de votre coeur est incontestable, et je la préférerais, s'il fallait opter" (337). Officially the family and society are thus obliged to recognize the legitimacy of Marianne's position. Marianne has been given a mother and this relation takes priority above all others.

During the trial itself, Marianne explicitly codes her filial attachment in the language of passionate devotion according to which the object of desire functions as raison d'être: "Je ne vivrais point si je vous perdais; je n'aime que vous d'affection; je ne tiens sur la terre qu'à vous" (335). And after the trial it becomes clear that Valville occupies a distinctly secondary place in Marianne's affective economy: "J'ai pourtant songé à M. de Valville; car s'il m'oubliait, ce serait une grande affliction pour moi, plus grande que je ne puis dire; mais le principal est que vous m'aimiez; c'est le *coeur de ma mère* qui m'est le plus nécessaire, il va avant tout dans le mien" (343; italics mine). Valville's subsequent disaffection and betrayal thus become highly predictable since he is no longer a condition of Marianne's quest.[11]

A new series of minor obstacles present themselves to the couple. Valville is to be given a post and the marriage is again postponed until the formalities are completed. The delay functions as a test for

Valville, which he fails by an excess of patience. With the full retrospective understanding of the dialectics of passion, Marianne explains
that Valville's gallantry was, in fact, proof of a change of heart: "Il
fallait apparemment que son amour ne fût plus ni sérieux, ni si fort;
et il ne me disait de si jolies choses qu'à cause qu'il commençait à
n'en plus sentir de si tendres" (348). If, however, the wisdom of the
narrator perceives the inevitability of Valville's betrayal, Marianne *in
situ* is taken unawares and responds like the sentimental heroine (she
then was) by falling desperately ill ("le transport au cerveau" [358]).
Indeed, when she learns that Valville loves another, she announces
her desire to die: "Eh! que ne me laissiez-vous mourir? Comment
voulez-vous que je vive? . . . Ah! je ne survivrai pas à ce tourment-
là, je l'espère; Dieu m'en fera la grâce, et je sens que je me meurs"
(367). But despite Marianne's determination to dramatize her misery,
her supporters refuse to see the defection as tragic; not to mention her
rival: "Quant à vous, je ne vous crois ni ambitieuse ni intéressée; et si
vous n'êtes que tendre et raisonnable, en vérité, vous ne perdez rien
. . . c'est comme si vous n'aviez point eu d'amant" (379). Mademoiselle Varthon, thus, essentially confirms the values of Marianne's
own system: since it is not *by* Valville that she can win (in) the world,
nothing is lost but misplaced feelings. And since these feelings are
not passionate, it is as though the connection had never existed. The
nun in the convent where Marianne is staying sees Valville's action
in a larger perspective: "Son infidélité est peut-être une grâce que le
ciel vous a faite; la Providence qui nous gouverne est plus sage que
nous, voit mieux ce qu'il nous faut. . . . Mettez vous bien dans
l'esprit que vous ne deviez pas épouser celui dont il est question, et
qu'assurément ce n'était pas votre destinée" (382). Although
Marianne is not entirely consoled by such reasoning, the vision of an
unknown future intrigues her: "Elle a raison . . . ceci ne décide encore de rien; je dois me préparer à d'autres événements" (385). However, what most appeals to Marianne is the effect the future will have
on Valville: "D'autres que lui m'aimeront, il le verra, et ils lui ap-
prendront à estimer mon coeur" (385). In other words, Marianne understands perfectly the fundamental principle of the game between
men and women; her only question is how to play it to best advantage.

From the beginning of her apparent defeat, Marianne senses the importance of tactics and maneuvers Valville into a position that leaves him humiliated and speechless. Her greatest satisfaction is to have made Valville regret her, so that her vengeance can appear as generosity. Although, like Merteuil, Marianne uses self-control as a means to control others,[12] she cannot aspire to self-sufficiency and must answer to Madame de Miran. It is here that Marianne's connection to her mother is consecrated, for Mme de Miran takes Marianne's part, rejects her own son ("Ah! voilà qui est fini, je ne l'estimerai de ma vie" [412]), and exclaims: "Songe que tu es pour jamais ma fille, et que je te porte dans mon coeur" (414). Once it has been clearly established that she can remain the daughter without being attached to the son, Marianne is able to embark on her own destiny: "Je suis née pour avoir des aventures, et mon étoile ne m'en laissera pas manquer" (418). Her adventures begin with a proposal of marriage from an aristocratic admirer of her virtue. But Marianne, "dégoûtée du monde" (425), contemplates the conventual life. The nun who had encouraged her before now takes over the narrative to relate her own life in order to show Marianne that she is not alone in her misery. Tervire's story, which occupies the rest of Marivaux's novel, is essentially a quest for a mother, and through that mother, security. The thematic play between the two stories—and their chiasmatic relation[13]—paradoxically confirms the reading of Marianne's trajectory as a text of filiation and af-filiation. For while Tervire's story ends when she finds her mother, the *end* of Marianne's adventures is promised but never delivered, except, of course, by her title—in the title.

Mme Riccoboni endeavors to conclude *Marianne.* In her version Valville reappears, penitent and tender, and Marianne toys with his confusion:

Mes doigts entrelacés dans les barreaux d'une grille fort noire allaient, venaient, se jouaient et ne perdaient rien à ce badinage, le bras suivait, comme de raison: ces charmes, relevés par l'air de négligence dont je les étalais, disaient à Valville: Je ne vous montre pas mes grâces pour vous les faire remarquer, je n'ai garde, je ne pense à rien; elles sont là pour tout le monde, mais elles y sont, profitez-en comme un autre (605).

This passage in fact reduplicates Marianne's initial appearance in church during which she displayed her charms, knowingly, for public consumption. The script is identical: feminine charms, specifically the hand and arm, are deliberately manipulated to entice and tantalize. What has changed is the audience: where before her performance was directed at men in general, and Valville's gaze distinguished him from all others, here Marianne is repeating her one-woman show for one man who is now the *same* as all the others. For Deloffre, "this Marianne has indeed come down in the world by lowering herself to *coquetteries* of this sort."[14] Despite Deloffre's regrets, Mme Riccoboni seems to have replicated the basic thematic structure of the novel.[15] Her Marianne leaves the reader, as did Marivaux's, with the promise of more to come: "Valville était venu, reparti; où me conduirait la démarche hardie de le renvoyer? . . . Mais avant d'entrer dans la partie la plus intéressante de ma vie, permettez-moi de me reposer un peu" (626).

The end of the novel, then, is encoded as a beginning: the point of departure for Marianne as *Mademoiselle*. And in this sense, it is plausible to imagine the terms of that career as a series of adventures in which Marianne, like the Marquise de Merteuil, would play with men to satisfy the needs of her vanity and pride. (After all, Valville *has* betrayed Marianne for another woman, and however generous she might appear, it is nonetheless revenge that she seeks.) Supported by a mother, whose sole function is to approve of her, without a constraining father or husband, possessed of an independent income, Marianne has the power to operate alone. And Marianne is an exemplary operator: "Woman," Robert Mauzi would have it, "with all her wiles, her intuition and her genius."[16] But if the Comtesse de *** demonstrates a "genius" for the analysis and manipulation of the intricacies of society's games as they are played out between men and women, young Marianne can afford only to experiment within the limits of virtuous behavior. The stamp of approval she has received from society is of too recent date to allow her the classy freedom the Marquise has inherited.

To invoke Laclos at this point, however, is to anticipate, both in our argument and historically. For if the Marivaudian universe is regulated by the equivocal, the equivocal aligns itself far more with the *équilibrisme* [17] of *Pamela* than with the irony of the *Liaisons*. [18] In the final analysis, moreover, Marianne's femininity is wedded to virtue rewarded. Although her attachment to virtue pales in comparison to Pamela's emphatic devotion, her capacity for vice is but a shadow of the real thing. Marianne is the stylish and stylized model of Rococo iconography: her most serious crime is a self-conscious wink. And we are conned into complicity if we enter the frame. The reader of Marianne's adventures, however, cannot but enter the frame, the space between promise and fulfillment. For when early in the novel Mme Dutour, counseling and consoling a distraught Marianne, recommends deferral—"promettre et tenir mène les gens bien loin"(47)—she does not only supply the maxim of the coquette, but the structure of the novel itself: each installment of the adventures explicitly or implicitly reiterates this premise of Marivaux's production. Marivaux/Marianne's promise to deliver binds the reader to the pleasure of postponement; an aristocratic pleasure which bypasses the banality of revelation, recognition, and the rules of proper closure. The enigma of origins remains intact; and the price of Marianne's "feminine" destiny, like the name of the female *destinataire* of her narrative, remains *en blanc*.

Chapter Three

THE REWARDS OF VIRTUE

Pamela

Who can find a virtuous woman? For her price is far above rubies.
The heart of her husband doth safely trust in her. . . .
                                                              —*Proverbs*

Nothing besides Chastity, with its Collateral Attendants, Truth,
Fidelity and Constancy, gives the Man a Property in the Person
he loves, and consequently endears her to him above all things.
                                        —Addison, *Spectator* no. 99

"*Tombera? tombera pas?*" Will she or won't she is the pleasure, Huysmans wrote with some lassitude, of the psychological text.[1] He was referring to the late nineteenth-century French novel of adultery starring a hesitant Marquise and a persistent Count. In the eighteenth-century English novel, the emblematic wavering is not a Marquise de Merteuil's, but Pamela's; and the Count, the would-be seducer, a less glamorous Squire B. Thus the central "psychological" suspense in *Pamela* is structured by an assiduous "courtship" of a lower-class heroine by a landed gentleman.[2] Pamela's narrative, like Marianne's, begins with an attempted seduction. And again like Marianne, Pamela refuses offers of fine clothing and financial protection in exchange for her favors, only to be rewarded for this refusal in the end by marriage and social elevation. Although Marianne's marriage takes place off the stage of the text, and to a man whose title is clearly more important than his person, the *dénouement* of her drama, no less than Pamela's, is dependent upon the external recog-

nition of an inner nobility which equalizes the prerogatives of superior rank.[3] Still, if Marianne in a 1765 edition is a *Nouvelle Paméla*,
in 1740, Richardson's Pamela is a new and very English type.[4]

Pamela's tribulations begin when she is fifteen. Working as a servant to help her family (impoverished country folk, fallen from earlier prosperity), Pamela's only experience of the world is the residence
of her employers. As the novel opens, Pamela's mistress has just died,
and she explains to her parents that as her lady had provided a
measure of education that made her "otherwise qualifed above my
degree,"[5] poor Pamela's *place* is now in question. Nonetheless,
Pamela can reassure the Andrewses; a protector will replace her
former protectress: "Well, but God's will must be done!—And so
comes the comfort, that I shall not be obliged to return back to be a
clog upon my dear parents! For my master said, I will take care of
you all, my good maidens: and for you, Pamela, (and took me by the
hand; yes, he took my hand before them all), for my dear mother's
sake, I will be a friend to you" (3–4). Mr. B. then specifies the
modalities of their friendship: Pamela is to take care of his linen. Although it is common enough for women servants to be associated
with underclothing and laundry, Pamela's handpicked assignment
will bind her inextricably to her master: her work on his waistcoat
will become the alibi for the delay that retains her in his presence.
Once the new *master/servant* relation is thus reestablished, Mr. B.
adds a personal touch: "And gave me with his own hand four golden
guineas, and some silver, which were in my old lady's pocket when
she died; and said, if I was a good girl, and faithful and diligent, he
would be a friend to me, for his mother's sake. And so I send you
these four guineas for your comfort; for Providence will not let me
want" (4). This particular sum (which Pamela with curious celerity
transfers to her parents), by its status as legacy, provides a legitimate
continuum of relations: the master's generosity appears to be motivated by simple respect for his mother. To insure the continued
exchange of money and services, Pamela has merely to prove herself
an exemplary servant ("faithful and diligent").

The postscript of her letter, however, tells a less edifying tale: the
master, Pamela relates with some distress, burst into his mother's
room where Pamela was writing, and demanded to see her letter.

First criticizing her for trying to hide the letter, then praising her handwriting and spelling, he ends this infringement upon her epistolary self by invoking his mother. Pamela's reaction is perplexity: "To be sure I did nothing but courtesy and cry, and was all in confusion, at his goodness" (5). Like Moll and Marianne before her, Pamela's initial response to mixed messages is to deny ambiguity (his) and ambivalence (hers) by citing the prerogatives of class-bound behavior.

Although Pamela's parents are separated from her in space, their moral universe is ubiquitous. Despite the fundamental impotence caused by their poverty, they are able to warn their daughter of impending danger, for they see her as a character in a well-known scenario of seduction and betrayal. Mr. Andrews, therefore, can interpret the text for his untutored daughter. The organization of his letter is a model of conventional wisdom: first an expression of regret—for the demise of the lady who had provided for Pamela in such a way that her clothing is now worthy of a "gentlewoman"—but then concern that harm could come from her being "set so above [her]self" (5). Paternal fear follows paternal pride: "Every body talks how you have come on, and what a genteel girl you are; and some say you are very pretty; and, indeed, six months since, when I saw you last, I should have thought so myself, if you was not our child" (5). Pointing out every ambiguity and drawing his own conclusions, he performs an *explication de texte*. First, the terms of the master's benevolence: "And oh, that fatal word! that he would be kind to you, if you would do *as you should do* almost kills us with fears" (6). "*As you should do*" in Mr. Andrews's rewriting, removes all doubt (Pamela's, not the reader's) as to Mr. B.'s definition of "good": Pamela is to benefit from Mr. B.'s generosity at the price of her favors. The prospect of that transaction accounts for the melodramatic lexicon of Mr. Andrews's response. Indeed, the Andrewses would prefer to "live upon the water, and, if possible, the clay of the ditches I contently dig, than live better at the price of our child's ruin" (6). And then a series of questions—why such attention, why take her hand, why read her letter, why praise her writing, why encourage her reading?—which are in fact one: why should a master take such interest in a servant. Disinterested paternalism is a contradiction in terms. The Andrewses are good hermeneuts (if Pamela isn't) and know how to interpret.

Abandoning allegory for metaphor, Mr. Andrews returns to his basic anxiety: "We *fear*—yes, my dear child, we *fear*—you should be *too* grateful,—and reward him with that jewel, your virtue, which no riches, nor favour, nor any thing in this life, can make up to you" (6). But Pamela's jewel is more than her own; it belongs, metonymically, to her family: "The loss of our dear child's virtue would be a grief that we could not bear, and would bring our grey hairs to the grave at once" (6). The economy is simple, as is the parable. The Andrewses prefer Pamela's death to their dishonor: "For we had rather see you all covered with rags, and even follow you to the churchyard, than have it said, a child of ours preferred any worldly conveniences to her virtue" (6–7). The morbid concern for appearances articulates the violence implicit in the ecology of middle-class morality: if as parents they are the authors of her life, as daughter she can be the author of their death.

When Pamela replies to her parents, she acquiesces to their rhetoric: "I will die a thousand deaths, rather than be dishonest any way . . . for although I have lived above myself for sometime past, yet I can be content with rags and poverty, and bread and water, and will embrace them, rather than forfeit my good name, let who will be the tempter" signed, "Your dutiful DAUGHTER till death" (7). She thus reinscribes their hyperbole, preferring "a thousand deaths" to the possibility of transgression, and rejecting her vestimentary elevation. The invocation of "rags," "poverty," and "bread and water"—familiar metaphors for abstinence and punishment—anticipates the allegory of the *secular* fall. It is not surprising that Pamela should end by opposing her good (parental) name and reputation to any challenger (the "tempter"), coding the worldly contest in conventional Christian paradigms.

For the time being, however, Pamela is far from wearing rags. Indeed, Mr. B. begins his campaign by giving her fine clothing. The first time, he presents her with hand-me-downs, his mother's clothing, but even so she finds it "too rich and too good for me, to be sure" (10). Still, since Mrs. Jervis, housekeeper and (apparently) protective mother figure, receives gifts of this nature as well, Pamela rationalizes the acquisition when she relates the occurrence to her parents: "O how amiable a thing is doing good!—It is all I envy great

folks for" (11). Despite her benevolent interpretation of Mr. B.'s generosity, Pamela, as did Marianne, experiences some discomfort at the
next and more intimate installment of "fine things" which includes
shoes and stockings. This gift is made in private: "I was quite as-
tonished, and unable to speak for a while; but yet I was inwardly
ashamed to take the stockings; for Mrs. Jervis was not there: If she
had, it would have been nothing" (11–12). Her surprise and silence
are but a variant of her original behavior: she does not know how to
act or what to say in the presence of so generous a master. But her
inner feelings are reflected on her face, which leads Mr. B. to re-
mark: "Don't blush, Pamela: Dost think I don't know pretty maids
should wear shoes and stockings?" (12). Confronted with proof of her
transparency, like Moll, Pamela is "confounded": ". . . So, like a
fool I was ready to cry; and went away courtesying and blushing, I am
sure, up to the ears; for, though there was no harm in what he said,
yet I did not know how to take it" (12). For reassurance, Pamela
rushes to Mrs. Jervis who explains that she is being outfitted to look
the part of a waiting maid, the place Mr. B. has promised her with
his sister. Pamela transmits that version to her parents. Nonetheless,
the reader is left with the fact of Pamela's involuntary response. Her
blushing indicates that on some level she is reading the other message. Although Mr. B. has not declared himself explicitly, Pamela,
forewarned by her parents, cannot help but wonder why he wants to
dress her and why it bothers her that he does.

   If Pamela perceives Mr. B.'s initial attempts at seduction with wary
confusion, she continues to grant him the benefit of the doubt. Ambiguity, however, is erased by certainty when he finally makes a
direct assault upon her virtue. Mr. B. finds Pamela alone, isolated
from the activity of the main house, sewing in the summer-house.
He begins, characteristically, by taking her hand, which in itself in-
duces fear and trembling. When she recovers her powers of speech,
Pamela explains that being alone in his presence, in the absence of
official business violates her sense of place. Mr. B., however, inter-
rupts her explanations to justify his position: "*Because* you are a little
fool, and know not what's good for yourself. I tell you I will make a
gentlewoman of you, if you be obliging, and don't stand in your own
light; and so saying, he put his arm about me and kissed me!" (16).

He interprets their relation in the name of (his) superior understanding, arrogating the power of discrimination in her system of values. In his perspective, Pamela has only to put herself in his hands, so to speak, and her confusion will be removed. He seals his proposition with a kiss, confirming what is implicit in "obliging" beyond the shadow of a doubt. Pamela, again as if anticipating her parents' reaction, condemns Mr. B.'s behavior and at the same time justifies her own: "I struggled and trembled, and was so benumbed with terror, that I sunk down, not in a fit, and yet not myself; and I found myself in his arms, quite void of strength; and he kissed me two or three times, with frightful eagerness" (16). The verbs describing Pamela's response to Mr. B.'s attack indicate a sequence of diminishing movement, from activity to passivity, mobility to immobility: her struggle ends with the passage to another confusing state, in which she finds herself—inexplicably—debilitated. Pamela, clearly, succumbs to the first kiss only because of the violence of the surprise attack. When she frees herself from Mr. B.'s overwhelming embrace, however, she refutes his verbal taunts ("What a foolish hussy," "foolish slut" [16–17]) with moral energy and self-assurance: "You have taught me to forget myself and what belongs to me, and have lessened the distance that fortune has made between us, by demeaning yourself, to be so free to a poor servant. Yet, sir, I will be bold to say, I am honest, though poor: and if you was a prince, I would not be otherwise" (17).

If Mr. B.'s earlier and more devious messages rendered Pamela mute, directness elicits an articulate response. Her conviction of spiritual equality (in the face of a threat to it) leads to a vigorous verbal defense that contrasts sharply with the ineffectuality of the physical one. Pamela's argument is that Mr. B. has defied the social conventions governing their relations. By his actions, the master has momentarily removed the barrier that separates him from his servant. The physical rapprochement of the literal distance between them has threatened the vertical or hierarchical axis. Mr. B. has lowered himself to Pamela's level. At the same time, Pamela claims that her own *place* (what belongs to her) has been disturbed, reiterating her confession to her parents that she had been set above herself and had lived above herself. Forgetting herself means, then, having fantasized a higher status. To Mr. B.'s perversion of values, Pamela presents a moral corrective and a reordering of priorities: spiritually, at least, the servant contains her own superiority. The master, however, persists in his self-defense: "Who would have you otherwise, you foolish slut! Cease your blubbering. I own I have demeaned myself; but it was only to try you" (17). He replies to Pamela with her own words, accepting her coding ("otherwise")—only to justify his conduct and reassert his prerogatives in the name of the power built into their relations. Finally, Mr. B. resorts to canonical behavior by trying to buy Pamela's silence with gold: in exchange for her silence, he accepts to "forgive" her. Pamela thus has another opportunity to assert herself and refuse, which she does: "I won't take the money, indeed, sir, said I, poor as I am: I won't take it," thus anticipating the signature of her letter home: "Your dutiful and honest DAUGHTER" (17).

The signatures of the letters vary according to local pressure (dutiful, distressed, afflicted) but essentially repeat "poor and honest," the lexical matrix of Pamela's text. Although those virtues are passive, Pamela is active in protecting them.[6] Obedient to her parents and obsequious with Mr. B., Pamela nonetheless prevails intact: Mr. B. continues to surprise Pamela and take liberties; she continues to protest, weep, write to her parents, and seek consolation from Mrs. Jervis. The novel is constructed on the repetition of this supervising sequence until, that is, Mr. B. recognizes that Pamela's "epic resistance"[7] has conquered him.

If the novel, as we have seen it, builds upon obvious contrasts of class and sex, that double polarization plays itself out within an equally oppositional structure of moral and sentimental values. Pamela, for her part, finds those aspects of her master's behavior he attributes to "love" perplexing: "Is it not strange, that love borders so much upon hate? But this wicked love is not like the true virtuous love, to be sure: *that* and *hatred* must be as far off, as *light* and *darkness*. And how must this hate have been increased, if he had met with such a base compliance, after his wicked will had been gratified" (49). Pamela consciously resists the collapsing of these polarities, shoring up the potential inadequacy of her personal vision with reference to the only reliable book in her library: the "Holy Writ," as she puts it, and the story of Amnon and Tamar (49).[8]

Nonetheless, in the face of Mr. B.'s incorrigibility, Pamela at last resolves to return home. At this turning point in the narrative, the author intervenes to summarize, anticipate, and point the moral: "Thus every way was the poor virgin beset: And the whole will shew the base arts of designing men to gain their wicked ends; and how much it behoves the fair sex to stand upon their guard against artful contrivances, especially when riches and power conspire against innocence and a low estate" (91). This commentary redundantly inscribes the central conflict within the eighteenth-century ritual drama of innocence and worldliness, the grammar of the *exemplum*. Each pole of the axiological opposition, of course, is subsumed by the couple *victim/victimizer*. In the sequences that follow, as Pamela becomes a prisoner on Mr. B.'s Lincolnshire estate, the question to be resolved is whether the sheer resources of her innocence can resist and overcome his strategies of corruption: "By G-d I will have her!" (56). Will he or won't he?

A persecuted maiden, Pamela begins by passively enduring her fate, consoling herself with pen and paper. But frustration and despair finally lead her to try more than letter writing in secret: she decides to escape. After successfully climbing out of a window but unsuccessfully maneuvering a brick wall, and getting hurt in the process ("My left hip and shoulder were very stiff, and full of pain, with bruises; and, besides, my head bled, and ached grievously" [179]), Pamela finds herself in front of a pond: "I crept along, till I could raise myself on my staggering feet; and away limped I!—What to do, but to throw myself into the pond, and so put a period to all my griefs in this world!" (179). The drama of her effort is underlined by its physical difficulty—the effort being all the more remarkable for her previous wounds. Here we see that delicate, blushing, and swooning Pamela can rise to the occasion when the threat is great enough; the reader's faith in her indomitability is revitalized.[9] The pond, however, offers a tempting and nonheroic solution. But before Pamela decides to reject the option of suicide for religious reasons, she indulges in a gratifying fantasy: she imagines Mr. B. finding her dead body and feeling remorse at having used her so badly:

And my master, my angry master, will then forget his resentments, and say, O, this is the unhappy Pamela! that I have so causelessly persecuted and destroyed! Now do I see she preferred her honesty to her life, will he say, and is no hypocrite, nor deceiver; but really was the innocent creature she pretended to be! Then, thought I, will he, perhaps, shed a few tears over the poor corpse of his persecuted servant (180–81).

Instead of being outraged by Mr. B.'s cruel pursuit, Pamela accepts the *legitimacy* of his behavior to the extent that she interprets his anger from and within the fixed hierarchy of power. Her death alone, by removing her from his domain, can force him to give up his anger, to take her seriously, and on *her* terms. Only on seeing her corpse will Mr. B. grant credibility to his *servant*. (The last word of her scenario completes the polarization generated by *master*.) Despite the momentary gratification afforded by this imagined revolution in sexual power politics, however, Pamela abandons what she considers a solution of weakness for a loftier vision: servitude to divine will. (Like Sade's Justine, Pamela trusts in Providence.)

This episode clearly marks a turning point in the struggle between Pamela and her master. On the one hand, Pamela begins to articulate ambivalent feelings about Mr. B. ("O what an angel would he be in my eyes yet, if he would cease his attempts, and reform!" [187]),[10] thus reversing the terms in which she habitually casts their relation; on the other, Mr. B. changes his tack: he offers Pamela a settlement. The settlement is a contract, which is reproduced as such in the text. A series of seven articles stipulates the terms of an agreement according to which Pamela would live with Mr. B. as his wife. She would reap all the benefits such an arrangement might bring for a year, after which time he would marry her if she were still satisfied. Pamela refutes the proposal point by point in favor of "the more solid ornaments of a good fame, and a chastity inviolate!" (201). Pamela's refusal stimulates Mr. B.'s final assault on her virtue in which he comes very close to rape. (He dresses himself as the servant Nan and thereby comes to bed with Pamela disguised as a woman.) But Pamela faints dead away—and so convincingly[11]—that Mr. B. is quite thoroughly discouraged.

Pamela's genuine terror seems to move Mr. B. and he devises a new strategy which, however, Pamela recognizes as such: he would *"melt"* her, she protests, "by kindness" (226). Thus, in heart-to-heart talks Mr. B. explains to Pamela how socially impossible marriage is, even though he loves her. Pamela here begins to suspect the truth of her *tolerance*: "And now I begin to be afraid I know too well the reason why all his hard trials of me, and my black apprehensions, would not let me hate him" (224). She cares for her jailer. Pamela's dilemma is both hers and her virtuous sisters': a split between official feelings—rejection, in this instance, of Mr. B.'s illicit demands—and unofficial ones—reciprocation of desire. But the refusal to acknowledge her own sexuality is not a simple matter. On one level supported by religious and conventional morality, Pamela denies the very possibility of an illicit sexual *exchange*; on another, despite her "confusion" and blushes, she denies the existence of desire in herself.[12] Such denial corresponds to the ideology governing the representation of femininity in the period: the positive heroine acknowledges sexuality slowly and reluctantly, if at all. Like the discovery of love, desire is perceived as a shock to the system, a reversal of accepted values and *idées reçues*. (It is only within the safety of imminent death, for example, that Julie confesses to her passion for Saint-Preux; and in the battle between Valmont and Mme de Tourvel, Tourvel is the last to recognize the true nature of her feelings.) Nevertheless, while it is possible to decipher the text of Pamela's inner conflict, the structure of the novel is dominated by the *externalized* struggle between Pamela and Mr. B., between virtue and vice. Since the title announces that virtue is to be rewarded, narrative resolution must come from the force opposed to Pamela. Until that transformation occurs, Pamela remains prisoner not only of Mr. B., but of her own ignorance.

Unlike Marianne, whose first brush with sexual aggression leaves her heart intact, Pamela has the difficult task of reconciling sexuality and love. *Pamela* (in this more like *Julie*) can be divided thematically into two parts: the first dominated by a daughter's confrontation with (aggressive) male sexuality, the second by her transformation from daughter to wife and the testing of marriage as integrator of sexuality.[13] Pamela's recognition of her true feelings for Mr. B. proceeds by stages but is stimulated by her release as a prisoner from Mr. B.'s estate: "I think I was loath to leave the house. Can you believe it?—What could be the matter with me, I wonder?—I felt something so strange, and my heart was so lumpish!—I wonder what ailed me!—But this was so *unexpected!*" (256). The alternation of rhetorical questions and exclamations signals the confusion of first love, and specifically its surprise. When Mr. B. writes to reveal the extent of his feelings for her (*his* surprise [258–59]), Pamela is provided with a clue to her discomfort: "For I know not *how* it came, nor *when* it began; but crept, crept it has, like a thief, upon me; and before I knew what was the matter, it looked like love" (260). For Pamela, then, love made her its victim by a sneak attack, and she maintains the alibi of ignorance: literally, she did not see it coming. Like Julie, she overestimated her ability to defend herself as she perceives, for the first time, her own vulnerability: "I am sorry to find this trial so sore upon me; and that all the weakness of my weak sex, and tender years, who never before knew what it was to be so touched, is come upon me, and too mighty to be withstood by me" (260–61). Pamela's acknowledgement of her change of heart, her acceptance of the existence of positive feelings for Mr. B., initiates the transformation that Mr. B's second letter will complete. It is only by having gone so far within herself that she can make the decision to trust her master.

Even before the actual marriage takes place (the *official* resolution of the social opposition), the polarization that opposed Pamela and Mr. B. sexually begins to be neutralized upon Mr. B.'s initiative. He announces the change that has taken place in him: "I do own to you, my Pamela, said he, that I love you with a purer flame than ever I knew in my whole life; a flame to which I was a stranger" (279).[14] Thus while he takes Pamela into his world socially, morally he accedes to hers: "Your virtue was proof against all temptations, and was not to be awed by terrors: Wherefore, as I could not conquer my passion for you, I corrected myself, and resolved, since you would not be mine upon my terms, you should upon your own: and now I desire you not on any other, I assure you" (315). Despite reassurances of this sort, Pamela fears marriage both because she feels unworthy of her master and because marriage represents the unknown, independence, and implicitly, the sexual connection: "To be left to my own conduct, a frail bark in a tempestuous ocean, without ballast, or other pilot than my own inconsiderate will" (349–50).[15] It is precisely Pamela's *distrust* of herself (once betrayed), that must be corrected before the marriage takes place.

Mr. B., confronted with Pamela's "sweet confusion" (351) in the face of their impending marriage, tries to assure her that the terms of their relation have been reversed: "You have a generous friend, my dear girl, in me; a protector now, not a violator of your innocence" (351). Mr. B. becomes that which he once claimed to be. And suspecting that it is in Pamela's sexual fears that the problem lies, he restates the change that she has worked in him: "After having been long tossed by the boisterous winds of a more culpable passion, I have now conquered it, and am not so much the victim of your beauty, all charming as you are, as of your virtue" (360). Saint-Preux expresses himself in similar terms to explain the change that has occurred in him: "J'ai vécu dans l'orage, et c'est toujours vous qui l'avez excité. . . . Toujours vous exercez le même empire, mais son effet est tout opposé; en réprimant les transports que vous causiez autrefois, cet empire est plus grand, plus sublime encore." In both cases the object of desire is perceived to have a dual empire, the capacity to evoke passion through beauty and admiration through virtue. The repression of the effects of the first in favor of the second is presented as a victory of which the subject is proud and as a tribute to the source of inspiration. Thus the conversion of guilty passion to sublimated admiration is the process that finally makes a positive relation possible for the first time. From Pamela's point of view, however, this transformation is not a function of her power but of Divine will: "And thus the dear, once naughty assailer of her innocence, by a blessed turn of Providence, is become the kind, the generous protector and rewarder of it" (364). Marriage as sacred confirmation of a superior plan thus allows the continuance of innocence.

Between the wedding ceremony and the wedding night—"This happy, yet awful moment" (372)—Pamela takes a walk with Mrs. Jewkes (now her servant and ally) and reflects upon the change that has occurred in her life: "What a different aspect every thing in and about this house bears now, to my thinking, to what it once had! The garden, the pond, the alcove, the elm-walk. But, oh! my prison is become my palace; and no wonder every thing wears another face!" (369). In the face of the definitive transition she is about to undergo, Pamela redundantly states her perception of maximum difference. Her recognition that what once was threatening is not only defused, but a source of protection, is the necessary preparation for her new state. Once Pamela is married and the sexual initiation a (euphemized) fact, the social adjustment remains the only obstacle to perfect happiness. Pamela has yet to be accepted by the society she has married into. The social opposition is mediated by the person of Lady Davers, Mr. B.'s sister. In one very long scene, whose function is analogous to Marianne's trial, Pamela is subjected to humiliations until Mr. B. intervenes, forcing his sister to desist. His arguments are based on two interlocking premises: that his marrying Pamela automatically raises her—"a man ennobles the woman he takes, be she *who* she will; and adopts her into his *own* rank, be it *what* it will" (447)—and that Pamela contains her own nobility: "For beauty, virtue, prudence, and generosity too, I will tell you, she has more than any lady I ever saw. Yes, Lady Davers, she has all these *naturally*; they are *born* with her; and a few years' education, with her genius, has done more for her, than a whole life has done for others" (448). Mr. B.'s energetic defense of Pamela, when contrasted with Valville's passivity toward and eventual detachment from Marianne, underscores the difference in the ideological orientation of the two novels: Pamela's destiny is to be installed in marriage, her virtue to be rewarded by the man who threatened it. For Marianne, virtue is also rewarded by the man who threatened it but that man is M. de Climal and not her prospective husband. Her destiny is to be recognized by aristocratic society so that she can reap the benefits of her merits independently. However, in both cases rewards begin with society's recognition of the heroines' *spiritual* superiority.

Pamela's ascent is consolidated by the return to the Bedfordshire house where her narrational life began. Once servant to the mistress of the estate, she returns as its mistress: "And oh, what a delightful change was this journey, to that which, so contrary to all my wishes, and so much to my apprehensions, carried me hence to the Lancashire house! And how did I bless God at every turn, and at every stage!" (486). It only remains for Pamela to make a solitary visit to the summerhouse—the scene of Mr. B.'s first violence to her virtue—to measure the distance she has come. The places of danger are now neutralized by the transformational properties of legitimacy, of marriage.[16]

The programmatic status of Richardson's fiction announced in the title—*Pamela: or Virtue Rewarded*—is recapitulated at the end of the novel in a series of "brief observations" designed to "serve as so many applications of its most material incidents to the minds of YOUTH of BOTH SEXES" (530). The reader is summoned by the author to an exegesis, an elucidation of the parable, and exhorted to model his or her behavior accordingly. The efficacy of the *exemplum*, of course, is dependent (tautologically) upon the exemplary trajectory of its hero: if one is to reap Pamela's rewards, one must emulate Pamela herself. Nothing (to return to our point of departure), it would seem, could be further from Marivaux's "intention" in publishing *Marianne*. Her life and name are given as equivalent to *adventures* and that rubric, we may infer from the "avertissement" which frames the novel, evokes the frivolous. Taking a stand against the public taste which "ne veut dans les aventures que les aventures mêmes," however, the publisher promotes his writer for her *reflexive* posture, due, he speculates, to her retreat from the world: "situation qui rend l'esprit sérieux et philosophique." Unlike Richardson's overtly authorial interventions, if there is a message adumbrated in Marivaux's novel, it is inseparable from the code delivering it, from a discourse of sociability in turn inseparable from Marianne's voice: "d'une écriture de femme." That voice of feminine experience, moreover, pronounces on the ways of the world less to reform it than elegantly to mock it. But whatever the modalities of register, the graphs of the two destinies are symmetrical by the clarity of their upward curves. In the face of obstacles, Marianne looks to her destiny and Pamela looks to Providence; nevertheless, secular or Christian, elevation structures both patterns. Trial by humiliation is at last compensated by the rewards of innocence; Marianne and Pamela emerge as Cinderella figures: Marianne gets the fairy godmother, Pamela the prince.[17] These optimistic fairy tales that chart, we like to think, the daydreams of servant girls, that celebrate the victory of what Richardson calls at the end of *Pamela* the "social virtues," invited instant parody. *Pamela*, of course, more than *Marianne* (protected by its unfinished status and the ambiguous wit of its morality) became an immediate target for Fielding, Cleland, and Sade. Although Pamela's success has not been rewritten as serious literature, it remains the blueprint for bestsellers: programs for women only.

Chapter Four

A HARLOT'S PROGRESS: II

Fanny Hill

> *Nous vivons tous, depuis bien des années, au royaume du prince
> Mangogul: en proie à une immense curiosité pour le sexe, obstinés
> à le questionner, insatiables à l'entendre et à en entendre parler,
> prompts à inventer tous les anneaux magiques qui pourraient
> forcer sa discrétion.*
>   —Michel Foucault, *La volonté de savoir.*

Unlike *La Vie de Marianne* and *Moll Flanders*, where prefatory material provides a summary of the story to come and the key to its *mode
d'emploi*, *Fanny Hill* offers the reader no more than a name and a
suggestive subtitle: *Memoirs of a Woman of Pleasure.*[1] Consequently,
as narrator, Fanny herself must account for the authenticity of her
text. And so she begins with what one might call the standard operating procedures of the fictional memoir. Just as Marianne writes to a
female friend "dont le nom est en blanc" as an obligation ("Mais
enfin, puisque vous voulez que j'écrive mon histoire, et que c'est une
chose que vous demandez à mon amitié, soyez satisfaite: j'aime encore mieux vous ennuyer que de vous refuser"), and with some reluctance, fearful that to transcribe her story will undercut its impact ("Il
est vrai que l'histoire en est particulière, mais je la gâterai, si je
l'écris; car où voulez-vous que je prenne un style?"), Fanny writes to
an anonymous "Madam" to fulfill a request—"I sit down to give you
an undeniable proof of my considering your desires as indispensable
orders"[2]—promising to adopt a style that reproduces her life *mimetically*: "I shall . . . use no farther apology, than to prepare you for

seeing the loose part of my life, wrote with the same liberty that I led it" (15). But where Marianne, like Moll, withholds her own name ("N'oubliez pas que vous m'avez promis de ne jamais dire qui je suis; je ne veux être connue que de vous"), Fanny announces hers: "My maiden name was FRANCES HILL. I was born at a small village near Liverpool in Lancashire, of parents extremely poor, and, I piously believe, extremely honest" (16).

Honesty would seem to run in the family. Fanny's attachment to the truth requires the revelation of all pertinent details: "I will not so much as take the pains to bestow the strip of a gauze wrapper on it, but paint situations such as they actually rose to me in nature, careless of violating those laws of decency that were never made for such unreserved intimacies as ours" (15). Fanny justifies the relation of "the scandalous stages" of her life because she is privileged in having "emerged, at length, to the enjoyment of every blessing in the power of love, health, and fortune to bestow" and this "whilst yet in the flower of youth" (15).[3]

Fanny's story begins as that of many a poor-but-honest maiden:

> My education, till past fourteen, was no better than very vulgar; reading, or rather spelling an illegible scrawl, and a little ordinary plain-work composed the whole system of it: and then all my foundation in virtue was no other than a total ignorance of vice, and the shy timidity general to our sex, in the tender stage of life when objects alarm or frighten more by their novelty than anything else: but then this is a fear too often cured at the expense of innocence, when Miss, by degrees, begins no longer to look on a man as a creature of prey that will eat her (16).

Like Moll, Fanny's education in matters or morals is a non-education; innocence is only a function of ignorance. And like Moll again, Fanny codes the vicissitudes of her own experience within the text of the feminine condition in general.

The moral vacuum might not have been disastrous if Fanny had not lost her natural protectors, but: "I was now entering my fifteenth year, when the worst of ills befell me in the loss of my fond tender parents, who were both carried off by the smallpox, within a few days of each other; my father dying first, and thereby hastening the death of my mother, so that I was now left an unhappy friendless orphan . . ." (16). One misfortune engenders another: thus, when Fanny goes to London to "SEEK MY FORTUNE" (17) in the company of a more experienced friend, she is soon betrayed: "left thus alone, absolutely destitute and friendless" (19).

Though twice abandoned, Fanny is spurred on by the story of Pamela's success[4] as reported by the worldly-wise Esther Davis:

As how several maids out of the country had made themselves and all their kin forever, that by preserving their VIRTUE, some had taken so with their masters that they had married them, and kept them coaches, and lived vastly grand, and happy, and some, mayhap, came to be duchesses: Luck was all, and why not I as well as another (17).

Needless to say, although poor and honest like Pamela to begin with, this is not the text of Fanny's success. A penniless orphan, her adventures begin with a search for employment. As we saw with Marianne, not only are the opportunities for work extremely restricted, but the job search itself is an obstacle course to the preservation of virtue. Fanny, for her part, less proud than the "virtuous orphan," looks for a place as a maid, and in her naiveté is hired by the madam of a brothel. With these givens, and the anticipatory information of the title of her memoirs, the advent of her sexual initiation is highly predictable. But where Moll draws the curtains of modesty, restricting the reader's view of her sexuality to its *consequences*, Fanny exposes the *process* of her sexualization. In fact, the text itself is precisely a text of exposure: it reveals what is covert in the more polite fiction of the period.[5]

Like Marianne and Pamela, Fanny is given a set of clothing appropriate to her new role, provided by her prospective protector and seducer: the man who is to take possession of that "perishable commodity . . . a maidenhead" (29). When the "rigging . . . out" (29) process is completed Fanny contemplates her new self: "When it was over, and I viewed myself in the glass, I was, no doubt, too natural, too artless, to hide my childish joy at the change; a change, in the real truth, for much the worse, since I must have much better become the neat easy simplicity of my rustic dress than the awkward, untoward, tawdry finery that I could not conceal my strangeness to" (29). Fanny, like Marianne, with the ironic distance of retrospection, can perceive the superimposition of the two selves: the rustic innocent dressed as sophisticated woman of the world.[6] But at this moment of the narrative, young Fanny is not in a position to revel in the pleasures of the sophisticated narrator: "Well then, dressed I was, and little did it then enter into my head that all this gay attire was no more than decking the victim out for sacrifice whilst I innocently attributed all to mere friendship and kindness in the sweet good Mrs. Brown" (30). For, despite her initial exposure to sexuality at the hands of Phoebe (Mrs. Brown's assistant), Fanny is still operating as an innocent.

Mrs. Brown encourages Fanny to accept her new provider: "That he would make my fortune if I would be a good girl and not stand in my own light . . . that I should trust his honour . . . that I should be made forever" (33). These are exactly the terms and the language of Mr. B.'s proposition to Pamela; and again the verbal cliché announces the narrative cliché. Fanny fights off the first attack on her virginity, but as she explains: "Neither virtue nor principles had the least share in the defence I had made, but only the particular aversion I had conceived against the first brutal and frightful invader of my virgin innocence" (37). Fanny, like Moll, in the mimesis of truthful narration, is careful to separate the motives of her behavior; distinguishing, as it were, unflattering fact from flattering fiction. As an innocent, however, Fanny casts her seducer in the canonically negative terms of his role; and as if to justify her fragility, falls ill: "into a kind of delirious doze, out of which I waked late in the morning, in a violent fever: a circumstance which was extremely critical to relieve me, at least for a time, from the attacks of a wretch, infinitely more terrible to me than death itself" (38). Still a virgin, Fanny is entitled to the privileges of literary virtue: the brain fever of the pathetic, oppressed heroine. And she can articulate the vision of sexual aggression as a fate worse than death that sustains Pamela in her struggle.

Fanny makes a rapid recovery, however, and soon comes to desire "the ceremony of initiation" (39). As she explains, her attitude changed: "Conversation, example, all, in short, contributed, in that house, to corrupt my native purity, which had taken no root in education; whilst now the inflammable principle of pleasure, so easily fired at my age, made strange work within me, and all the modesty I was brought up in the habit (not the instruction) of, began to melt away like dew before the sun's heat; not to mention that I made a vice of necessity, from the constant fears I had of being turned out to starve" (39). Now faced with examples of immodest behavior, her mind cannot refute the evidence of her body; and her temperament further undermines her flimsy moral preparation. Fanny's use of metaphor here as elsewhere functions in direct counterpoint to the banality of the event at hand, dramatizing (and sentimentalizing) her maidenhood. Finally, however, and almost as an afterthought, Fanny adds to the euphemic tableau of innocence the logic of poverty: like Moll's "but that by the way." But the benefit of hindsight undercuts an overly self-righteous stance as she confesses: "Nothing . . . was wanting to . . . prevent my going out anywhere to get better advice. Alas! I dreamed of no such thing" (40). Fanny, by now, is hooked; and like Moll, she rushes to her ruin.

Her first complete experience of heterosexual intercourse is vicarious: she watches with her initiatrix through a crevice in a panel:

For my part, I will not pretend to describe what I felt all over me during this scene; but from that instant, adieu all fears of what man could do unto me; they were now changed into such ardent desires, such ungovernable longings, that I would have pulled the first of that sex that should present himself, by the sleeve, and offered him the bauble, which I now imagined the loss of would be a gain I could not too soon procure myself" (49).

This voyeuristic prelude marks the beginning of Fanny's career as a woman of pleasure. Although Fanny will continue to account for her experience in the rhetoric of both sentimental and preromantic fiction, the valorization of the underlying premises of those fictions undergoes a radical transformation. Here, for example, her precious jewel, her maidenhood, is now a trinket she would gladly give up. Loss is transformed into gain, however, since her jewel can buy other treasures and pleasures which, like Mme de Merteuil in her youth, Fanny is burning to *know*. The sight of passion has turned her into an insatiable flame. Phoebe tries to relieve her but as Fanny puts it: "For my part, I now pined for more solid food, and promised tacitly to myself that I would not be put off much longer with the foolery of woman to woman" (51). Fanny's instinctive penchant for pleasure reads as a euphoric text of *libertinage*; her sexuality is not *bound* to an antisocial *system* of eroticism. As a result, throughout the novel a tension between two competing poles—sentimental (Richardsonian) teleology and fantasmatic (Sadian) repetition—is maintained.

Fanny, therefore, is saved from receiving the "essential specific" from just any male: "Love itself took charge of the disposal of me, in spite of interest, or gross lust" (51). She comes upon her man at dawn where he is sleeping off the effects of a night of reveling and it is love at first sight: "No! no term of years, no turn of fortune could ever erase the lightning-like impression his form made on me. . . . Yes! dearest object of my earliest passion, I command forever the remembrance of thy first appearance to my ravished eyes . . . it calls thee up, present; and I see thee now!" (52). Like Psyche fascinated by the beauty of sleeping Cupid's form, Fanny is compelled by the enchanting beauty of her Adonis (as she calls him).

Until the actual moment of her defloration, then, Fanny speaks the language of love's victim: "Past or future were equally out of the question with me. The present was as much as all my powers of life were sufficient to bear the transport of without fainting. . . . I was drove to it by a passion too impetuous for me to resist, and I did what I did because I could not help it" (56). Love as *fatum* prepares the inevitable end, which Fanny alternately fears and yearns for: "I wished, I doted, I could have died for him; and yet, I know not how or why, I dreaded the point which had been the object of my fiercest wishes; my pulses beat fears, amidst a flush of the warmest desires. This struggle of the passions, however, this conflict betwixt modesty and lovesick longings, made me burst again into tears" (57). As we saw with Marianne, the sentimental heroine struggles with the double bind of fear and desire. For Fanny, although the dilemma is manifested in physiological terms, the conflict between opposing forces is nonetheless resolved by tears. In most eighteenth-century novels, the act of defloration, while the event toward or away from which the narrative moves, is euphemized, often to the point of silence. In *Fanny Hill*, on the contrary, the act is uncovered and indeed exploited.

Although readers like Leo Braudy describe the erotic topography of *Fanny Hill* as an "unspoiled Eden," and thus as "part of the natural,"[7] the parallels between Cleland's text and Sade's deliberately unnatural (or at least supernatural) universe are difficult to ignore. To the extent that both Cleland and Sade make explicit what is implicit in the sentimental inscription of the war between the sexes, it seems appropriate to zero in briefly on a moment in its unveiling. Below are juxtaposed Fanny's account of her defloration, and Justine's.[8]

And, drawing out the engine of love assaults, drove it currently, as at a ready-made breach. Then! then! for the first time, did I feel that stiff horn-hard gristle, battering against the tender part. . . . Applying then the point of his machine to the slit, . . . then driving on with fury, its prodigious stiffness, thus impacted, wedgelike, breaks the union of those parts. . . . He improved his advantage, and . . . forcibly deepens his penetration; but put me to such intolerable pain, from the separation of the sides of that soft passage by a hard thick body, I could have screamed out. . . . At length, the tender texture of that tract giving way to such fierce tearing and rending, he pierced somewhat further into me: and now, outrageous and no longer his own master, but borne headlong away by the fury and over-mettle of that member, now exerting itself with a kind of native rage, he breaks in . . . and one violent merciless lunge sent it, imbrued, and reeking with virgin blood, up to the very hilt in me. . . . I screamed out, and fainted away with the sharpness of the pain (58–59).

In his fury the monster lashes out against the altar at which he cannot speak his prayers. . . . [T]he chastened flesh yields, the gate cedes, the ram bursts through; terrible screams rise from my throat; the entire mass is swiftly engulfed, and darting its venom . . . the snake gives ground. . . . Never in my life have I suffered so much. . . . His weapon is raised and trained upon me . . . in a fury, he rattles the temple's porticos, he is soon at the sanctuary. . . . Not content to be master of the place, he wishes to reduce it to a shambles. Such terrible attacks, so new to me, cause me to succumb; but unconcerned for my pain, the cruel victor thinks of nothing but increasing his pleasure. . . . I fall back upon the throne which has just been the scene of my immolation, no longer conscious of my existence save through my pain and my tears . . . my despair and my remorse.[9]

In both accounts, the description of penetration is coded—no one is surprised—by martial metaphors. In a series of cruel assaults, the aggressor wreaks destruction upon his female adversary by deploying a weapon of propulsion. The feminine response, symmetrically, is coded as a military topography: the vulnerable territory under attack gives way to the invader. But if Cleland's epic favors the glory of the battlefield—once more unto the breach—by superposing the language of sacrilege on the language of military violence, Sade underscores the symbolic stakes of the intervention: his gates are not only the gates of war, but the entrance to the *temple*, which contains the altar and the sanctuary. Defloration becomes desecration. Justine never recovers from her immolation, but Fanny is saved by profane love. Unlike Justine, who remains the passive object of a masculine will to domination by the powers of the phallus, Fanny becomes a desiring subject animated by the "longitudinal fallacy."[10] For Charles, despite the violence he has done Fanny, is not a Sadian libertine: "When I recovered my senses, I found myself undressed and in bed, in the arms of the sweet relenting murderer of my virginity, who hung mourning tenderly over me, holding in his hand a cordial, which, coming from the still dear author of so much pain, I could not refuse" (59–60). Fanny has been mutilated and murdered, but the metaphor is converted from negativity to positivity since the murderer is antonymically sweet and penitent. The death of virginity, moreover, soon is viewed as rite of passage to another realm: ". . . after a few enjoyments had numbed and blunted the sense of the smart . . . I arrived at excess of pleasure through excess of pain. But, when successive engagements had broke and inured me, I began to enter into the true unallayed relish of that pleasure of pleasures" (61).

If, however, in the effusion of first love, Fanny seizes the day with sublime confidence—"Or, what were all fears of the consequence, put in the scale of one night's enjoyment, of anything so transcendently the taste of my eyes and heart, as that delicious, fond, matchless youth?" (62)—in time she becomes subject to the literary laws of feminine anxiety: "I could not dispel the gloom of impatience and tender fears which gathered upon me, and which our timid sex are apt to feel in proportion to their love" (69). Fanny gives herself over completely to the love of her life: "He was the universe to me, and all that was not him was nothing to me" (72). And Charles demonstrates his acceptance of such a role by molding Fanny to his taste: he instructs her not only in the ways of love, but "in a great many points of life that I was, in consequence of my no-education, perfectly ignorant of" (73). In her eagerness to please her man, Fanny is the perfect pupil. Under Charles's tutelage, she loses her country ways. True to the economy of romance, Fanny is ready to sacrifice all in gratitude for her lover's affections: "I could have made a pleasure of the greatest toil, and worked my fingers to the bone, with joy, to have supported him" (73). Illicit love, however, must be punished. At the height of the idyll, "the barbarity of . . . fate" deals the "mortal, the unexpected blow of separation" (74). Charles's family removes him from Fanny's presence so that he might pursue a more appropriate path of fortune.[11] Fanny, again in her role as sentimental heroine, "fainted away, and after several successive fits, all the while wild and senseless, I miscarried of the dear pledge of my Charles's love: but the wretched never die when it is fittest they should die, and women are hard-lived to a proverb" (76). True to another proverb of the feminine text, a long illness ensues. But Fanny (to her regret) recovers: "My health returned to me, though I still retained an air of grief, dejection, and languour, which, taking off the ruddiness of my country complexion, rendered it rather more delicate and affecting" (76–77).

Fanny, now looking the victim's part as a result of her double loss, enters the cycle of retribution that follows wrongdoing in eighteenth-century novels of vice and virtue. The motherly landlady, who nursed Fanny back to health, insists on payment, threatening Fanny with prison and providing her with the means (a man) to discharge her debt. Fanny accepts him with a sense of fatality—"lifeless and indifferent to everything" (80). After he makes love to her for the first time, she is seized with remorse "for having suffered, on that bed, the embraces of an utter stranger. I tore my hair, wrung my hands, and beat my breast like a madwoman" (81). Fanny, however, survives this bereavement too; for as she comments: "Violent passions seldom last long, and those of women least of any" (81). Like Moll, Fanny often seeks to explain and justify behavior which she herself recognizes as reprehensible in a woman: "But our virtues and our vices depend too much on our circumstances; unexpectedly beset as I was, betrayed by a mind weakened by a long and severe affliction, and stunned with the horrors of a jail, my defeat will appear the more excusable, since I certainly was not present at, or a party in any sense, to it" (81).

The second time, however, having taken an aphrodisiac, Fanny has a more sophisticated dilemma to resolve:

All my animal spirits then rushed mechanically to that centre of attraction, and presently, inly warmed, and stirred as I was beyond bearing, I lost all restraint, and yielding to the force of the emotion, gave down, *as mere woman*, those effusions of pleasure, which, in the strictness of still faithful love, I could have wished to have kept in. Yet oh! what an immense difference did I feel between this impression of a pleasure merely animal, and struck out of the collision of the sexes by a passive bod-

ily effect, from that sweet fury, that rage of active delight which crowns the enjoyments of a mutual love passion . . . (84–85; italics mine).

Fanny distinguishes carefully between the biological urge experienced as *mere woman*, the uncontrollable part of herself, and the true
passion of *love*. (Similarly, though in a loftier register, Marianne
compared the instinctual coquetterie of all women to please, with her
specific desire to please Valville. In both cases, however, the natural
impulses of women as a sex are negatively coded.) Fanny castigates
herself for her failure to be more than mere woman. And having betrayed the bonds of fidelity by base pleasure, she accepts the implications of an inferior destiny: "As soon as he was gone, I felt the usual
consequence of the first launch into vice (for my love attachment to
Charles never appeared to me in that light). I was instantly borne
away down the stream, without making back to the shore" (86).
"The first launch into vice" produces an inevitable trajectory.

Fanny becomes a kept woman: "And by this means I got into a
circle of acquaintance that soon stripped me of all the remains of
bashfulness and modesty which might be yet left of my country education, and were, to a just taste, perhaps, the greatest of my charms"
(88). In her new incarnation, Fanny remains faithful to her protector
until she is betrayed; then takes revenge by indulging herself with a
local messenger boy. But "imprudent neglect" (108) leads to discovery. Her contract is revoked and she is, for the first time, on her own
"turned loose upon the town, to sink or swim, as I could manage
with the current of it" (113). Fanny prepares to embark on a "new
profession" and with this ends the first letter.

For the first half of the novel, Fanny is primarily characterized as a
sentimental heroine whose experience of sexuality by ever increasing
degrees makes her typologically different from her counterparts. Nevertheless, her sexual appetite and capacity for pleasure are maintained
formally within the thematic structure of the sentimental education
in which a young girl from the provinces is initiated into society.
Until this point Fanny has been in protected situations (kept by
men). The division of the novel into two parts, two installments of a
long letter, underscores the change to come. The second letter, as in
La Vie de Marianne, begins by a *re*motivation. The narrator sepa-

rates herself from the object of the narration and comments on the
problems of describing her sort of life "whose bottom, or groundwork
being, in the nature of things, eternally one and the same . . . there
is no escaping a repetition of near the same images, the same figures,
the same expressions" (115). But if the courtesan's text inevitably becomes redundant, it is redundant in a particular way. The reader is
invited to perceive difference within the sameness because Fanny registers a sense of progress before each adventure. Although the educative component of sexual exploration is a *topos* in the novel of erotic
Bildung, in Fanny's case the impulse to self-knowledge seems more
than rhetorical strategy. Braudy writes: "Fanny is fascinated by the
physiology of sexual reactions not merely because Cleland wants to
stimulate his readers but also because, in the development of her own
character, she wants to know. Sexuality is a possible and much ne-
glected way into knowledge of the self."[12]

Fanny must *learn* about "this new stage of my profession . . .
passing thus from a private devotee to pleasure into a public one"
(116). This phase of her education takes place under the auspices of
Mrs. Cole, her "gouvernante" (113) and "faithful preceptress" (203),
from whom Fanny discovers that it is the tradition of the trade to enter
as a "virgin," that, "in the loss of a fictitious maidenhead, I should
reap all the advantages of a native one" (116). On the evening during
which Fanny is to be introduced to the habitués of the house, the
program consists of each woman's relating to the audience the manner in which "she first exchanged the maiden state for womanhood"
(121). (Fanny is exempt by virtue of her "titular maidenhead" and
Mrs. Cole by her age.) Each girl tells her story, after which she and
her partner of the evening make love in front of the audience. By the
time it is Fanny's turn to be introduced to her companion, she has,
like the first time, been stimulated by voyeurism. When she stands
undressed, on display, she explains: "I had not, however, so
thoroughly renounced all innate shame as not to suffer great confusion at the state I saw myself in" (149). The enthusiastic response,[13]
however, restores her composure: "I might flatter myself with having
passed my examination with the approbation of the learned" (149).
Again initiation is cast as education; the brothel becomes an institution of higher learning. Having completed the entrance require-

ments, she is admitted in good standing: "for that time, or indeed any other, unless I pleased, I was to go through no further trials, and that I was now consummately initiated, and one of them" (152).

Fanny's gallant of the night wants to take care of her but, in a replay of the first situation, his father sends him away. Although Mrs. Cole looks out for Fanny in her "widowhood," Fanny feels "fated to be my own caterer in this, as I had been in my first trial of the market" (154). Thus the structure of Part II self-consciously replicates that of Part I. This time, however, while waiting to be supplied with a provider, Fanny goes out on the street and attracts one. Still it is the landlady who arranges the counterfeit defloration. When her lover awakes, he finds the bedsheets stained: "The illusion was complete, no other conception entered his head but that of his having been at work upon an unopened mine; which idea . . . redoubled at once his tenderness for me, and his ardour for breaking it wholly up" (165). This lover, then, reenacts the behavior of Charles, the true initiator; and the recurrence of the same expression (the mine to be destroyed) reiterates the original polarization. The male is "like a cock clapping his wings over his downtrod mistress;"[14] the female, "the deep wounded, breathless, frightened, undone, no longer maid" (166). Fanny admits to a "faintish sense" of pleasure but maintains professional detachment: "I had no taste for the person I was suffering the embraces of, on a pure mercenary account; and then, I was not entirely delighted with myself for the jade's part I was playing, whatever excuses I might plead for my being brought into it; but then this insensibility kept me so much the mistress of my mind and motions, that I could the better manage so close a counterfeit, through the whole scene of deception" (166). Fanny, by now, can make many distinctions in her experience of sexuality: the passion of true love which is reserved for Charles; the exercise of animality, sheer pleasure when she has chosen her companion; and then her professional responsibilities which make sex a mere physical performance for which she has little enthusiasm and some guilt.

With time, however, Fanny accepts (indeed embraces) the vicissitudes of her destiny: "no condition of life is more subject to revolutions than that of a woman of pleasure" (172). Nevertheless, she establishes a hierarchy among her companions in vice and would separate herself in spirit from the literal truth of the stereotype. If, for example, her companions indulge in "criminal" acts, Fanny—with hindsight—indulges in self-serving moral commentary: "It will add, too, one more example of thousands, in confirmation of the maxim, that when women get out of compass, there are no lengths of licentiousness that they are not capable of running" (190). Fanny thus reinscribes the ideology of the text: the first step leads directly to the path of insatiable vice. But Fanny's attention to self-preservation—"I found a secret satisfaction in respecting myself, as well as preserving the life and freshness of my complexion" (184)—is an attempt to defy the maxim, to control her destiny despite the rigors of the scenario.

Indeed, Fanny's final incarnation as a woman of pleasure does not take place under Mrs. Cole's (that "severe enemy to the seduction of innocence" [203]) protection; she retires to the country. With money put aside, Fanny sets herself up with a "new character of a young gentlewoman, whose husband was gone to sea," and waits "without impatience for what the chapter of accidents might produce in my favour" (204). Fanny, like Moll, establishes the potential for a scene, but then waits for it to happen. However resourceful and experienced as adventuresses, they both claim to need a man in order to attain independence. Inevitably, moreover, the status of (autonomous) subject proves to be a doubly mediated one: Fanny and Moll cease to circulate as objects only when they are integrated within the family; neutralized by the bourgeois and Protestant morality that officially underwrites the English memorial novel as genre: the "spiritual" autobiography.

For Fanny, integration begins when in the face of prosperity loneliness leads to a reordering of values, a change of heart which terminates in marital bliss and familial harmony. Fanny's last adventure as a woman of pleasure occurs with an older gentleman. (He resembles Moll's gentleman from Bath, with the difference that Fanny, consistently luckier than Moll, obtains from him the financial security she had been seeking.) This relationship, as was the initial one with Charles, is doubled by an educative process: "From him it was I first learned, to any purpose, and not without infinite pleasure, *that I had such a portion of me worth bestowing some regard on;* from him I received my first essential encouragement and instructions, how to put it in that train of cultivation, which I have since pushed to the little degree of improvement you see it at" (206; italics mine). When the "rational pleasurist" (206) dies, and leaves Fanny at the head of a large fortune,[15] when she seems to have everything she ever wanted personal happiness becomes her concern: "My regret was a mighty and just one, since it had my only truly beloved Charles for its object" (207). Fanny here returns to her original vision of Charles and maintains, as does Manon to Des Grieux, that despite "all my personal infidelities, not one had made a pin's point impression on a heart impenetrable to the true love-passion, but for him" (207). Dismissing the contingencies of the flesh, Fanny celebrates the integrity of the spirit. In this Fanny, like Manon, demonstrates the time-worn paradox of the prostitute: the gold digger has a heart of gold.

Fanny's last adventure takes her to the country, where she hopes to fulfill two goals—to show off her success and to be a benefactress to distant relations—thus confirming her new socialization. But the journey is never completed. It is interrupted by a surprise meeting with Charles.[16] Beyond the satisfaction of love renewed, Fanny is particularly pleased at Charles's distress: "Charles reduced, and broken down to his naked personal merit, was such a circumstance, in favour of the sentiments I had for him, as exceeded my utmost desires" (212). Fanny can enjoy her love without any concern for money, that is to say, she can enjoy a heroine's destiny.[17] But despite the return of the "true refining passion" (213), Fanny and Charles are still joined in a posture of illicit desire. Charles, however, insists that Fanny allow him to *raise* her: "to receive his hand, by which means I was in pass, among other innumerable blessings, to bestow a legal parentage on those fine children you have seen by this happiest of matches" (219). Whereas in the initiatory sequence of illicit love, Fanny miscarries of Charles's child, the legal sanction of marriage results in healthy reproduction. The clichés of bourgeois happiness overcode the message of "happily ever after."

The tale of Fanny's exploits ends here, but in addition to this tribute to local morality, Fanny concludes her memoirs as a universal allegory: "Thus, at length, I got snug into port, where in the bosom of virtue, I gathered the only uncorrupt sweets" (219). Aware that some might find "this tail-piece of morality" (219) implausible, Fanny nonetheless pursues her literary prerogatives: "If I have painted Vice in all its gayest colours, if I have decked it with flowers, it has been solely in order to make the worthier, the solemner sacrifice of it to Virtue" (220). Thus the end of the narrative, by celebrating the victory of virtue over vice, officially delimits Fanny's destiny within the confines of the genre, the obvious violations it has incurred in the course of narration notwithstanding.

Although it can be argued that the content and recurrence of the violations are so extreme as to throw into question the pertinence of formal solidarity, if my reading of *Fanny Hill* has any validity at all, it will have shown the power of the eighteenth-century intertext to overdetermine the *shape* of a given fiction. For if books like Cleland's *Memoirs* "live . . . because they touch the dream life of men," [18] nonetheless, when one reads *Fanny Hill* with two hands, so to speak, one cannot but recognize its very local color. At the very least as a linear *mapping*, *Fanny Hill* conforms to the pattern of a certain eighteenth-century narrative, of female *Bildung*.

Looking back, Fanny, no less than Marianne or Moll, can assess the road traveled: her progress and her mastery of self in the world. In the end, she can play with the metaphors of theatricality which, in eighteenth-century rhetoric, are the measure of mastered experience. Anticipating (and bypassing) her interlocutor's doubts as to the genuineness of her conversion from Vice to Virtue: "just as if one was to fancy one's self completely disguised at a masquerade, with no other change of dress than turning one's shoes into slippers," (220) Fanny would prove her case by reinstituting the principle of education. Her last words tell of her husband's initiation of his son, the better to "form him to virtue, and inspire him with a fixed, a rational contempt for vice." She thus marks her own distance from the very "scenes of debauchery" she once knew so well.

The disastrous downward curve of the harlot's progress is, in the final analysis, averted, indeed reversed, in favor of the "happy end" of virtue rewarded. As she had wished in the beginning, Fanny reaps Pamela's recompense: she moves from rags to riches, the bottom of the social ladder to the top. Such is the telic power of the structure of ascent in the English novel.

The success of these female apprentices—Moll, Marianne, Pamela

and Fanny—is the euphoric versant of what I have called the
heroine's text. In the next chapters, we will see the negative obverse
of the paradigm: the exclusion of the heroine from (and through) the
social violence of the world; the scenario of illicit love fatally punished.

Part Two
The Dysphoric Text

Chapter Five

LOVE FOR A HARLOT

Manon Lescaut

> *La femme, avec son génie de bourreau, ses talents pour la torture,
> est et sera toujours la perte de l'homme.*
> —Balzac, *Splendeurs et misères des courtisanes*

Moll Flanders and Fanny Hill, the memorialists of the euphoric text, enjoy literary control over the fiction of their erotic encounters. Having lived to tell the tale, they observe with remorse or delight past scenes of victory or defeat. At the same time they are the stars of an essentially one-woman show. For if Moll and Fanny are always coupling—in pursuit of the ultimate and legitimate couple—their narrative is the performance of a relatively autonomous "I." Manon, however, like that other perfidious "Fatal Woman," Mme de Merteuil, always exists for the reader through the mediation of the illicit couple she forms with a single lover. Despite the resistance of both Manon and Merteuil to a system that would contain them exclusively within that couple, the text of these destinies is inseparable from its bonds. It is literally through the correspondence between Mme de Merteuil and Valmont that the reader has access to Merteuil's story, and through the transcription of Des Grieux's "oral" account that Manon lives. But more important than the narrative implications of the bond are the ideological ones. Manon and Merteuil are punished for their erotic indulgences, I would suggest, because their couplings call into question the integrity of an individualized male life, and through that masculine destiny, the laws of an economy of circulation intended to protect phallic identity. Despite her final repentance, Manon goes too far in destroying Des Grieux's name and place to be redeemed by marriage.

The story of Manon is the story of Des Grieux's love for a harlot called Manon.[1] In that love story the signifying trajectory is the hero's, the apprenticeship of the world through sexual encounters again his. Unlike the "memorandums" of Moll Flanders, the adventures of Marianne, the memoirs of Fanny Hill, this text of recollection is first and by its title the story of the Chevalier Des Grieux. But literary history has revised the novel's title, retaining above all the name of Manon, and detaching the novel from the *Mémoires d'un homme de qualité* to which it belonged originally. In this sense, the heroine's text, despite its formally subordinated status, has displaced the hero's.

To read Manon, and through Des Grieux's eyes, is to read a fragment of a life, a perplexing life that ends inconclusively. Manon's death brings the novel to a close, but prematurely; before, that is, the mystery of her character is elucidated: we will never know, for example, whether Manon's taste for pleasure would have been eclipsed in the end by her conversion to virtue. In this irresolution, Prévost's novel would seem to be defined by the hermeneutic implications of what Naomi Schor has called the "hieratic code" according to which "a female character has only to be named and she poses a riddle whose answer will not necessarily coincide with the closure of the text."[2] For Schor, the riddle of femininity operates as a structuring theme in the feminocentric novel. Of *Manon Lescaut* we might then say that the organizing narrative principle is Des Grieux's (and after his, the reader's) attempt to unravel the mystery of "cette étrange fille," as he calls her. Because this obscure object of desire is at the same time the object of narration, the hermeneutic process is inevitably short-circuited by the codes of eternal femininity. In the final analysis, then, and particularly in the later edition, Manon's life makes only stereotypical sense: as the story of illicit love punished, and as a harlot's progress.

Unlike Moll Flanders, who finds life in the New World, Manon—banished from circulation—meets death. She first appears to the reader through the "author's" eyes as a beautiful prisoner in chains about to be transported to America:

Parmi les douze filles qui étaient enchaînées six à six par le milieu du corps, il y en avait une dont l'air et la figure étaient si peu conformes à sa condition, qu'en tout autre état je l'eusse prise pour une personne du premier rang. Sa tristesse et la saleté de son linge et de ses habits l'enlaidissaient si peu que sa vue m'inspira du respect et de la pitié. Elle tâchait néanmoins de se tourner, autant que sa chaîne pouvait le permettre, pour dérober son visage aux yeux des spectateurs. L'effort qu'elle faisait pour se cacher était si naturel, qu'il paraissait venir d'un sentiment de modestie.[3]

Manon, who has not yet been named, is thus defined by her very physical connection to a degraded class, but that physical link to the group serves primarily to reveal her psychological disjunction from it. Indeed, our innocent bystander is so taken with this extraordinary prisoner that he confesses that in other circumstances he might have mistaken her for a gentlewoman. Before leaving the scene of such a pathetic gathering, the author speaks to this astonishing apparition: "Elle me répondit avec une modestie si douce et si charmante, que je ne pus m'empêcher de faire, en sortant, mille réflexions sur le *caractère incompréhensible des femmes*" (15; italics mine). The Marquis's esteem and estimation of Manon as an impartial observer prepare and underwrite Des Grieux's reaction: "Elle me parut si charmante que moi, qui n'avais jamais *pensé à la différence des sexes*, ni regardé une fille avec un peu d'attention, moi, dis-je, dont tout le monde admirait la sagesse et la retenue, je me trouvai enflammé tout d'un coup jusqu'au transport" (19; italics mine). This incarnation of femininity may not be entirely innocent—she does tell him, after all, that she is being sent to a convent because of her "penchant for pleasure"—but Des Grieux fails, or refuses, to decipher the danger implicit in that message because of his urgent desire to succor. The pathos of Manon's situation stimulates Des Grieux's newly discovered masculinity and he undertakes her rescue.[4]

The lovers enjoy a brief moment of bliss (by Des Grieux's father's accounting, no more than twelve days) punctuated by Manon's betrayal and terminated by Des Grieux's house arrest brought about by paternal authority. This pattern of events conforms to the narrative cliché referred to earlier as "illicit love punished."[5] The sequence, which will be repeated three more times in the course of the novel, constitutes the matrix of *Manon Lescaut*: fleeting happiness, followed by Manon's betrayal,[6] in turn followed by retribution from paternal authority. The inevitability of the sequence is built into the social and psychological structure of the couple's relation. The change effected in Manon's social registration—a Manon "point de qualité, quoique d'assez bonne naissance" in 1731 becomes a Manon "d'une naissance commune" in the 1753 edition—underlies disparity of birth as a cause of instability, and has been seen as a regrettable concession to an increasingly moralizing taste:[7] as *common*, Manon's behavior is not only plausible to an eighteenth-century audience, but overdetermined;[8] her punishment ideologically appropriate. But if the relationship between the lovers becomes more predictable because more stereotypical—*Pamela*, we should recall, appears midway between the two editions, and Prévost translated *Clarissa* in 1751—the accentuated disparity "qualité"/"naissance commune" is not without narrative advantage. It serves to legitimize what might otherwise appear to be idiosyncratic and arbitrary opposition to the legitimization of the couple on the part of Des Grieux's father, and more generally underscores the eccentric position of the romantic couple as a literary phenomenon: "just as the illicit is the trembling attraction of the novel," Elizabeth Hardwick writes in *Seduction and Betrayal*, "so is the illicit between persons of different rank, different natures, a variation that stirs our sense of the dramatic instabilities and violations of love."[9] More important, perhaps, than class difference in the consistent failure of the couple is the disparity in their affective economies. Immediately following Des Grieux's account of his first tryst with Manon, he comments: "Il est sûr que, du naturel tendre et constant dont je suis, j'étais heureux pour toute ma vie, si Manon m'eût été fidèle" (25). Later on in their adventure, and only slightly the wiser for his experience, Des Grieux declares: "Manon était passionnée pour le plaisir; je l'étais pour elle" (50). Both statements inscribe a fundamental disparity. Manon, by definition, cannot be faithful to Des Grieux within *his* economy. While his desire is susceptible to fulfillment by Manon alone, her desire for him (at least until they enter the New World) requires *supplementation*. Because of these two major disjunctions, Des Grieux and Manon are condemned to repeat this dysphoric sequence until social alienation and death rewrite it in another key.

Despite Manon's unworthy behavior (as related to him by his father), Des Grieux is still entranced: "Il est certain que je ne l'estimais plus; comment aurais-je estimé la plus volage et la plus perfide de toutes les créatures? Mais son image, ses traits charmants que je portais au fond du coeur, y subsistaient toujours" (36). Perfidy, of course, is built into the paradigm of fatal female attraction. Manon is thus both stereotype and archetype; and it is entirely predictable that when she reappears two years later, after Des Grieux's imprisonment at home and his seclusion in the seminary, Des Grieux will be reseduced by her ineffable charm: "C'était elle; mais plus aimable et plus brillante que je ne l'avais jamais vue. Elle était dans sa dix-huitième année. Ses charmes surpassaient tout ce qu'on peut décrire. C'était un air si fin, si doux, si engageant, l'air de l'Amour même. Toute sa figure me parut un enchantement" (44). Manon comes, then, to Des Grieux, claiming that his love is vital to her existence: "Je prétends mourir, répondit-elle, si vous ne me rendez votre coeur, sans lequel il est impossible que je vive" (45). The hyperbole of her diction, with its echoes of *l'amour-passion*, is designed to rewrite her infidelity and justify—by the logic of reciprocity—Des Grieux's attachment to her in the reader's eyes.

Manon must now reintegrate Des Grieux into her world, which she does, as usual, by the language of love: "Elle m'accabla de mille caresses passionnées. Elle m'appela par tous les noms que l'amour invente pour exprimer ses plus vives tendresses" (45). By her very excess, by her manipulation of the rhetoric of desire, Manon binds Des Grieux to her. Des Grieux, recaptured and persuaded against all reason, reiterates his initial commitment to Manon—abandonment of all that defines him (fortune and reputation). His loss in love's economy will be transformed into gain: "Je lis ma destinée dans tes beaux yeux; mais de quelles pertes ne serai-je pas consolé par ton amour!" (46). Manon's admission that she had left him because she was dazzled by the promises of another protector is not lost upon Des Grieux. But moved by her repentance despite the disaster he reads in her eyes, he lets himself believe again. Manon assumes control, dresses him, and they attempt to replicate their first happiness. When they set up a *ménage* outside Paris in an effort to avoid the temptation of worldly things, Manon momentarily displays the submissive side of herself: "la douceur et la complaisance même" (49). The alternation between Manon's compliant domesticity and her pursuit of headier pleasures is fundamental to her characterization. If there were not these two sides to her, then Des Grieux would not remain so vulnerable. But Manon always holds out the promise of conforming to his ideal. Then, too, although the prostitute in literature always manifests a potential for redemption, if Manon were purely and consistently *fille*, her final incarnation as the *amante incomparable* would lack retroactive plausibility. Moreover, the heroine of the masculine imagination is always essentially a double figure: the incarnation of contradiction. As Simone de Beauvoir has said: "There is no figurative image of woman which does not call up at once its opposite: she is Life and Death, Nature and Artifice, Daylight and Night . . . we always find the same shifting back and forth. . . . In the figures of the Virgin Mary and Beatrice, Eve and Circe still exist." [10] This coexistence of polarities results in cliché-characters, figures of stereotypical dimensions whose behavior follows a sequence as overdetermined as the fixed pattern of a verbal cliché. [11]

In the case of Manon, the reader anticipates that given Manon's taste for pleasure (explicitly announced as etiology in the early pages of the novel), the tenure of domestic tranquility is destined to be brief. Indeed, when a fire destroys their entire fortune while they are seeking pleasure in Paris (just as money burns a hole in their pockets), Des Grieux tries to hide the disaster from Manon: "Je connaissais Manon; je n'avais déjà que trop éprouvé que, quelque fidèle et quelque attachée qu'elle me fût dans la bonne fortune, il ne fallait pas compter sur elle dans la misère. Elle aimait trop l'abondance et les plaisirs pour me les sacrifier" (53). He, like the reader, knows that the dissipation of funds will precipitate, with fatal logic, the dissolution of the couple. The connection between love and money (or love and lack of money) functions here as it does in *Moll Flanders*; the relation is formulaic. Because Manon is an expensive habit, Des Grieux finds himself bending his notions of moral integrity to support it. In order to do so, however, he must legitimize, not to say rationalize, his need (desire) for her and her needs for money. In the first instance, Des Grieux proceeds by tautology: Manon is worthy of love because she is worthy of love. Thus, after a fleeting moment of doubt and bad conscience, he declares: "Je m'étonnai, en me retrouvant auprès d'elle, que j'eusse pu traiter un moment de honteuse une tendresse si juste pour un objet si charmant" (61). The power of her charms invalidates all scruples, cancels all other values. In the second case, Des Grieux relies upon hyperbole and euphemism: "Manon était une créature d'un caractère extraordinaire. Jamais fille n'eut moins d'attachement qu'elle pour l'argent, mais elle ne pouvait être tranquille un moment, avec la crainte d'en manquer. C'était du plaisir et des passe-temps qu'il lui fallait" (61). By placing Manon in a class by herself, Des Grieux would bypass the rules of the stereotype; he would also divest her of responsibility by reading her as a childlike victim of the pleasure principle.

Manon, however, shatters that comforting interpretation. Faced again with the prospect of misery, she leaves Des Grieux. This incident reproduces the first rupture, but this time Manon provides an explanation, and in writing: "Je t'adore, compte là-dessus; mais laisse-moi, pour quelque temps, le ménagement de notre fortune. Malheur à qui va tomber dans mes filets! Je travaille pour rendre mon Chevalier riche et heureux. Mon frère t'apprendra des nouvelles de ta Manon, et qu'elle a pleuré de la nécessité de te quitter" (69). The note is designed to leave no room for reply. In each sentence Manon affirms her connection to Des Grieux, but establishes the principle of separation: thus in the first part of the first sentence Manon guarantees her love, and in the second she requests the permission to operate alone for their couple. In the second sentence she casts herself as the Fatal Woman, using the metaphor of entrapment appropriate to that archetype. Justifying the means by their end, reversing the courtly roles of the couple wherein the lady will work for her knight, she separates herself finally from her lover by establishing her brother as intermediary: *he* will form the couple with Manon, who is, nonetheless *ta* Manon (to *mon* Chevalier), granting him ultimate and eventual possession. She concludes with a tribute to thwarted love, the invocation of her tears functioning as a proof of feeling.

The arrangement Manon's brother has made is (perversely) familial: G . . . M . . . is a paternal figure; Manon (young enough to be his daughter) is to be kept by him with Des Grieux living there too as a "brother." Manon, however, is not to accord the father her final favors, but to use him to provide for the lover/brother. This family, needless to say, is not built for survival. The deception is revealed and as a result Manon finds herself at "l'Hôpital." Des Grieux too goes to prison but it is Manon's fate alone that worries him: "A l'Hôpital, mon Père! O Ciel! ma charmante maîtresse, ma chère Reine à l'Hôpital, comme la plus infâme de toutes les créatures!" (86). Confronted with the dethronement of his idol, Des Grieux acts with heroic energy; he escapes from prison to save Manon, to restore her to her rightful place. Even in such sordid circumstances, however, Manon's remarkable qualities are apparent. And when Des Grieux's new protector, M. de·T., visits Manon, he adopts Des Grieux's rhetoric: "Pour le lieu . . . il ne faut plus l'appeler l'Hôpital; c'est Versailles, depuis qu'une personne qui mérite l'empire de tous les coeurs y est renfermée" (104). Her ability to transform emerges then not only as a function of the alchemy of love (as in *Fanny Hill:* "Had it been a dungeon that Charles had brought me to, his presence would have made it a little *Versailles*"), but as proof of autonomous magical powers: being Manon changes the world. Touched by the pathos of the star-crossed lovers, M. de T. resolves to help.

After Manon's escape, the couple returns to rustic isolation at Chaillot in the hope of reliving their first idyll. Des Grieux is again faced with the problem of supporting Manon in style, both to make her happy and to bind her to him. Although for Des Grieux having Manon is having everything ("J'étais plus fier et plus content avec Manon et mes cent pistoles, que le plus riche partisan de Paris avec ses trésors entassés" [117]), Manon does not exist, is nothing to herself without the trappings of the elegant life ("elle n'était plus rien, et elle ne se reconnaissait pas elle-même, lorsque, ayant devant les yeux des femmes qui vivaient dans l'abondance, elle se trouvait dans la pauvreté et dans le besoin" [110]). Manon can only be had by Des Grieux (and this prefigures the Manon of the final phase of the novel) when she is not herself. The obvious drawback of such an equation, as we noted at the beginning of this chapter, is that it is not symmetrical. In Manon's perspective, Des Grieux means happiness only when wealth is *added* to the formula; worse yet, the source of wealth is indifferent to her: it can come from Des Grieux, *or* from another.

At this juncture in the novel occurs the episode of the Italian prince which was added to the text in the 1753 edition. It has been objected that the inclusion of this incident in the definitive version weakens the representation of Manon. That would be true if Manon were only "volage" and not "sincère." But we have seen that Manon is a contradiction in terms: neither the one, nor the other, but both. What is, then, the function of this episode? First of all, it serves to allay Des Grieux's anxiety just before Manon's third and cruellest betrayal, and thus provides an element of contrast and suspense; secondly, it increases the reader's perception of Manon as enigmatic because unpredictable[12] (she does not perform according to type); finally, it constitutes a break in the mechanism of sequences and (paradoxically) reinforces the effect of repetition. Des Grieux, then, has learned that during his absence in Paris, where he was procuring money for Manon, she has been flirting with a rich foreigner. His suspicions are reinforced by Manon's mood: "A mon retour, je retrouvais Manon plus belle, plus contente, et plus passionnée que jamais" (118). He speaks of her "humeur folâtre" (119) and wonders what it means: "Etrange fille! me disais-je à moi-même; que dois-je attendre de ce prélude?" (121). Manon's excited behavior is now a sign system he can decipher: Manon is about to move. And Des Grieux, underscoring the obvious interpretation, adds: "L'aventure de notre première séparation me revint à l'esprit" (121). The scene, from beginning to end, is orchestrated by Manon: at her request, the couple spend the day alone in the intimacy of their apartment. Manon has Des Grieux sit at her dressing table while she plays with his hair. Then, in a curious inversion of the Delilah story, when the prince appears, Manon literally drags Des Grieux to meet him at the door, ("elle empoigna d'une main mes cheveux") as proof of *his* power: "Tous les princes d'Italie ne valent pas un des cheveux que je tiens" (123), converting metaphor to catachresis. Convinced by the demonstration, Des Grieux reads Manon's behavior as a tribute to their love.

But Manon thrives on the complicated situations of theatrical comedy, whatever their content, so that *formally* this episode is not radically different from the scenes of betrayal. Thus, when Manon learns that G . . . M . . .'s son is infatuated with her, she is determined to play *that* scene out, again including Des Grieux in the act. She needs him as a player: "G . . . M . . . est le fils de notre plus

cruel ennemi; il faut nous venger du père, non pas sur le fils mais sur
sa bourse. Je veux l'écouter, accepter ses présents, et me moquer de
lui" (128–29). Over and above the attraction of financial gain, it is dramatic irony that seduces Manon. Des Grieux was to have played a
role in this little play, but instead receives a note of dismissal. This
time the text of the note is given to the reader indirectly: "Il l'avait
comblée de présents; il lui faisait envisager un sort de reine" (134).
It is another man, a real provider, who gives Manon precisely what
Des Grieux himself thinks she deserves. As a final poetic twist, the
note ends: "*Signé*, votre fidèle amante, MANON LESCAUT" (135).

Undaunted by so painful a repetition of (their) history, Des Grieux
pursues Manon: "Je m'avançai à la porte de mon infidèle, et malgré
toute ma colère, je frappai avec le respect qu'on a pour un
temple" (140). Despite his rage, he is intimidated before he even sees
her. Prisoner of his cult, he continues to worship. Manon, beloved
infidel, again contradicts his expectation: "Manon était occupée à
lire. Ce fut là que j'eus lieu d'admirer le caractère de cette étrange
fille" (140). Once more, her *strangeness* is a measure of the discrepancy between the (sexual) perspectives of the two lovers: Des Grieux
is suffering from a broken heart, while Manon is reading peacefully
as though nothing had happened. In a reiteration of the terms of his
first statement, Des Grieux vents his anger only to fall to his knees,
asking for forgiveness; Manon is thus reinstated as supreme being to
Des Grieux's repentant adoration: "Toute-puissante Manon!" (144).

Thus assured that her power is intact, Manon explains her reasons
for breaking her word, and accepting to send Des Grieux a surrogate
mistress as a consolation prize. Her rationale is based upon a distinction between sex and love: "La fidélité que je souhaite de vous est
celle du coeur" (147). It is, moreover, this very principle that allows
Manon to admit that she would not have spent the night as a "ves-
tale." Des Grieux is too entranced to be humiliated by this professional attitude and agrees to Manon's final scene: "Vous aurez son
couvert à souper, me répétait-elle, vous coucherez dans ses draps, et,
demain, de grand matin, vous enlèverez sa maîtresse et son argent.
Vous serez bien vengé du père et du fils" (149–50). Just as Merteuil
describes her adventures with Belleroche to flatter and provoke Valmont, Manon uses G . . . M . . . the younger to stimulate Des

Grieux: *you* will replace *him*. The refinement of the revenge is demonstrated by the progression of violation: from eating on his rival's dishes to sleeping between his sheets. In this final sequence of illicit love the stakes are dangerously high and Des Grieux—with his characteristic flair for cliché—dramatizes disaster: "Nous étions dans le délire du plaisir, et le glaive était suspendu sur nos têtes. Le fil qui le soutenait allait se rompre" (151). It is at the very moment of pleasure hyperbolized, the ultimate ephemerality, that old G . . . M . . . arrives and surprises the lovers *in flagrante delicto*. The deception is exposed and punishment ensues as the lovers are conducted separately to their prisons.

Again, Des Grieux is concerned only with Manon's fate: "Venez, ma chère reine, lui dis-je, venez vous soumettre à toute la rigueur de notre sort. Il plaira peut-être au Ciel de nous rendre quelque jour plus heureux" (156–57). This elegiac tone introduces the final phase of the novel: Manon enslaved, the "amante incomparable" of the New World. Manon was "reine" while in prison, a fate considered unworthy of her then; she was "reine" for G . . . M . . . the younger; finally she is Des Grieux's queen for her last trial. The illicit lovers are to be punished definitively; separation is again the condition of their punishment. Manon's departure for the New World is marked narrationally by the reinscription of the tableau with which the novel opened (this time from Des Grieux's point of view). Manon has come full circle, with the difference that her degradation has been rationalized. The reader now knows why "cette figure capable de ramener l'univers à l'idolâtrie, paraissait dans un désordre et un abattement inexprimables" (178). Manon is the victim of her own victimization—the punishment commensurate with her tyranny. But if society (the old world) is closed to the lovers, Des Grieux feels that all is not lost, because having Manon to himself at last ("J'étais maître du coeur de Manon, le seul bien que j'estimais" [180]), he can reconstitute a world of their own: "Tout l'univers n'est-il pas la patrie de deux amants fidèles? Ne trouvent-ils pas l'un dans l'autre, père, mère, parents, amis, richesses et félicité?" (180). It is this assumption that the couple can replace the family, reproduce and contain the dimensions of the world, that has been, from the beginning, Des Grieux's fantasy; untenable until now, he imagines that he can will its realization. This construct in no way differs from Saint-Preux's original projection of idyllic life alone with Julie: it is a function of the dialectic of desire according to which frustrated possession of the love object in the face of "idées fantastiques de l'honneur" (180) imposed by the father, generates the fantasy of a community *à deux* beyond the reach of authority.[13]

But "romantic love overflows beyond its source, into the world around it; it needs the recognition and support of a wider community. In the world as it is, however, there is no community that will provide this support, nowhere romantic lovers can belong authentically."[14] Manon does not feel possessed of the strength necessary to perform heroically: "Mourons, me répéta-t-elle; ou du moins, donne-moi la mort, et va chercher un autre sort dans les bras d'une amante plus heureuse" (182). But in the face of Des Grieux's persistence in linking his destiny to hers at whatever cost, she responds to his energy in the language of love with which she first charmed him: "C'était, entre elle et moi, une perpétuelle émulation de services et d'amour" (184). Faced with the disintegration of her own system of independence, Manon accedes finally to Des Grieux's vision of the couple. His claim that they are married temporarily affords them protection and a place to live; but even in the New World the old values prevail: unmarried, Manon would be expected to circulate on the (slave) market. Thus retroactively Des Grieux's lie is justified for when the marriage is revealed to be a wish and not reality, Manon's status is immediately degraded. Their shabby surroundings mark the opposition to the glamour of their previous life together, but Des Grieux has faith in Manon's power to transform: "Et puis, tu es une chimiste admirable . . . tu transformes tout en or" (187), and a hut becomes a palace. The alchemy of love brings the recognition of change to Manon herself: "Je n'étais qu'une ingrate. Mais vous ne sauriez croire combien je suis changée" (187–88). Realizing the injustice of her past behavior toward Des Grieux, Manon resolves to dedicate herself to the new version of the couple, accepting the principle of exclusivity.

Nonetheless, it is Des Grieux who seeks to institutionalize the change from disorder to virtue, to complete the neutralization of disruptive sexuality through marriage: "Elle était droite et naturelle dans tous ses sentiments, qualité qui dispose toujours à la vertu. Je lui fis comprendre qu'il manquait une chose à notre bonheur" (190). But since what is *missing* has always defined the dynamic of the couple,[15] it is inevitable that the attempt to fill that lack should bring about its dissolution. Thus, when Des Grieux reveals to the governor that Manon is not in fact his wife, she automatically becomes a source of disorder, an object of desire. The function of the father as oppositional force to the life of the couple is assumed by the governor through his nephew; and the couple finds itself in a reduplication of the original structure. The primitive social order of the new world proves to be as inimicable as that of the old. It remains, then, to the lovers to seek refuge beyond "civilization" in a natural world inhabited by "savages." It is at this point that Manon assumes in Des Grieux's eyes the stature of "amante incomparable" anticipated in the episode of the Italian prince. Reversing roles, Manon seeks to assert herself as protector: "Je me soumis durant quelques moments à ses désirs. Je reçus ses soins en silence et avec honte" (198). By taking care of his wound, and striving to make Des Grieux comfortable, Manon denies him his paternal function and becomes a maternal figure. Des Grieux's shame at the reversal of roles, a reduplication of his discomfort during the Italian prince episode, generates a frenzy of self-sacrifice on his part. He divests himself of his clothing to provide her with a bed on the earth and his passion ("ardeur"/"baisers ardents"/"la chaleur de mes soupirs") serves as a substitute for fire. Despite his care, he cannot infuse Manon with his life, and death brings "la fin de ses malheurs" (199).

The reader is not given her dying words, but her death grants Des Grieux what he sought from her in life: "Je la perdis; je reçus d'elle des marques d'amour, au moment même qu'elle expirait" (199). In death, Manon is entirely his and receives the last proof of his desire; he breaks his sword—the symbol of his class and his virility—in an attempt to prepare the earth for Manon's grave; then wraps the idol of his heart in his own clothing: "Je ne la mis dans cet état qu'après l'avoir embrassée mille fois, avec toute l'ardeur du plus parfait amour" (200). Manon dead, Des Grieux's love is at last consummated. Des Grieux, despite his desire for death, survives the loss of his incomparable mistress; and the novel ends with his reinsertion

into the social life from which his liaison with Manon had excluded
him. Their story thus has a double ending: the death of the heroine
and the "reform" of the hero. The two trajectories, of course, are in-
tertwined: if Manon's existence disrupted the social order (by whose
rules Des Grieux defines himself through rebellion or conformity),
her death brings about, or rather, allows for the reestablishment of
social continuity. The power of illicit sexuality *incarnated* by Manon
is defused and neutralized by her death. Only *after* her death does
their love become "perfect" and therefore redemptive: secularly re-
generative.

To the extent that this novel is the story of an education—analogous to the social initiations experienced by Marianne or
Moll—it is, in the final analysis, a very costly one for it requires a
dead body. We are far, in Prévost's fiction, from the optimistic closure of the novels considered in the first half of this study that I have
called the euphoric text. With Prévost we have a distinctly pessimistic
model. As English Showalter writes, grouping Prévost as do I with the
novelists of the second half of the century: "The authors view the
outcome with varying degrees of sadness, but the one result that seems
impossible is a happy ending. In every case, the heroine dies, and
only this tragic emancipation can permit the hero to contemplate his
experience with some detachment and reconcile himself to
failure."[16] In *Clarissa, La Nouvelle Héloïse* and *Les Liaisons
dangereuses*, this expensive paradigm holds true as well, although in
the first and last instances, the hero's "reconciliation" (in Lovelace's
case, "expiation") entails his death as well. In none of these novels,
in sharp contrast to the earlier ones, does marriage as an index of
social optimism (even muted or parodied) offer itself as a *plausible*
fictional solution[17] to the problematics of self and desire that under-
lie the plots of most if not all feminocentric eighteenth-century
fiction. Without marriage as *telos*, there can only be death; or so it
seems.

Chapter Six

THE MISFORTUNES OF VIRTUE: I

Clarissa

> *Tout ce que Montaigne, Charron, La Rouchefoucauld et Nicole*
> *ont mis en maximes, Richardson l'a mis en action.*
> —Diderot, *L'Eloge de Richardson*

Clarissa, Dorothy Van Ghent states in the opening sentence of her essay on that young lady's history, "is the antithesis of Moll Flanders, as heroine."[1] Indeed, the destinies of these two feminine types appear so radically different from each other that at first blush it seems difficult to see how one might oppose them in a meaningful polarity. It is far easier, for example, to show that Sade's *Justine* is the "nightmare obverse"[2] of *Pamela*: the positivities of the one being each time cancelled out, or rather negated by the reiterative degradation of the other. In what sense, then, can one read Clarissa's tragic tale of private life as the dark side of Moll's (ultimately) euphoric account of fortune and misfortune? Van Ghent places the "chief idiosyncracy of Moll Flanders' world" in its "tendency to externalize life"; of Clarissa's, obversely, "to convert the external forms of life . . . into subjective quality and spiritual value."[3] This *environmental* opposition is true enough: Moll navigates with ease and all deliberate speed in a universe controlled by the flow of cash; whereas Clarissa is buffeted about "by the high winds of passionate control," unable to "steer" the course she desires.[4] But if the two trajectories differ in the way they can be seen to move through the space against which they are articulated, and in the *economy* of that space, they are also—and more important—different in the delineation of focus. By this I do not mean simply those incidences of form—a single voice, recollected and tranquil as opposed to an anxious plurality of register, and that "to the moment"—which determine narrative point of view. I mean, rather, the focus or emphasis given to the facts of the life at hand. As Van Ghent has seen: "The central action of Clarissa's story is a rape, an experience which might have assumed a position of minor importance among Moll's adventures in adultery, bigamy, and incest— conceivably an incident that Moll might even have forgotten to make a 'memorandum' of."[5] Clarissa, precisely, could not possibly forget the singular event that forces her to exist in the world as a sexual personality *on its terms*. Unlike Moll, whose narrative and heroine-ism depend upon the inclusion, even the incorporation, of sexual event, Clarissa's private sense of plot requires its exclusion.[6] She is not willing to assume a sexual identity that must be negotiated in a marketplace of competing desires. She cannot, like Moll, move on after the fact; she cannot, in the final analysis, move at all. It is perhaps this paralyzing insistence, this paradoxically hypertrophic reduction of human identity to sexual definition, that separates Defoe's fictions of the self from Richardson's.[7] With Richardson, and after him, the war between the sexes in the eighteenth-century novel changes from comic skirmishes to tragic violence;[8] everyone can be said to lose, but the signifying casualties are female.

In the first-person retrospective—as we saw with Moll, Marianne, and Fanny—the "I" justifies the *why* of its tenure. Epistolary fiction, however, must, as the mimesis not of a life but of a *moment* in a life, insinuate its legitimacy; above all it must justify its historicity. While the task of fictional memoirs is to account for a life and thus begins with a summary of origins, a point of departure in time past, the epistolary novel is grounded in the present. The significance of this distinction for the trajectory that interests us here is that the heroine of fictional memoirs embarks on a quest which provides a context for sexual confrontation, and her history reveals the stages that precede her first conflict (the innocence of "before"); whereas the virtuous heroine of the epistolary novel is first presented to the reader as already engaged in erogenous combat. Thus, as was true for Pamela, Clarissa's letters are generated by the opening moves of a seduction. In the epistolary novel of a feminine destiny, the exchange of letters concretizes a dialectics of desire already in place.

To guarantee the reader's belief in a fable of seduction, the first letters must establish rapidly the heroine's title to innocence. *Clarissa,* for example, opens with a letter addressed to that young lady by her best friend and confidante, Miss Howe, through which the reader (whose apprehensions and admiration were already stimulated by the preface) immediately perceives Clarissa's exemplary vulnerability:

> I AM extremely concerned, my dearest friend, for the disturbances that have happened in your family. I know how it must hurt you to become the subject of the public talk; and yet upon an occasion so generally known, it is impossible but that whatever relates to a young lady, whose distinguished merits have made her the public care, should engage everybody's attention. I long to have the particulars from yourself; and of the usage I am told you receive upon an accident you could not help; and in which, as far as I can learn, the sufferer was the aggressor (I, 1).

Within the first paragraph, then, the key terms of this heroine's text are announced: Clarissa is defined by her exceptionality; her reputation belongs to the public domain; the order of family life has been disrupted; and Clarissa is the source of disorder.

Although it is not immediately clear what role Lovelace is to play in Clarissa's life, he is presented (along with Clarissa's brother) as being responsible for her current unhappiness. Moreover, the prospect that any contact should exist between the two is cautioned against: "My mother will have it that you cannot now, with any decency, either see him or correspond with him" (I, 2). The special pertinence of Mrs. Howe's caveat only becomes evident as the novel develops; at this point, however, as a representative of conventional and high-minded morality (like Mme de Volanges), her remarks serve to delimit Clarissa's options within the prevailing system of values. By the second letter (the first installment of Clarissa's explanation as requested) the reader learns that Lovelace is noble and handsome: an eligible (though "wild") bachelor and a desirable party. By the third we learn that Lovelace's suit had been "rejected" by Clarissa's sister Arabella and that he had turned his attentions to Clarissa. Despite Mrs. Harlowe's wariness of "his reputed faulty morals," the family tenders tentative approval: "My Uncle Harlowe, that his *daughter* Clary, as he delighted to call me from childhood, would reform him if any woman in the world could" (I, 9). With the word *reform*, the key to the fundamental opposition (and law of attraction) between Clarissa and Lovelace is set in place: the God-fearing Christian daughter of the middle classes versus the godless aristocratic rake. This gamble proves an impossibility; an impossibility at least as long as the two combatants exist in the world.

In the week that separates Clarissa's first letter from the sixth, Clarissa's father (upon the urgings of Clarissa's adversarial brother) has prohibited further contact with Lovelace and a new marriage prospect has been proposed: "This is Mr. Solmes; *Rich* Solmes you know they call him" (I, 25). Thus despite the extraordinary length and complexity of this novel, the heart of the drama is exposed rapidly, and from Clarissa's viewpoint. Clarissa, like Julie, must confront her father's will in the matter of marriage. And while Clarissa is not initially (at least not to her knowledge) in love with Lovelace as Julie is with Saint-Preux, both heroines are caught in a doubly triangular configuration: daughter/father/lover, young woman/*senex amans*/young lover. Just as Julie immolates herself to her father's will, Clarissa's itinerary returns her to her father: "As the story progresses, it is not the daughter's rebellion that is thematically paramount, but the daughter's obedience; for her father's curse is far more effective emotionally upon her than the attraction of the lover."[9]

Her first desire is to remain as a daughter with her father: "But, upon the whole, this I do repeat—that nothing but the *last* extremity shall make me abandon my father's house, if they will permit me to stay" (I, 291). Indeed, it is only despair over her father's intractability that leads her to her fatal error of judgment: "To be carried away on Thursday—to the moated house—to the chapel—to Solmes! How can I think of this! They will make me desperate" (I, 314). The language itself mimes her panic; the telegraphic style corresponds to the urgency of the message: lines merely appended to the original text (her uncle's letter) included for Miss Howe's perusal. The specificity of the date functions as a life sentence; and Clarissa, while hoping for favorable resolution, prepares to escape if all else fails. Anticipating negative public reaction, Clarissa justifies her projected action by exposing her dilemma:

Only one thing must be allowed for me; that whatever course I shall be *permitted* or be *forced* to steer, I must be considered as a person out of her own direction. Tossed to and fro by the high winds of passionate control (and, as I think, unreasonable severity) I behold the desired port, the *single state*, which I would fain steer into; but am kept off by the foaming billows of a brother's and sister's envy, and by the raging winds of a supposed invaded authority; while I see in Lovelace the rocks on one hand, and in Solmes, the sands on the other; and tremble lest I should split upon the former of strike upon the latter (I, 345–46).

This passage anticipates Clarissa's negative odyssey: the journey not homeward bound, but away from the household and her place. Like Odysseus, Clarissa's will is countered by an angry and inexorable authority; but unlike him, she is not destined (from above) to navigate the impossible space between Scylla and Charybdis. This metaphoric summary of a victim's trajectory, a destiny imposed from without, is both a brief and a defense; a disclaimer of responsibility; a legal fiction. "Out of her own direction," kept off course, Clarissa can no longer answer for herself. For the heroine confronted with impossible alternatives, the inevitable solution is flight, or in a more violent register, escape into death. Thus Clarissa declares in the presence of Solmes himself: "I will undergo the cruellest death—I will even consent to enter into the awful vault of my ancestors, and to have that bricked up upon me, rather than consent to be miserable for life" (I, 380). But having affirmed, with Gothic rhetoric, her willingness to die ("*This* or *any* death" [I, 380]), Clarissa explores the possibility of flight. She seeks protection from Miss Howe's mother: "Place me anywhere, as I have said before—in a cot, in a garret; anywhere—disguised as a servant—or let me pass as a servant's sister—so that I may but escape Mr. Solmes on one hand, and the disgrace of refuging with the family of a man at enmity with my own on the other; and I shall be in some measure happy!" (I, 411).[10] Unfortunately for Clarissa, Mrs. Howe refuses to extend her motherly guardianship to so unworthy a daughter, and deprived of a surrogate family, Clarissa is forced to fend for herself. Clarissa thus agrees to enter into a "treaty" with Lovelace according to which she promises to marry no other man so long as he remains single: it is "a compliment

I am willing to pay him in return for the trouble and pains he has taken, and the usage he has met with on my account" (I, 444). By giving him "room to hope" (I, 474), Clarissa plans to temporize, in the hope that time itself will accomplish her ends. She agrees, therefore, to a secret meeting in the summerhouse; but when she finds that Lovelace intends to deliver her physically from her plight, Clarissa high-mindedly rebels: "Shall *I*, to promote your happiness, as you call it, destroy all my future peace of mind?" (I, 479). Ever resourceful, Lovelace then assumes the role of the knightly protector: "Remember only that I come at your appointment, to redeem you, at the hazard of my life, from your jailers and persecutors, with a resolution . . . to be a father, uncle, brother, and, as I humbly hoped, in your own good time, a *husband* to you, all in one" (I, 480). By casting Clarissa as a persecuted maiden, Lovelace can cast himself as an heroic deliverer; and tempering romance with middle-class fiction, proposes domestic salvation. Then, as if trapped himself by his own flair for plot, Lovelace carries Clarissa off against her will.

Retroactively, Clarissa laments her mistake, and its inevitability: "This last evil, although the *remote* yet *sure* consequence of my first—my prohibited correspondence! by a father *early* prohibited" (I, 486). Clarissa, like Julie, situates her original and fatal error in the exchange of letters. She "despises" herself for her "crime" and castigates herself to Miss Howe (as Julie does to Claire) since "better things were expected from me than from many others" (I, 487). Once again, the heroine of great expectations is betrayed by the seducer's "deluding arts" (I, 487).[11] Above all, Clarissa resents that in her "folly," she allowed herself to be tricked: "out of *myself*" (I, 487) and into the double bind of the divided self.

From the abduction by Lovelace (at the end of volume I), the narrative obeys a "basic formal division . . . [which is the] expression of the dichotomisation of the sexual roles."[12] For as a rake, Lovelace is committed (onomastically) to possessing women without love. In pursuing Clarissa, he acts out the maxims of the stereotypical masculine role, justifying his behavior in terms of the corresponding feminine role of hypocritical resistance: women accept/expect to be taken by an aggressive male. For despite Clarissa's spotless fame, Lovelace is skeptical about its authenticity: "Is not, may not, her virtue be founded rather in *pride* rather than in *principle?* . . . If impeccable how came she by her impeccability? The pride of setting an example to her sex has run away with her hitherto, and may have made her till *now* invincible" (II, 35–36). Though attracted to the "divine Clarissa" for her exemplary femininity, in order for Lovelace to respect Clarissa (i.e., marry her and renounce his freedom) he must *himself* experience her uniqueness: "Then who says Miss Clarissa Harlowe is the paragon of virtue?—is Virtue itself? . . . Has her virtue ever been *proved?* Who has dared to try her virtue? . . . To the test then . . . since now I have the question brought home to me whether I am to have a wife?" (II, 36). If Clarissa should fail in her trial, prove to be a woman and not divine, Lovelace will have had the satisfaction of destroying her myth and maintaining his: "But if she resist—if nobly she stand her trial? Why then I will marry her, and bless my stars for such an angel of a wife" (II, 41). Entrapped by the logic of gender, Lovelace makes a mistake of genre: he fails to perceive that Clarissa is not made for comedy.

For Lovelace it is Clarissa's egregious superiority that makes her a worthy adversary: "Thou knowest that I always illustrated my eagle-ship, by aiming at the noblest quarries" (II, 253). The metaphor of male sexual prowess in which the woman functions as prey is not unconscious on Lovelace's part; it constitutes the founding myth of his system:

There may . . . be some *cruelty* necessary: but there may be *consent in struggle;* there may be *yielding in resistance.* But the first conflict over, whether the following may not be weaker and weaker, till *willingness* ensue, is the point to be tried. I will illustrate what I have said by the simile of a bird new-caught. We begin, when boys, with birds, and, when grown up, go on to women; and both, perhaps, in turn, experience our sportive cruelty (II, 245).

The real "point," then, is not the violence of the original assault but its potential carry-over, its initiatory quality. It is less a question of breaking down than breaking *in:* "Now, Belford, were I to go no further than I have gone with my beloved Miss Harlowe, how shall I know the difference between *her* and *another* bird? To let her fly now, what a pretty jest would that be! How do I know, except I try, whether she may not be brought to sing me a fine song, and to be as well contented as I have brought other birds to be, and very shy ones too?" (II, 247). The goal is to make Clarissa accept and like her cage, to respond to training, to respond in a sexually positive way. The assumption Lovelace makes, like Valmont, is not only that any woman can be had, but that secretly she is waiting only for the right man to unlock her sexuality. Thus, while it is true that "sadism is . . . the ultimate form which the eighteenth-century view of the masculine role involved,"[13] the phallocentric pretentions of Lovelace and Valmont are complicated and infirmed by both their own involvement and entrapment, by their need to form their victims, to *attach* them to pleasure: the Sadian victim/heroine never progresses beyond violation. Lovelace dramatically misjudges Clarissa, however: unlike Mme de Tourvel, Clarissa refuses to recognize an erotic self within the terms of a *masculine* definition of desire.

Lovelace proceeds to operate according to his principles of subjugation, although they are continually undermined by his own intimidation: "As my trembling hands seized hers, I soon made fear her predominant passion. And yet the moment I beheld her, my heart was dastardized; and my reverence for the virgin purity so visible in her whole deportment, again took place. Surely, Belford, this is an angel" (II, 375). Lovelace consistently represents Clarissa as though she actually belonged to another world, complete with dazzling halo; she appears to him as a *vision* in which her charms are sacralized, and as such temporarily neutralize his sexuality. Thus when a fire he has set in the house where he holds her a virtual prisoner, gives Lovelace the opportunity to penetrate legitimately into her room, Clarissa anticipates (quite justly) the advent of the "last extremity" (II, 502) and attempts a Lucretia-like defense: "Redoubling her struggles to get from me, in broken accents, and exclamations the most vehement, she protested that she would not survive what she called a treatment so disgraceful and villainous; and looking all wildly round her, as if for some instrument of mischief, she espied a pair of sharp-pointed scissors on a chair by the bedside, and endeavoured to catch them up, with design to make her words good on the spot" (II, 502). Lovelace again, and despite his advantage, is deterred from acting on his own violent impulses by the emergence of Clarissa's mystical power:[14] "By my soul, thought I, thou art, upon full proof, an angel and no woman!" (II, 504). This near-violation is followed by an abortive escape and the sequence will be replicated in the course of the narrative with increasing intensity, until, that is, the fiasco becomes fulfillment.

The last image the reader has of Clarissa before her trial by force is that of a broken flower: "And down on her bosom, like a half-broken-stalked lily, top-heavy with the overcharging dews of the morning, sunk her head, with a sigh that went to my heart" (III, 193). And abruptly, after this Iliadic simile, Lovelace's strangely succinct report: "I can go no farther. The affair is over. Clarissa lives" (III, 196). After the rape, locked inside her room, making herself safe through voluntary confinement, Clarissa drafts and destroys letters, fragments of which are reconstituted by Lovelace. In the "papers" to Miss Howe, her father, and her sister, Clarissa denigrates herself and proclaims her unworthiness. With Lovelace, she alternates between anger and despair: "Thou pernicious caterpillar, that preyest upon the fair leaf of virgin fame, and poisonest those leaves which thou canst not devour! . . . Thou eating canker-worm, that preyest upon the opening bud, and turnest the damask rose into livid yellowness!" (III, 207). Clarissa's "defloration," anticipated in the simile of the broken lily by Lovelace, is taken up metaphorically by the possessor of the flower herself. But where Lovelace sees violation as breaking, Clarissa sees it as infection. Even where the leaf is not mutilated, the disease penetrates.[15]

Clarissa also writes a longer statement to Lovelace in which she explains her view of the situation and communicates her desires for the future: "I shall never be what I was. My head is gone. I have wept away all my brain, I believe; for I can weep no more" (III, 210); "Alas! you have killed my head among you" (III, 211). Clarissa's head (and her maidenhead) is the place of death where before it was the place of reason and pride. Clarissa's pride[16] makes it impossible for her to accept Lovelace, and to accept through him, her flesh, her womanliness: "I never shall be myself again: I have been a very wicked creature—a vain, proud, poor creature—full of secret pride . . . and now I am punished" (III, 212). Her pride allowed her to think she could conquer Lovelace, convince her family, determine her life. Defeated, no longer herself, her only desire is to be locked up in a madhouse. But Lovelace does not exult: "She is invincible!

Against all my notions, against all my conceptions (thinking of her as a woman, and in the very bloom of her charms), *she is absolutely invincible"* (III, 229). And would claim his bride.

Still unable to see Clarissa for what she is, Lovelace is baffled by her sense of irremediable destruction: "That her will is not to be corrupted . . . she has hitherto unquestionably proved. . . . What nonsense, then, to suppose that such a mere *notional violation* as she has suffered, should be able to cut asunder the strings of life?" (III, 242). But it is precisely the *idea* of violation that revolts Clarissa; the violence has been done to her sense of self.[17] Her revulsion, however, finally energizes her, and in a scene which reduplicates that of the scissors, Clarissa, penknife in hand, defends herself against Lovelace's approach: " 'Stop where thou art! Nor, with that determined face, offer to touch me, if thou wouldst not that I should be a corpse at thy feet!' " (III, 288). Again, Clarissa's instinct is to protect herself through self-destruction, although her suicide is postponed: " 'Thank God! said the angel—delivered *for the present*; for the *present* delivered—from myself!' " (III, 290); and she escapes, as she had planned initially, disguised as a servant.

Free from Lovelace's control, Clarissa's project is to suppress her "vile" self and to restore her *"best self"* (III, 321).[18] This therapy is to be private. But Mrs. Howe (from first to last, the voice of convention) calls for public rehabilitation. If Clarissa was a model daughter, and a representative of exemplary femininity ("The whole sex is indeed wounded by you: for who but Miss Clarissa Harlowe was proposed by every father and mother for a pattern for their daughters?" [III, 323]), then reparation must be made *socially*—and metonymically—to compensate for the *sexual* violation of all women: by the prosecution of Lovelace through legal channels (vindication through justice) or marriage. Clarissa refuses both options; the first out of a sense of futility, the second, from a sense of revulsion: "Do you think your Clarissa Harlowe so lost, so *sunk*, at least, as that she could, for the sake of patching up, in the world's eye, a broken reputation, meanly appear indebted to the generosity, or perhaps *compassion*, of a man who has, by means so inhuman, robbed her of it?" (III, 519–20). Penitent but still proud, Clarissa seeks a symbolic transformation that would take her *beyond* the judgment of this world, would resolve and therefore dissolve the social and sexual polarization that opposes her both to her family and Lovelace. Once she recognizes, as Julie ultimately does, the impossibility of a secular resolution, death becomes the only plausible outcome.

Clarissa refuses to live in a world in which she is no longer esteemed:

But since my character, *before* the capital enormity, was lost in the eye of the world; and that from the very hour I left my father's house; and since all my own hopes of worldly happiness are entirely over; let me slide quietly into my grave; and let it not be remembered, except by one friendly tear, and no more, dropped from your gentle eye, mine own dear Anna Howe, on the happy day that shall shut up all my sorrows, that there was such a creature as   CLARISSA HARLOWE (III, 374).

This passage provides the reader with Clarissa's abridged version of her history. CLARISSA HARLOWE became a fiction once she left her father's house. And she looks to death as an *eradication* of that past.

The only challenge left to Clarissa is to learn to forgive Lovelace: "And I hope, clasping her hands together, uplifted, as were her eyes, my dear *earthly* father will set me the example my *heavenly* one has already set us all; and, by forgiving his fallen daughter, teach her to forgive the man, who then, I hope, will not have destroyed my eternal prospects, as he has my temporal!" (III, 501). Having left her father's house and having found no substitute for his protection, Clarissa's last efforts are to return. But in order for her to return, that is, to die and enter the house of the heavenly father feeling "qualified for the state" (III, 500), the earthly father must relent. Mr. Harlowe, deeming that her present punishment is sufficient, at last accepts to withdraw the curse, but forgiveness is withheld: "For the rest, he will never own you, nor forgive you; and grieves he has such a daughter in the world" (IV, 57). Clarissa nonetheless writes to Lovelace that she is optimistic: "I have good news to tell you. I am setting out with all diligence for my father's house. I am bid to hope that he will receive his poor penitent with a goodness peculiar to himself; for I am overjoyed with the assurance of a thorough reconciliation. . . You may possibly in time see me at my father's; at least, if it be not your own fault" (IV, 157). Lovelace takes the letter literally and imagines that it means Clarissa is not only confessing her love, but agreeing to marriage.[19] Even Belford, who is in constant attendance on Clarissa, is at a loss to decipher the text properly and she must explain: " 'Read but for my *father's house, heaven*' " (IV, 213).

Indeed, while suffering from no diagnosable ailment, Clarissa is nonetheless perishing, and preparing for death. She arranges to have a coffin delivered to her room. The coffin is decorated with ornaments and inscriptions; Belford mentions specifically the presence of "the head of a white lily snapped short off, and just falling from the stalk"[20] and the choice of date: "The date, April 10, she accounted for, as not being able to tell what her *closing-day* would be; and as that was the fatal day of her leaving her father's house" (IV, 257). In Clarissa's symbolic chronology she has already died twice, so that her real death, like Julie's,[21] is not frightening. However, Julie's exaltation in the face of death is motivated by her anticipated reunion with Saint-Preux; Clarissa sees her death as more heavenly bliss: "As for me, never bride was so ready as I am. My wedding garments are bought . . . the *happiest* suit, that ever bridal maiden wore, for they are such as carry with them a security against all those anxieties, pains, and perturbations which sometimes succeed to the most promising outsettings" (IV, 303). Death provides Clarissa with the security that she could never have in life: infallible protection against disruptive sexuality.[22] Her sense of happiness and pleasure comes from the guarantee of stasis: "To be so much exposed to temptation, and to be so liable to fail in the trial, who would not rejoice that all her dangers are over!" (IV, 339). But this triumph over temptation through transcendence was not the only ending to the story of the maiden and the rake Clarissa had imagined. As she explains from the safety of her death bed: "And yet, my dear Mrs. Norton, I will own to you *that once I could have loved him—ungrateful man! had he permitted me to love him. I once could have loved him*. Yet he never deserved my love. And was not this a fault?" (III, 345). Her fault would seem to be a poor choice, an error of judgment about the object of her affection that would in fact antedate (as it compounds) the "capital enormity" of leaving her father's house; her fault was to have overestimated Lovelace's worth. But in a subsequent confession to Belford this fault proves to be even more clearly bound to Lovelace's failure to understand her (retroactive) willingness: "Poor man, said she! I once could have loved him. This is saying more than ever I could say of any other man out of my own family! Would he have permitted me to have been a humble instrument to have made him good. I think I could have made him happy!" (IV, 306). Although Clarissa's self-castigation—owning her "fault"—seems to be an uncharacteristically mellow rewriting of what might have been, the power of her conviction is not seriously mitigated by her desire, in the past conditional tense, to serve, and humbly; she could have loved Lovelace had she been able to bring him to love her on her terms.

In this need to maintain the correctness of her plot, Clarissa's mistake is thus not so different from Lovelace's: "Clarissa is as enslaved to the moral attitudes of others in her desire to become an example as Lovelace is enslaved to older forms of literary character."[23] Trapped by the constraints of representation, they are unable to read their own subtexts; and this blindness kills. But Lovelace (ultimately and like Valmont) has a better time of it, for he is allowed a moment of insight before he dies. Clarissa, so often luminous in Lovelace's eyes, and despite the brilliance of her last days, is not. To the end (and unlike that Catholic reader of *Clarissa*, Mme de Tourvel), Clarissa Harlowe remains in the dark about the nature of her desire. This is necessarily so because the self of her body has become tied to the rape, and beyond that, because the rape itself is the hyperbole of a loathing for female sexuality as it has been inscribed for her by Lovelace and her father. Clarissa will have nothing to do with that definition of her life: "this vile, this hated *self!*" (III, 321). Unable, despite her gift for letters, to unwrite the text which keeps her prisoner, Clarissa must, like Julie, die to be restored to the self of her exemplarity.

Chapter Seven

THE MISFORTUNES OF VIRTUE: II

La Nouvelle Héloïse

> *Qu'est-ce que la vertu? C'est, sous quelque face qu'on la considère, un sacrifice de soi-même. Le sacrifice que l'on fait de soi-même en idée, est une disposition préconçue à s'immoler en réalité.*
>
> —Diderot, *Eloge de Richardson*

No reader of eighteenth-century novels needs to be convinced of the importance of Richardson's fictions—especially *Clarissa*—for the French novelists of the heroine's text in the second part of the century. In particular, it is impossible not to read *La Nouvelle Héloïse* in the penumbra of the "caverns" celebrated by Diderot. By the same token, however, the novelistic stereotypes so clearly delineated by Richardson are to a great extent blurred and even subverted within Rousseau's more philosophical writing of the passions and their relations to social institutions. My own reading nevertheless will focus on that strand in Rousseau's text which, by the insistence of its language, links and unlinks the tragic heroines of the dysphoric plot to and from each other. I do not propose to circumscribe Rousseau in this brief essay, only to trace the representation of Julie's heroine-ism.

Like *Clarissa*, *La Nouvelle Héloïse* unfolds under the sign of the paternal metaphor. Although the power of the father's law was already contested in Prévost's earlier *Manon Lescaut*, the measure of that power was taken by the bonds, and the violence of those bonds, connecting father to son. In *Clarissa* and *La Nouvelle Héloïse*, the family romance within which the "love stories" are framed is a scenario that engages fathers and daughters. Julie's first love, no less than Clarissa's, is her father. For both heroines their drama is that desire—acknowledged or denied—threatens their place in the father's house by the challenge it brings to their exemplary filiality, to their primary and privileged definition of self.

The liminary letters of the novel—three letters of passionate pursuit from Saint-Preux—open the scene of a daughter's seduction. When Julie finally answers, however, it is as though the seduction had already been accomplished: "Il faut donc l'avouer enfin, ce fatal secret trop mal déguisé! . . . Que dire? comment rompre un si pénible silence? ou plutôt n'ai-je pas déjà tout dit, et ne m'as-tu pas trop entendue? Ah! tu en as trop vu pour ne pas deviner le reste."[1] Her reply demonstrates a basic rule in the semiotics of female vulnerability: in the silent exchange of first love, a woman's eyes reveal involuntarily what her voice refuses. Breaking the silence, therefore, is less a confession than a reiteration, redundancy confirmed by the rhetoric of repetition: "trop mal déguisé," "trop entendue," "trop vu." But if Julie finally admits in words to what her lover already knows by virtue of his powers of penetration, it is only in response to his threats of suicide and flight, and from the beginning she casts herself as the unwitting victim of a plot: "Entraînée par degrés dans les pièges d'un vil séducteur, je vois, sans pouvoir m'arrêter, l'horrible précipice où je cours" (12). For although Saint-Preux has presented himself as love's and Julie's victim, his hopeless devotion is not without its violence. As Christie Vance has commented, "though Saint-Preux appears to be vowing obedience to Julie's authority, the simple act of confessing his love is a kind of aggression."[2]

In the idiolect of the text, the code of seduction by entrapment leads to the central metaphor of moral collapse: the fall into the abyss. The horror of the imminent brink, however, seems irresistibly attractive, for Julie's static moral self passively watches her dynamic immoral impulsion carry her away. Indeed, the disaster implicit in "fatal secret" is translated here as *inevitability* and underlines the chain reaction of the *coup de foudre*: "Dès le premier jour que j'eus le malheur de te voir, je sentis le poison qui corrompt mes sens et ma raison; je le sentis du premier instant, et tes yeux, tes sentiments, tes

discours, ta plume criminelle, le rendent chaque jour plus mortel"
(13). Love at first sight, then, is not ecstasy but contamination.
Seeing Saint-Preux is equivalent to absorbing the love philter—the
potion/poison that takes immediate and irremediable effect, infecting
the body and the mind. But if the destructive potential of love is established by metaphor, the characterization of Saint-Preux as its vehicle is achieved through metonymy, each element articulating the
sequence of love's progress: eyes→feelings→words. Words, however, find expression in two modes, "discours" and "plume": the pen,
the instrument which records love, is the more dangerous, and
"plume" is the only term to be modified by an adjective other than
the possessive: "criminelle." All these hostile agents reinforce the
deadliness of the poison: "mortel" confirms the diagnosis of *l'amour-
passion* as a terminal disease:

Je n'ai rien négligé pour arrêter le progrès de cette passion funeste. Dans l'impuis-
sance de résister, j'ai voulu me garantir d'être attaquée; tes poursuites ont trompé ma
vaine prudence. Cent fois j'ai voulu me jeter aux pieds des auteurs de mes jours,
cent fois j'ai voulu leur ouvrir mon coeur coupable; ils ne peuvent connaître ce qui
s'y passe; ils voudront appliquer des remèdes ordinaires à un mal désespéré: ma mère
est faible et sans autorité; je connais l'inflexible sévérité de mon père, et je ne ferai
que perdre et déshonorer moi, ma famille, et toi-même. Mon amie est absente, mon
frère n'est plus; je ne trouve aucun protecteur au monde contre l'ennemi qui me
poursuit; j'implore en vain le ciel, le ciel est sourd aux prières des faibles. Tout
fomente l'ardeur qui me dévore; tout m'abandonne à moi-même, ou plutôt tout me
livre à toi; la nature entière semble être ta complice; tous mes efforts sont vains, je
t'adore en dépit de moi-même (13).

Having no secular allies, Julie looks to heaven, but there is no reply.
Delivered sacrificially to her persecutor, she can only yield to the inevitable, repudiating responsibility. Since all of Julie's efforts to be
"moral" fail, her passionate self takes over: "Je t'adore en dépit de
moi-même." With self-fulfilling prophecy, Julie thus confesses to
complicity in the very process of denial.

Fearing the future, she looks back to the past: "Ah! le premier pas,
qui coûte le plus, était celui qu'il ne fallait pas faire; comment m'ar-
rêterais-je aux autres? Non; de ce premier pas, je me sens entraîner
dans l'abîme, et tu peux me rendre aussi malheureuse qu'il te
plaira" (13). The drama of "premier" is reactivated. Previously used

in a punctual sense ("the first time"), here it is sequential, the beginning of a series of which the final term is always in implicit abeyance. "Le premier pas" was the step not to take; and having taken the most costly one, the others are inevitable. It remains only for Julie to acknowledge her impotence, which she does by inviting Saint-Preux to recognize his victory and his victim. Pleading for mercy from her persecutor, continuing to abdicate responsibility, Julie leaves the resolution of the problem to Saint-Preux: "Tu seras vertueux ou méprisé; je serai respectée, ou guérie. Voilà l'unique espoir qui me reste avant celui de mourir" (14). This proposition ends Julie's second letter. Despite the despairing language through which Julie has cast herself as a victim, she has not, in fact, been captured. But she has established the oppositional poles within which the narrative sequences unfold: the beginning contains the end, love contains death, Julie must deny herself to live, Saint-Preux must deny himself if Julie is to be cured. She has assumed the role of the persecuted maiden for whom there is no help, barring the transformation of her self-inflicted persecutor.

Saint-Preux, transported by the thought of being loved by Julie, assures her of the purity of his intentions: "Je frémirais de porter la main sur tes chastes attraits plus que du plus vil inceste, et tu n'es pas dans une sûreté plus inviolable avec ton père qu'avec ton amant" (15–16). Saint-Preux thus guarantees the containment of desire by the fear of contamination. By referring to the restrictions of the incest taboo, he at the same time asserts the possibility of a functional equivalency between himself and Julie's father. The novel, however, is founded on the very incompatibility of the lover and the father (indeed, this phase of the correspondence takes place in the *absence* of the father, who from the beginning is hostile to Saint-Preux). The implications of "unnatural" violation (sexuality as crime) thus are promoted by Saint-Preux as well.

Although Saint-Preux assures Julie that she purifies the flames of the passion she inspires, Julie remains frightened by the disruption love has caused in her. The split, the divided self, is described to Claire as *another* self: "C'est à toi de me rendre à moi-même" (17). Julie is *already* nostalgic for an original and lost innocence. Thus when Saint-Preux, restless in the conditions of their arrangement, seeks a reward for his sacrifice, Julie reconstructs the history of her feelings and invalidates his claims: "Mon imagination troublée confondait le crime avec l'aveu de la passion; . . . les combats de la modestie me parurent ceux de la chasteté; je pris le tourment du silence pour l'emportement des désirs" (24). She read too literally the signs of the text, taking the word for the reality it represented. The first misreading of erotic discourse led to a second: taking the emergence of defenses to mean the presence of real danger. In retrospect, these false interpretations can be corrected by a reappraisal of reality: "Deux mois d'expérience m'ont appris que mon coeur trop tendre a besoin d'amour, mais que mes sens n'ont aucun besoin d'amant" (24). Where Saint-Preux now wants sensual recognition, Julie proposes a soulful embrace: "Nos âmes se sont pour ainsi dire touchées par tous les points, et nous avons partout senti la même cohérence. . . . Le sort pourra bien nous séparer, mais non pas nous désunir" (28). The principle of platonic love reorganized by the strictures of courtly love functions as the ideological basis of Julie's revised version of their relationship.

Having found a satisfactory superstructure, Julie can now reassume control of their mutual destiny. And it is the fact of her *virginity* that serves as justification for her supremacy: "Nous nous trouvons dès le premier âge chargées d'un si dangereux dépôt, que le soin de le conserver nous éveille bientôt le jugement; et c'est un excellent moyen de bien voir les conséquences des choses, que de sentir vivement tous les risques qu'elles nous font courir" (29). Julie defines the psychological and ethical evolution of the female character as a function of an original guardianship. Feminine organization is thus fundamentally constituted by a strategy of *protection* in the face of potential harm: "*dangereux dépôt.*" Until Julie is in fact deflowered, the totality of the correspondence is implicitly or explicitly centered on this issue: who is to govern the protectorate; and her chastity polarizes the narrative as obsessively and consistently as does Pamela's or Clarissa's.

Julie then plans the stages of their affair, including the scheduling of the first kiss (directly before the first separation, also scheduled by Julie). The description of the "petite surprise," the mark of generosity to be accorded in the neutralizing presence of Claire, "*l'inséparable cousine,*" is supplied by Saint-Preux: "Le feu s'exhalait avec nos soupirs de nos lèvres brûlantes, et mon coeur se mourait sous le poids de la volupté, quand tout à coup je te vis pâlir, fermer tes beaux yeux, t'appuyer sur ta cousine, et tomber en défaillance" (38). In this representation of the kiss, passion again becomes a progression toward death. For if Saint-Preux's "volupté" is explicitly connected with dying, Julie's swoon is no less a "petite mort." Saint-Preux concludes his letter with an analysis of the implications of this "fatal moment": "Je ne puis plus vivre dans l'état où je suis, et je sens qu'il faut enfin que j'expire à tes pieds . . . ou dans tes bras" (39). The kiss of death, interrupted by Julie's faint, has left Saint-Preux in a zone of frustrated irresolution that can be mediated only by death or consummation, both now equivalencies opposed to life.

Julie, however, is more preoccupied with her father's kisses than with Saint-Preux's: "Ne conçois-tu point quel charme c'est de sentir, dans ces purs et sacrés embrassements, le sein d'un père palpiter d'aise contre celui de sa fille?" (45). In Julie's hierarchy, the father supplants the lover. His embrace belongs to the sacred sphere. The role of the daughter takes precedence over the role of the mistress. The return of the father, "le meilleur des pères," realizes Claire's prediction, opposition to Saint-Preux on the basis of his birth ("un petit bourgeois sans fortune!"). Through Claire, the reader learns the extent of Julie's misery: "L'aimable Julie est à l'extrémité, et n'a peut-être pas deux jours à vivre. L'effort qu'elle fit pour vous éloigner d'elle commença d'altérer sa santé; la première conversation qu'elle eut sur votre compte avec son père y porta de nouvelles attaques" (68). Julie, victim of the nameless fever that afflicts the heroine in the turmoil of conflicting emotions, obsessively invokes Saint-Preux in her delirium. Her rationalized defenses (as they retroactively appear) break down. Julie's mother, in the face of her daughter's imminent danger, allows Saint-Preux to return via Claire's mediation and without the knowledge of the father.

The oppositions of Saint-Preux to Julie and Julie to the father, predicted in Julie's first letter, are activated. While Saint-Preux prepares to take Julie away, her father promises her to another: "Enfin mon père m'a donc vendue! il fait de sa fille une marchandise, une esclave!" (68–69). But so negative a version is immediately renounced: "C'est le meilleur des pères; il veut unir sa fille à son ami, violà son crime" (69). This short letter, with its elliptical, unfinished sentences, rhetorical questions, and repeated exclamations, mimetically reproduces Julie's sense of ineffable doom: "C'en est fait, c'en est fait, la crise est venue. Un jour, une heure, un moment, peut-être . . . qui est-ce qui sait éviter son sort?" (69). Julie is again the persecuted maiden helplessly awaiting her fate. The letter functions as an alibi, justifying her fall—the account of which immediately follows.

Claire, the guardian of the kiss, was absent during its ultimate realization, and Julie, unprotected, succumbs to its promise: "Où étais-tu, ma douce amie, ma sauvegarde, mon ange tutélaire? Tu m'as abandonnée, et j'ai péri!" (69). After reproaching Claire for having recalled Saint-Preux and vilifying Saint-Preux for his barbarity, Julie assumes the blame, asserts her guilt: "Tous mes malheurs sont mon ouvrage, et je n'ai rien à reprocher qu'à moi" (70). Her first version gives pity as her motive. Seeing Saint-Preux agonizing at her feet (one of the two alternatives he had projected, death at her feet or in her arms), Julie yields: "Peut-être l'amour seul m'aurait épargnée; ô ma cousine! c'est la pitié qui me perdit" (70). Indeed, from the beginning Julie had anticipated the dangers of pity, her own guilt in the face of the strictures she had imposed. When confronted with a choice in which the stakes have escalated to deadly proportions, the hierarchy of values defies Julie's powers of reason. Guilt and anxiety confuse priorities: "Tout abattait mon courage, tout augmentait ma faiblesse, tout aliénait ma raison; il fallait donner la mort aux auteurs de mes jours, à mon amant, ou à moi-même" (70). Since each element of the first proposition is subverted by the verb that governs it (courage is dis-couraged, weakness strengthened, reason un-reasoned), the corresponding relations—Julie/parents, Julie/Saint-Preux, (immoral) Julie/(moral) Julie—are given equal value. Moreover, since each is marked with the potential of *death*, Julie annuls the component of alternative implicit in the concept of choice: "Sans savoir ce que je faisais, je choisis ma propre infortune; j'oubliai tout, et ne me souvins que de l'amour" (70). "Choosing," then, means succumbing to an irrational act of love, an irresponsible impulse that commits the "je" of the daughter to death, to eternal dishonor. And *that* self survives the disaster only to be narrated as negativity: "Je suis tombée dans l'abîme d'ignominie dont une fille ne revient point; et si je vis, c'est pour être plus malheureuse" (70). Like Clarissa, Julie has lost her "best" self.

Saint-Preux tries to console Julie by translating her behavior into a positive paradigm: Julie has become his "natural" wife, which transforms and sacralizes her fall into the abyss. But Julie regrets paradise lost: "Un feu pur et sacré brûlait nos coeurs; livrés aux erreurs des sens, nous ne sommes plus que des amants vulgaires" (76). Pure and sacred, she remained within the embrace of the father; profaned, she is disinherited. Only incorporating Saint-Preux or, rather, assimilating herself to him can repair that loss: "Sois tout mon être, à présent que je ne suis plus rien" (77). As Simone de Beauvoir has said of the woman in love, Julie, having experienced annihilation through sexualization, seeks to restore her abolished ego in the "dream of ecstatic union"; by being integrated with her lover's existence, she "will share his worth, she will be justified."[3]

Passive submission, however, is just one phase in the dialectic of love: for the woman in love, "her abdication of self saves her only on the condition that it restores her empire."[4] Thus Julie rebuilds her lost empire through a twofold process of manipulation: mystification and titillation. She begins by alluding to a secret solution to the dilemma of illicit love, projecting a future and at the same time demanding that Saint-Preux swear fidelity to her for a nonfuture: "Donne-moi, dans tes engagements pour *un avenir qui ne doit point être*, l'éternelle sécurité du présent" (84; italics mine). Withholding vital information from her lover (that she thinks she is expecting a child, that her father has promised her to another), she controls Saint-Preux through the ambiguity of the mixed message. Julie can then unambiguously bind him to her through the metaphor of courtly love: "C'est là, mon féal, qu'à genoux devant votre dame et maîtresse, vos deux mains dans les siennes, et en présence de son chancelier, vous lui jurerez foi et loyauté à toute épreuve" (86). This "chancelier" is Julie's other half, Claire, whose protection neutralizes passion.

Since Julie's parents are to be absent, Claire forms the third term of the triangle. Julie can then project a replication of the first kiss by proposing a lovers' meeting in the country. But in a love affair defined and nourished by obstacles, the rewards of chivalric devotion are often postponed. Saint-Preux is again deprived of what he was promised until frustration finally stimulates Julie as well, and she proposes the ultimate romantic encounter, a night in her room: "Loin de rebuter mon courage, tant d'obstacles l'ont irrité; je ne sais quelle nouvelle force m'anime, mais je me sens une hardiesse que je n'eus jamais; et, si tu l'oses partager, ce soir, ce soir même peut acquitter mes promesses, et payer d'une seule fois toutes les dettes de l'amour" (120). The invitation is thus profered as a challenge, a contest of courage in the name of *contractual* love. Its motivation is double: on the one hand, it is designed to prove to Saint-Preux the inadequacy of sexual desire: "Viens avouer, même au sein des plaisirs, que c'est de l'union des coeurs qu'ils tirent leur plus grand charme" (121). On the other, impatient with the irresolution of the situation, the static opposition of irreconcilable terms, Julie seeks to force a transformation. Thus Julie, who feels that she has no control over her destiny ("Je suis désormais à la seule merci du sort" [111]), acts to precipitate the inevitable, even or especially if it involves disaster: "Mais songe pourtant que cet instant est environné des *horreurs de la mort*; que l'abord est sujet à *mille hasards*, le séjour *dangereux*, la retraite d'un *péril extrême*; que *nous sommes perdus* si nous sommes *découverts*" (120; italics mine).

The danger implicit in the challenge to Saint-Preux's courage is thus made explicit. Indeed, Julie has planned their final tableau: "Si nous sommes surpris, mon dessein est de me précipiter dans tes bras, de t'enlacer fortement dans les miens, et de recevoir ainsi le coup mortel pour n'avoir plus à me séparer de toi, plus heureuse à ma mort que je ne le fus de ma vie" (121). The agent of death will be Julie's father, who, separating the lovers in life, will unite them in death. Star-crossed lovers, they will die together. Illicit sexuality will be punished by the legitimate representative of the family, of social order: the patriarch. And since loss of innocence has already condemned Julie to a non-life (by the violation of her existential values), her death will become the instrument of happiness.

Their night is spent undiscovered. Julie's father harms the lovers definitively, but not according to the scenario Julie had fantasized.[5] Outraged at the idea of a marriage between Julie and Saint-Preux, the baron slaps and beats Julie until she falls and bleeds. Forgiveness, however, follows anger; through his anger and authority the father reclaims his daughter: "Ici finit le triomphe de la colère et commença celui de la nature" (149) ("nature" for Julie means positive relations between the father and the daughter). The baron does not excuse himself but acts out his remorse: "Il cherchait les occasions de me nommer sa fille, et non pas Julie, comme à l'ordinaire" (150). In paternal reaffirmation, he has Julie sit on his lap: "Douce et paisible innocence, tu manquas seule à mon coeur pour faire de cette scène de la nature le plus délicieux moment de ma vie!" (151). Thus, lack of innocence (erotic feelings for Saint-Preux) subverts *natural* and familial order.

The following morning, the father enters his daughter's room, sits next to her bed (recently occupied by the lovers), and declares his immutable opposition to Saint-Preux. Immobilized by the violence of the competition, Julie turns to Claire: "Sépare-moi pour jamais de moi-même, donne-moi la mort s'il faut que je meure, mais ne me force pas à me percer le coeur de ma propre main" (152). This representation of Julie as divided self, where the division is equatable with death, is a reduplication of Julie's original vision. Early in the narrative the self-status she wished to return to was innocence, wholeness, daughterhood; here she would escape from the illicit, but being so far engaged, the "separation" involves a mutilation, an annihilation.

While the concept of death by her own hand was already operative in her decision to make love with Saint-Preux (70), sexuality did not bring the "death" she had anticipated. Her father's *will* does. The postscript to this letter announces that her father's blow caused her to miscarry. Indirectly, the father murders the child she hoped would be the term of transformation:[6] "Ainsi tout est fini pour moi; toutes mes espérances m'abandonnent en même temps" (153). The opposition remains unresolved. Claire, having summoned Saint-Preux to save Julie from death, now sends him away for the same reasons: "Le danger augmente incessamment: de la main de son père ou de la sienne, le poignard, à chaque instant de sa vie, est à deux doigts de son coeur" (158–59). Since Saint-Preux and the father cannot occupy the same place at the same time, Saint-Preux can save Julie by leaving, for Julie declares that she must stay: "Je ne déserterai jamais la maison paternelle" (185). She thus chooses the father over the lover, insisting, however, that her decision comes not from reason but from the heart. And she proposes a loving compromise: "Je ne t'épouserai jamais sans le consentement de mon père, mais je n'en épouserai jamais un autre sans ton consentement" (202). Thus through a rhetorical crisscross, she assumes again the impossibility of the double bind. But since she knows her father to be implacable and her lover submissive, she in fact establishes the possibility of another marriage.

When Claire marries, Julie retrieves the letters of her secret correspondence with Saint-Preux which Claire had been hiding, and unwittingly prepares the discovery that marks the final episode of Julie as daughter. For it is the mother, from whom Julie might have gained support, who finds the letters of criminal love: "La honte, l'humiliation, les cuisants reproches . . . j'ai tout mérité; je supporterai tout. Mais la douleur, les larmes d'une mère éplorée . . . ô mon coeur, quels déchirements!" (285). Just as pity for Saint-Preux generated Julie's fall, compassion for her mother motivates reparation. When her mother dies, Julie perceives this death as a function of her connection with Saint-Preux: "Vous par qui je plongeai le couteau dans le sein maternel, gémissez des maux qui me viennent de vous, et sentez avec moi l'horreur d'un parricide qui fut votre ouvrage" (295). The combinatory sex/death/family which overdetermined the narrative from the beginning takes its least ambiguous form here. As we have seen, in the idiolect of the text, sexual desire ("feu") finds expression through that instrument of communication ("plume criminelle") which in Julie's words/hands becomes the dagger ("poignard") of her immolation. Here "poignard" is replaced with the more domestic "couteau" responsible for her mother's death. The pen/dagger/phallus that kills Julie's filial innocence thus indirectly destroys the maternal principle as well.

The threat to Julie's existence as daughter temporarily rends the fabric of the family. The father seeks to repair that damage by giving Julie to a substitute of himself, an older man—a friend who had saved his life. Claire, as mediatress, recommends to Saint-Preux that he withdraw, since Julie betrothed is a Julie unavailable to him. Acceding to Claire's wisdom, Saint-Preux gives Julie permission to marry and Julie accepts her father's arrangement. But first she succumbs to smallpox, the heroine's disease par excellence. The fever and delirium and the obsession with Saint-Preux reproduce the conditions of her first illness. In the first illness, however, Julie emerged sexually committed to Saint-Preux. This time it marks her separation from him.[7] No longer seeking to escape her destiny, she accepts the marriage while reserving her "heart" for Saint-Preux. Claire announces the marriage/death of Julie in these terms: "Votre amante n'est plus; mais j'ai retrouvé mon amie, et vous en avez acquis une dont le coeur peut vous rendre beaucoup plus que vous n'avez perdu. Julie est mariée" (318). Claire has repossessed Julie's other half; the primacy of Saint-Preux's relation is reabsorbed in yet another process of triangulation. The cycle comes to an end with Julie's marriage to M. de Wolmar, which is posited as a new beginning. Julie is the rare heroine in the eighteenth-century novel whose saga involves a double incarnation and a double trial: as adolescent heroine and as married woman (Pamela, of course, passes the marriage threshhold to preside as matron, but marriage ends her sexual tests). During the second phase of Julie's life history, despite virtuous resistance supported by the bonds of marriage, the renascence anticipated is subverted by the reemergence of repressed desire for Saint-Preux.

After her marriage, Julie writes to Saint-Preux to give him an account of the transformation through which "his" Julie became Mme de Wolmar, and her program for the future: "Liée au sort d'un époux, ou plutôt aux volontés d'un père, par une chaîne indissoluble, j'entre dans une nouvelle carrière qui ne doit finir qu'à la mort" (319). In relating the chain of events that led up to this historic moment, Julie rewrites their novel according to the logic of fatal love. The first letter, like the first step, was the one to have avoided: "Au lieu de jeter au feu votre première lettre ou de la porter à ma mère, j'osai l'ouvrir: ce fut là mon crime, et tout le reste fut forcé" (320). Like Clarissa, Julie places the origin of the crime in correspondence; the first letter starts an irrevocable chain reaction. The second stage was the kiss: "Un instant, un seul instant embrasa . . . [mes sens] d'un feu que rien ne put éteindre; et si ma volonté résistait encore, dès lors mon coeur fut corrompu" (321). Once exposed, she fell victim to the illness she hoped would save her from herself; "mais la cruelle mort m'épargna pour me perdre. Je vous vis, je fus guérie, et je péris" (322): there is a fate worse than death. Forced to live, she thought destiny might still save her: "Le ciel rejeta des projets conçus dans le crime; je ne méritais pas l'honneur d'être mère" (324). After her mother's death, her father's emotional blackmail almost brought about her surrender to his will: " 'Ma fille, respecte les cheveux blancs de ton malheureux père; ne le fais pas descendre avec douleur au tombeau, comme celle qui te porta dans son sein; ah! veux-tu donner la mort à toute ta famille?' " (327), but Saint-Preux's heroic visit to Julie during her bout with smallpox revived her guilty passion: "Ainsi tous mes bons sentiments achèverent de s'éteindre, toutes mes facultés s'altérèrent, le crime perdit son horreur à mes yeux, *je me sentis tout autre au dedans de moi*" (330; italics mine). In this state of alienation from virtue, Julie prepared for marriage: "J'aurais vu les apprêts de ma sépulture avec moins d'effroi que ceux de mon mariage. . . . Dans l'instant même où j'étais prête à jurer à un autre une éternelle fidélité, mon coeur vous jurait encore un amour éternel, et je fus menée au temple comme une victime impure qui souille le sacrifice où l'on va l'immoler" (332). But the ceremony itself cannot resolve the conflict embedded in the very *language* of the dilemma ("éternelle fidélité" vs. "amour éternel"); resolution must come from transformation on another level. It is only the epiphany Julie experiences in the church that makes the transformation possible: "Une puissance inconnue sembla corriger tout à coup le désordre de mes affections et les rétablir selon la loi du devoir et de la nature" (333). This "correction" is, in fact, the reestablishment of the original hierarchy in which Julie obeyed the law of the father, the natural law of the sacred family. The illumination allows her to recover her Edenic integrity so that her new state is essentially the old; by becoming a wife she regains the status of the daughter: "liée au sort d'un époux, ou plutôt aux volontés d'un père."

Indeed, her illumination is presented consistently as rebirth: "Je crus me sentir renaître: je crus recommencer une autre vie" (334). The *new* Julie is the Julie that was lost: "La main secourable qui m'a conduite à travers les ténèbres est celle qui lève à mes yeux le voile de l'erreur, et me rend à moi malgré moi-même" (335). The clichés that invoke the work of Providence, the signs, then, of *revelation* redundantly confirm the radical conversion. The change of personality

results automatically from the mystical discovery; at the end of the es-
oteric quest is a new beginning. No longer *anima perambulans in
tenebris,* Julie's two selves, until this point split in a psychological
stalemate, are now reintegrated on a higher level. What Claire was
asked but failed to do (recover Julie's lost self for her), Providence
brings about.

Married, Julie is irrevocably Other, by belonging to another: "Julie
de Wolmar n'est plus votre ancienne Julie . . . il ne vous reste que
le choix de faire honneur de ce changement au vice ou à la vertu"
(342). For the transformation to be complete, Saint-Preux must
change as well; like Mr. B., he must transcend his disruptive maleness. Julie returns to the premises of their original situation, and
proposes that he content himself with being the lover of her soul
(343). Continuing to interpret desire as an obstacle to happiness, she
finally expresses relief at having been delivered from its threat
through the ties of marriage: "Ce lien si redouté me délivre d'une
servitude beaucoup plus redoutable, et mon époux m'en devient plus
cher pour m'avoir rendue à moi-même" (344). This other bondage is
precisely the price of desire, the burden of sexuality that Julie consistently experienced as oppression in the first phase of the novel. Marriage releases her from the demands of a desire that she regarded as
alienation from her true self.

But Julie's tribulations are not over; she is to be tried a second
time. In her incarnation as a married woman, desire banished reappears and its sublimation retroactively appears as repression, revelation as self-delusion. The perfect love, heroically sacrificed once
("immolé . . . à la vertu" [342]) through a marriage of self-denial, will
have to be immolated again, definitively, through death. That obstacles to Julie's program for happiness should reoccur is inevitable because the dialectic of *l'amour-passion* ends only in death; also because
its continuance is reinscribed in Julie's letter of farewell. By pointing
out to Saint-Preux the presence of tears on what is to be her *final* letter, she plays Mme de Tourvel's dangerous game of declining passion
while underscoring its existence. Moreover, while banishing Saint-
Preux from further direct communication, she establishes the principle of an exchange of letters with Claire. As a result, the original and
"safe" triangle remains. Nevertheless, in the first of many repeat per-

formances, Saint-Preux must leave in order to return in his new self and the necessity of his departure is sealed by the announcement of Julie's maternity: "Votre amie a donc ainsi que vous le bonheur d'être mère! Elle devait donc l'être? . . . Ciel inexorable! . . . O ma mère, pourquoi vous donna-t-il un fils dans sa colère?" (376–77). This legitimate child consolidates Julie's connection to another, a second family to which Saint-Preux cannot belong.

By the next letter in the sequence of the novel, four years later, Julie has two children. And by the third letter of this section, Saint-Preux has returned to visit with Julie in his new capacity as friend of the family: "C'était une mère de famille que j'embrassais" (404). Julie, for her part, finds her old lover changed for the better: "Au lieu de la soumission d'un esclave, il a maintenant le respect d'un ami qui sait honorer ce qu'il estime" (409). But despite Julie's claim that she admires the new Saint-Preux as an equal, she maintains a position of superiority from which (as in the past) she will test him. Saint-Preux's stay at Clarens begins with a process of trial and initiation; for he must learn by heart the geography of Julie's utopia of self-denial, her domain as Mme de Wolmar. Julie and her husband take Saint-Preux to her private sanctuary, a garden called Elysium, where nature is contained and controlled. After having been warned by Wolmar of the sacred nature of the place ("Apprenez à respecter les lieux où vous êtes; ils sont plantés par les mains de la vertu") as opposed to the groves of the past ("Jamais ma femme depuis son mariage n'a mis les pieds dans les bosquets dont vous parlez" [468]), Saint-Preux is given Julie's key so that he can return to the garden alone, to contemplate at his ease.

Wolmar thus articulates the conditions of the new relationship and acts to solidify it on his terms. Indeed, although Julie feels that it is up to her to convince herself and Wolmar that she is cured, it is Wolmar who in fact sets up the tests. He begins by taking the former lovers to the scene of their first kiss, the groves that Julie has avoided until now, since for her, it is in "ce même bosquet où commencèrent tous les malheurs de ma vie" (473). Wolmar insists that Julie and Saint-Preux reenact the kiss under his paternal supervision, and despite Julie's somber premonitions, she reports that the programmed version lacked the magic of the original: "Ce baiser n'eut rien de celui qui m'avait rendu le bosquet redoutable: je m'en félicitai tristement, et je connus que mon coeur était plus changé que jusque-là je n'avais osé le croire" (479). Wolmar feels that he has obtained his objective for he explains to Julie: "Ne craignez plus cet asile, il vient d'être profané" (479–80). Whereas for Pamela, revisiting the places of her traumatic past—the garden, the pond, the summer house—is salutary and celebrated as the consecration of progress toward psychic integration and future happiness, for Julie it is, rather, a perverse pilgrimage in which what was sacred is desecrated. Recognition of the transformation is less a subject of joy than resignation; at best the ambivalence of the bittersweet:[8] "félicitai tristement."

The premise of Wolmar's security is not, however, the illusion that Julie and Saint-Preux are no longer in love, but that *they* are convinced that they are not. Indeed, Wolmar's penultimate test—leaving the lovers alone with each other—is meant to demonstrate that Saint-Preux's love for Julie exists only "dans le temps passé"; that he loves Julie d'Etange, not Julie de Wolmar (492). Nonetheless, and despite the kissing trial, Julie fears the dangers of intimacy. Claire (absent herself) suggests another form of mediation: a boating excursion which would permit Julie "de jouir paisiblement d'un long tête-à-tête sous la protection des bateliers" (488). The outing, however, proves to contain its own dangers, for the boat almost capsizes in rough water, and an unexpected storm forces them to take shelter at Meillerie, the place of Saint-Preux's earlier exile. Saint-Preux seeks to relive those historic moments with Julie but she protests. His claim, however, that their hearts have maintained their special understanding is not denied: "Il est vrai, dit-elle d'une voix altérée; mais que ce soit la dernière fois qu'ils auront parlé sur ce ton" (504). In the conjugation of *l'amour-passion*, the future past must be read as the present tense.

Wolmar then imposes a third test on Saint-Preux: a final separation. While Saint-Preux is away, Julie imagines the means of a transformation that will afford total security to the prospective community: she would have Saint-Preux and Claire—now a young widowed mother—marry. Although Claire is reluctant, Julie perseveres and proposes the match to Saint-Preux: "Ne pouvant vous faire ange vous-même, je vous en veux donner un qui garde votre âme, qui l'épure, qui la ranime, et sous les auspices duquel vous puissiez vivre avec nous dans la paix du séjour céleste" (657). Julie, still fearing the excesses of Saint-Preux's sexuality, suggests (with Pauline high-mindedness) that it is better to marry than to burn. But the refinement of the proposition is, perhaps, less celestial; applying the established principles of inseparability (Julie equals Claire), Julie suggests, with a reasoning worthy of Manon, that Saint-Preux make love to her double: "N'est-ce pas aussi Julie que je vous donne? . . . Que votre coeur remplisse avec elle tous les engagements qu'il prit avec moi . . . je lui transmets cette ancienne dette" (658–59). The debt, Julie's term for sexual obligation (120), paid through mediation, reverses the terms of their original relation: where Claire witnessed Julie's sexuality with Saint-Preux, now Julie can enjoy Saint-Preux through Claire.

The rationalization of such an arrangement is supported by Julie's idealization of the family: "Voilà, mon ami, le moyen que j'imagine de nous réunir sans danger, en vous donnant dans notre famille la même place que vous tenez dans nos coeurs. Dans le noeud cher et sacré qui nous unira tous, nous ne serons plus entre nous que des soeurs et des frères" (659). Safe within the family, stability can be achieved, and Julie can have at last what she originally wanted: Saint-Preux (the brother she lost) and her father. This reconstructed family would resolve all the archaic oppositions. Saint-Preux, however, while acknowledging Claire's attractiveness, feels that he is cured of desire: "Non, non; les feux dont j'ai brûlé m'ont purifié; je n'ai plus rien d'un homme ordinaire" (666). He does not need or want a surrogate Julie; he has finally learned Julie's lesson. He has learned how to love without sensuality; he is already neutered.[9] Before Saint-Preux can return to take his adopted place in the family, however, Julie dies while trying to save her son from drowning. As Claire writes: "Jamais vous ne la reverrez . . . le voile . . . Julie n'est . . . " (691).

What remains is the answer to the enigma of Julie's heart: the final lifting of the veil. Earlier in the novel, when Wolmar seeks to justify leaving Saint-Preux and Julie alone for a week, he explains to Claire the "key" to his ostensibly "bizarre" behavior. The key to his confidence is an oxymoron: Saint-Preux and Julie love each other, but they are also "cured": which he calls an *enigma* (492). But this enigma is not equally puzzling: as it pertains to Saint-Preux, "le vrai mot de l'énigme," he writes, is that Saint-Preux loves a memory, "la mère de deux enfants n'est plus son ancienne écolière" (492). At best there is a family resemblance. For Julie, however, the case is less clear, for "un voile de sagesse et d'honnêteté fait tant de replis autour de son coeur, qu'il n'est plus possible à l'oeil humain d'y pénétrer, pas même au sien propre" (492). The impossibility of self-knowledge as it concerns the status of desire had already been put in place metaphorically by Julie herself at the moment of her epiphany in the temple; at that moment, the veil of human blindness had been lifted by the hand of Providence. That revelation had returned Julie to herself, had allowed Julie de Wolmar to come into being by obscuring the "ancienne Julie." It will take another illumination, that brought about by imminent death, for the veil covering her heart as Mme de Wolmar to be lifted.

That the veil is there to be noted and interpreted by the reader is assured by its recurrence as the novel moves to closure, resolution, death, and revelation. Saint-Preux is banished from Julie's presence by Wolmar's last test; and while Julie fantasizes a "séjour céleste" (657) for all parties, he sees Julie in a nightmare, her face covered by a veil. In this anticipated version of her death to him, Julie remains shrouded in mystery, despite Saint-Preux's efforts to penetrate: " 'Ami, calme-toi,' " she warns him, " 'le voile redoutable me couvre, nulle main ne peut l'écarter' " (603). Saint-Preux would rationalize the dream by making Julie's veil his own, and miming her epiphany— (". . . ce voile dont ma raison fut longtemps offusquée. Tous mes transports inquiets sont éteints. Je vois tous mes devoirs et je les aime" [606])—thus discovering that he too is capable of transcendence. But his "reading" neither erases the omens of death (Claire remains disquiet and morbid: "Ce voile! ce voile! . . . Il a je ne sais quoi de sinistre qui me trouble chaque fois que j'y pense" [607–08]) nor the fundamental *impenetrability* of Mme de Wolmar. Tony Tanner writes:

that veil subsumes in very clear symbolic form a great deal; all that has indeed separated Julie from her lover, all that she has allowed to come between them, and all that she has interposed between them herself—the inseparable cousin (at the beginning), the Word of the father, *la maison paternelle*, the *chaîne indissoluble* of her marriage, the rigid and powerful *cortège* in which she is fixed as the mother.[10]

The enigma, then, concretized through the veil, would seem to be bound up with an eighteenth-century version of a certain "unthinkable: the Mother's (sexual) pleasure."[11]

It is M. de Wolmar who gives the account of Julie's extraordinary last days (thirty-six pages): "Elle n'a point vécu comme une autre; personne, que je sache, n'est mort comme elle" (692). Wolmar himself is perplexed by Julie's tranquil agony: "Tout cela formait à mon sens une énigme inexplicable" (701). Like Clarissa, a faithful Protestant, Julie feels that she has made her peace with God the father, and that there is nothing left to fear: " 'Qui s'endort dans le sein d'un père n'est pas en souci du réveil' " (704). Julie generates her own halo, and confirms in dying the angelic essence that inspired the cult of her worshippers. The answer to the enigma, however, remains to be given and Julie explains to Wolmar that it is contained in a letter destined for Saint-Preux, a letter she gives him unsealed so that he can read it and determine whether it should be sent. In keeping with her vow, Julie bends, until the end, to the supremacy of the legitimate bond.

However, from the safety of conjugality and the imminence of her death, she is also free to tell the truth: "Je me suis longtemps fait illusion. Cette illusion me fut salutaire; elle se détruit au moment que je n'en ai plus besoin" (728). In death, her victory assured, her innocence maintained, Julie can confess to her vulnerability: "Un jour de plus peut-être, et j'étais coupable! qu'était-ce de la vie entière passée avec vous?" (729). Retroactively, Julie admits to the violence involved in repression: "Après tant de sacrifices, je compte pour peu celui qui me reste à faire: ce n'est que mourir une fois de plus" (729). Julie's "real" confrontation with death, then, replicates the sacrifice of her marriage, invalidating it as *illusion* in the terms in which it was conceived but reinscribing it in a higher code: "La vertu qui nous sépara sur la terre nous unira dans le séjour éternel. Je meurs dans cette douce attente: trop heureuse d'acheter au prix de ma vie le droit de t'aimer toujours sans crime, et de te le dire encore une fois!" (731).

Thus for Julie, the rewards of virtue are not a function of this world, but the next; the utopia she imagined, "le séjour céleste" (657), can only be realized in Christian paradise. Sexuality still synonymous with criminality can only be transcended definitively beyond the flesh. Only when the *word* is delivered from the grave can it remain innocent; Julie reminds Saint-Preux that when he is reading/hearing her last words "les vers rongeront le visage de ton amante" (731). Julie, then, dies giving herself to Saint-Preux, but in keeping with her character, remaining—as in his dream—beyond his touch in the ultimate nonconsummation. In death, Julie, like Manon, grants total and impossible possession.

It is Claire, Julie's other half, who ends the novel[12] (if we except the ultimate and authorial footnote)—not Saint-Preux, whom, in his grief, one can only imagine beyond words—Claire who cancels the future, preferring by far the past tense. Claire will have nothing to do with love, or marriage. In closing, she *names* her cousin only once, and by her *nom de jeune fille*, Julie d'Etange, curiously erasing the *mother* in whose memory Saint-Preux is to return as preceptor.

Through her death, then, Julie escapes finally from conjugality and bypasses motherhood to become again the daughter she always was. The secret desire of Mme de Wolmar is not a mother's pleasure, but a daughter's nostalgia.

Chapter Eight

THE MISFORTUNES OF VIRTUE: III

Les Liaisons Dangereuses

> Je ne sais pourquoi les hommes taxent les femmes de fausseté,
> et ont fait la Vérité femelle. Problème à résoudre. On dit aussi
> qu'elle est nue, et cela se pourrait bien. C'est sans doute par un
> amour secret pour la Vérité que nous courons après les femmes
> avec tant d'ardeur; nous cherchons à les dépouiller de tout ce que
> nous croyons qui cache la Vérité; et, quand nous avons satisfait
> notre curiosité sur une, nous nous détrompons, nous courons tous
> vers une autre, pour être plus heureux. L'amour, le plaisir et l'in-
> constance ne sont qu'une suite du désir de connaître la Vérité.
> —Duclos, *Oeuvres complètes*

Les Liaisons dangereuses is the only novel in this study whose title
does not announce the name(s) of its heroine(s). It announces instead
a plural focus and in that sense the primacy of plot over character, of
social event over any human singularity. By isolating two female destinies from the weave of intersecting letters, and thereby implicitly arguing for the inclusion of the novel as a heroine's text, I am doing
some small violence to Laclos's novel. It seems to me, however, that
the prefaces to the novel, despite their ironic manipulations of the
convention, justify my excision. Both the publisher's note and the
editor's preface identify female destiny as a crucial determinant in the
readability of the text. In the first instance we are told that in this
enlightened age it may be difficult for the reader to believe that a
doweried young lady should end her days in a convent, or a pretty

married young woman die of grief; in the second, that these same destinies are object lessons for readers of both sexes, but particularly for mothers and daughters. In this sense, the "literary" stakes of the genre—are these real letters, or is this only a novel?—and its ideological support—what is the moral justification for publishing this correspondence, real or not?—are intimately bound up with the feminine gender. The preface, moreover, articulates two maxims we have seen before guarantee the logic of the heroine's text: one, that "toute femme qui consent à recevoir dans sa société un homme sans moeurs, finit par en devenir la victime"; the other, that "toute mère est au moins imprudente, qui souffre qu'un autre qu'elle ait la confiance de sa fille."[1] These two important truths, as they are labeled, of course do not constitute the whole truth of the Liaisons.[2] They are, however, the grounding plausibility of its plots of seduction and betrayal, worldliness and innocence. The heroine's text in the Liaisons thus officially recapitulates the by now familiar premise of the dysphoric scenarios of the earlier novels: Laclos, his epigraph reminds us, has read La Nouvelle Héloïse; and Mme de Tourvel, we learn, Clarissa. Although the new attention to event implicit in the title, and to eventuality as ironized in the prefaces, might seem to suggest a dedramatization and a decentering of the feminine narrative, Laclos's novel, as I see it, does not so much undo the "old plot"[3] as unveil it. In that process, the heroine's story is at once reinscribed and rewritten. By approaching the Liaisons first as the text of its designated major female casualty, the Présidente, and then as the text of the female protagonist whose destiny is not announced in the prefaces, Mme de Merteuil, I propose to read the novel both as the feminocentric fiction it pretends to be and the feminocentric fiction it fails to be.

Like Clarissa, Mme de Tourvel is introduced to the reader as the reification of the attributes aligned in apposition to her name: "sa dévotion, son amour conjugal, ses principes austères" (17). In the eyes of their would-be seducers, what Clarissa stands for as a girl, Mme de Tourvel stands for as a woman: exemplary femininity and therefore the supreme challenge to the roué's standard script. Valmont's choice of the Présidente as the ideal type for his new project of seduction and betrayal, moreover, like Lovelace's, is based on the assumption that she is also *other* than her reputation, and that the truth of the prude is double. To Merteuil's claim that Mme de Tourvel, embarked as she is on a career of self-abnegation, can neither give nor experience real pleasure, at best "des demi-jouissances" (19), Valmont counters: "Elle est prude et dévote, et de là vous la jugez froide et inanimée? Je pense bien différemment. Quelle étonnante sensibilité ne faut-il pas avoir pour la répandre jusque sur son mari et pour aimer toujours un être toujours absent? Quelle preuve plus forte pourriez-vous désirer?" (21). Thus, if *Clarissa* is the novel of Lovelace's attempt and failure to prove the truth of the maxim, "Once subdued, always subdued," the *Liaisons* is Valmont's successful manipulation of another piece of conventional wisdom: "Le premier pas franchi, ces Prudes austères savent-elles s'arrêter? leur amour est une véritable explosion; la résistance y donne plus de force" (231). The Prude, like the Exemplar, fears, as Valmont puts it, "de sauter le fossé" (21–22). Lovelace must get Clarissa out of her father's house, since, as Anna Howe correctly observes, "Once you leave your father's house, punctilio is out the door." Valmont must get the Présidente to jump over the ditch: to let him into her fortress, her tower (as her name suggests). How does a libertine get a prude to take the proverbial first step? By talking about it; by talking about love. And this is perhaps the meta-maxim of seduction: "femme qui consent à parler d'amour," Valmont reminds Merteuil, "finit bientôt par en prendre" (155).

By the time the reader arrives at Mme de Tourvel's first letter the machinery for her seduction has already been established; and her defeat—from the publisher's note, if nothing else—overdetermined. Such prescience results in a necessarily slanted reading of Mme de Tourvel's text; her words are always filtered through a grid of information she herself can never possess. Her first letters, written to Madame de Volanges, correspond by the informal, polite, and humble tone to the mode of her type as announced, and establish the nature of her connection to the Volanges family. Mme de Tourvel characterizes Mme de Volanges's actions as "bontés vraiment maternelles," and her own feelings for Cécile as "l'amitié tendre d'une soeur" (25). With Mme de Rosemonde, Valmont's aunt, as a com-

panion, then, and an absent husband, she functions within a feminocentric "family." Valmont's presence in this world is thus a sexualized
intrusion, which she first perceives as familial and positive: "Notre retraite est égayée par son neveu le Vicomte de Valmont, qui a bien
voulu nous sacrifier quelques jours. Je ne le connaissais que de réputation, et elle me faisait peu désirer de le connaître davantage: mais il
me semble qu'il vaut mieux qu'elle" (25). In Mme de Tourvel's conscious perspective, Valmont's visit therefore is both a privilege and a
discovery: "Ici où le tourbillon du monde ne le gâte pas, il parle raison avec une facilité étonnante, et il s'accuse de ses torts avec une can-
deur rare. Il me parle avec beaucoup de confiance, et je le prêche
avec beaucoup de sévérité" (25). In retreat from the world, Mme de
Tourvel can listen to words she would otherwise have to reject—in
view of Valmont's reputation—and turn them to her advantage. Thus
the prude chastizes the rake, and the rake denigrates himself in the
face of purity. Finally, the Présidente draws the obvious conclusion
from her analysis: "Vous qui le connaissez, vous conviendrez que ce
serait une belle conversion à faire" (25). Tempted and, like Clarissa,
oblivious to her own vulnerability, Mme de Tourvel would convert
the epitome of worldliness while Valmont plays at reform in order to
facilitate his very secular intrusion. She does not understand the rules
of this game and Valmont does; but in the end both are captured.

Despite the Présidente's confident evaluation of the situation, Mme
de Volanges issues a warning, to which Mme de Tourvel replies with
some warmth: "Ce redoutable M. de Valmont, qui doit être la ter-
reur de toutes les femmes, paraît avoir déposé ses armes meurtrières,
avant d'entrer dans ce Château" (32). The source of her confidence
lies in the opposition she makes between *all women* and *this* chateau:
Mme de Tourvel is not other women, and this is her territory, her
fortress. Then, after having praised Valmont's unromantic behavior,
she concludes: "Enfin, si j'avais un frère, je désirerais qu'il fût tel que
M. de Valmont se montre ici" (32). This familial fantasy is crucial to
her justification for fraternization: "Peut-être beaucoup de femmes
lui désireraient une galanterie plus marquée; et j'avoue que je lui sais
un gré infini d'avoir su me juger assez bien pour ne pas me con-
fondre avec elles" (32–33). This is the key to the Présidente's relation-

ship with Valmont: she must feel that he perceives her as unique and superior to all other women; as long as he can convince her of that, everything is possible.

In the eighteenth-century novel, *any* heroine presented as virtuous and inexperienced inevitably confronts a would-be seducer. And this encounter can lead to only two possible outcomes, capitulation or victorious resistance. Within these options there are of course, as we have seen, variant forms characterized by degrees of irony or pathos according to context and register; and within these *modal* variations there are important contingencies of situation. Thus, while the erotic contest for Julie (as for Clarissa) is inscribed within the family and through the family society at large, Mme de Tourvel pursues her sexual destiny without the ("real") interference of the father. Adultery, obviously, constitutes a violation of the female social contract just as loss of virginity does. But the stakes of infidelity play themselves out less in relation to the husband[4]—who is an absent signifier—than in relation to a *private* definition of self. Mme de Tourvel circulates in the world according to her own values, however conventional they may be. Consequently, Valmont, as connoisseur of desirable objects, must subvert Mme de Tourvel's *self*-confidence if he is to add her to his collection. Only by forcing her to acknowledge a split between her public status and her private impulses can he successfully destroy her defenses.

Mme de Tourvel, like Julie, operates on the basis of pre-encoded principles.[5] From the beginning, we saw, the justification for her dialogue with Valmont—despite his reputation as a *dangerous* man—was his apparent respect for her pious status and social role. Valmont will now deliberately play to this image by performing a calculated act of charity—for her benefit. When Mme de Tourvel recounts the episode to Mme de Volanges, she reveals to the reader the *affective* value of such actions in her system: "C'est la plus belle vertu des plus belles âmes: mais, soit hasard ou projet, c'est toujours une action honnête et louable, et dont le seul récit m'a attendrie jusqu'aux larmes" (50). Valmont has activated the vital connection between good deeds and emotivity, and he accurately interprets the vehemence of her reaction to his performance ("On eût dit qu'elle prêchait le panégyrique d'un Saint" [51]) as a sign of the depth of emotion contained within her. Thus his game will be to continue to exploit the role of reformed rake by which Mme de Tourvel rationalized the initial encounter.

As long as Mme de Volanges remains Mme de Tourvel's confidante, it is Valmont's letters to *his* confidante, Mme de Merteuil, and *her* interpretation of his version of events that reveal to the reader the progression of Mme de Tourvel's feelings—feelings that she herself would rather not recognize. Whereas Julie exposes herself directly and completely in her letters to Claire and Saint-Preux, Mme de Tourvel must be deciphered through another consciousness. By this process, the reader knows more about Mme de Tourvel than she herself does, and this supplement of information serves to underscore her status as victim. For example, in the episode which marks the active launching of Valmont's campaign, the reader is given proof of Mme de Tourvel's inner life, her emotivity and vulnerability. Valmont makes a declaration of love on bended knee which leads her to confess her unhappy state—" 'Ah! malheureuse!' " (53)—and to burst into tears. These two words, which function as his leverage and justify both his first letter and her first step (her explanation), are communicated in Valmont's text. But what orients the reader is not so much the information as his reflection—his anger at the ease with which he has succeeded. His game requires recognition of the *price* of victory or loss on the part of the opponent: "Ah! qu'elle se rende, mais qu'elle combatte; que, sans avoir la force de vaincre, elle ait celle de résister; qu'elle savoure à loisir le sentiment de sa faiblesse, et soit contrainte d'avouer sa défaite. Laissons le Braconnier obscur tuer à l'affût le cerf qu'il a surpris; le vrai Chasseur doit le forcer" (53–54). The vocabulary of military strategy in which conquest is vaunted by indirection, by emphasis on defeat, is transcoded to a cynegetic metaphor worthy of Lovelace which expands upon the superiority of the hunter. The result is to mark the object of pursuit as doubly vulnerable—and the pursuer, doubly powerful.

The final element in the will to domination set in place by Valmont is that of Mme de Tourvel as love's victim. After observing her on her knees weeping and praying, Valmont boasts: "Quel dieu osait-elle invoquer? en est-il d'assez puissant contre l'amour? En vain cherche-t-elle à présent des secours étrangers: c'est moi qui réglerai son sort" (54). In his omnipotence fantasy, Valmont ascribes to himself total control over Mme de Tourvel's destiny: as agent of *fatum* and involuntary love. On every level, then, the description of their relationship depends upon a binary opposition—prude/libertine, quarry/hunter—which culminates here in the supervising polarization *victim/victimizer*, where the victim prays to be preserved from the sacrifice while the sacrificer prepares her immolation.

In her second letter to Mme de Volanges, Mme de Tourvel had defined the security of her position vis-à-vis Valmont, security based upon her moral superiority to other women and the walls of her fortress. Her problem now is to account for the apparent breach in her defense caused by Valmont's *error*: "L'étonnement et l'embarras où m'a jetée votre procédé; je ne sais quelle crainte, inspirée par une situation qui n'eût jamais dû être faite pour moi; peut-être l'idée révoltante de me voir confondue avec les femmes que vous méprisez, et traitée aussi légèrement qu'elles; toutes ces causes réunies ont provoqué mes larmes, et ont pu me faire dire, avec raison je crois, que j'étais malheureuse" (58). Her explanation to Valmont builds upon the connotations of "confusion": first, surprise and discomfort caused by the unexpected declaration of love; second, nameless fear resulting from a disorientation, from finding herself in someone else's script; and finally, the ramifications of that displacement: he has taken her for another, confused her with other (ordinary) women. It is a case of mistaken identity. The danger of his *false* perception caused in her the mental and emotional perplexity that erupts in tears and forces words to be uttered, words destroying the security of silence.

The rest of her letter develops the potential of this situation which, of course, belongs to the narrative cliché of first love. Mme de Tourvel, however, refuses that cultural metatext, refuses sentimental over-determination, and seeks to erase both the confusion and the words: "Vous ne me connaissez pas; non, Monsieur, vous ne me connaissez pas" (59). If he knew her, he would understand his mistake. Since his letter compounds his error by recording the outrage (like Saint-Preux's *criminal* pen), not only must silence ensue, but destruction of the evidence as well: "Je serais vraiment peinée qu'il restât aucune trace d'un événement qui n'eût jamais dû exister" (59). If the words cannot be taken back, their echo at least can be stifled, so that what ought not to have been will not be.

Mme de Merteuil, in her analysis of this letter, remarks on Mme de Tourvel's use of *words* and her understanding of their implications (70) and faults her only on the length of the letter, the sign of her self-betrayal. But she is optimistic for Valmont: "Je prévois qu'elle . . . épuisera [ses forces] pour la défense du mot, et qu'il ne lui en restera plus pour celle de la chose" (71). Indeed, the sexualizing power of the word we saw in Julie is operative here: to receive the word is to be penetrated by it. Defense against it is thus an act of *repulsion*, requiring an expenditure of energy that eventually weakens the ability to resist. When Mme de Tourvel discovers that she cannot stop the flow of words (Valmont's letters), she resolves to ask him to leave, citing his persistence in continuing the dialogue, in *articulating* feelings "que je ne veux ni ne dois écouter" (86). Valmont is flouting both her desire (*vouloir*) and her duty (*devoir*). But since Valmont has access to Mme de Tourvel's personal effects, he knows that she has not only saved all of his letters but also wept over one and recopied the first "d'une écriture altérée et tremblante" (96). The reader too knows that Mme de Tourvel cannot be taken at her word.

Indeed, her text soon reveals the signs of compromise. She accepts to discuss love: "Qui peut vouloir d'un bonheur acheté au prix de la raison, et dont les plaisirs peu durables sont au moins suivis des regrets, quand ils ne le sont pas des remords?" (105). Like Julie, Mme de Tourvel fears the costliness of passion. In the ideology of the French eighteenth-century novel, love as pleasure by definition cannot last, but its side effects are everlasting. And if the concept of illicit love per se evokes immediate negative associations, upon reflection Mme de Tourvel sees her own inexperience as a factor of additional misery: "Quel ravage effrayant ne ferait-il donc pas sur un coeur neuf et sensible, qui ajouterait encore à son empire par la grandeur des sacrifices qu'il serait obligé de lui faire?" (105). Love in Mme de Tourvel's system emerges both as alienation ("acheté au prix de la raison") and immolation (sacrifice being an oligatory function). Thus the very discussion of love disrupts the mind: "Il me semble que d'en parler seulement altère la tranquillité" (106). Love would bring change to her life, and change itself is seen as negative; Mme de Tourvel, like Julie, seeks to preserve the security of stasis.

Despite her avowed longing for silence, Mme de Tourvel continues to reply, insisting each time that she is writing for the last time and even then only to explain herself:

Chérie et estimée d'un mari que j'aime et respecte, mes devoirs et mes plaisirs se rassemblent dans le même objet. Je suis heureuse, je dois l'être. S'il existe des plaisirs plus vifs, je ne les désire pas; je ne veux point les connaître. . . . Ce que vous appelez le bonheur, n'est qu'un tumulte des sens, un orage des passions dont le spectacle est effrayant, même à le regarder du rivage. Eh! comment affronter ces tempêtes? Comment oser s'embarquer sur une mer couverte des débris de mille et mille naufrages? Et avec qui? Non, Monsieur, je reste à terre; je chéris les liens qui m'y attachent. Je pourrais les rompre, que je ne le voudrais pas; si je ne les avais, je me hâterais de les prendre. (117).

Mme de Tourvel, like Julie, founds her resistance to sexuality on temperamental incompatibility. Her version of happiness is based upon the inseparability of two notions: affectivity and worthiness. The "object" that permits the syncretism of both modes of existence is the husband. Her relationship with him guarantees serenity and good conscience. The bonds of the couple bind her safely to the earth, and this is a connection she would choose.

Opposed to that is Valmont's conception of happiness, posited on the existence of pleasures unknown to her. The description of *that* happiness ("ce que vous appelez le bonheur") is composed of terms related to the disruption of nature. The initial metaphor, "tumulte des sens," provides the matrix for the impassioned palinode on the dangers of desire.[6] Recoded as "orage des passions," the phenomenology of love as violence becomes a pathetic spectacle observed from the shore by a timorous spectator. The rhetoric of fear, introduced by "effrayant," is inspired by the dénouement of the drama: the "débris de mille et mille naufrages." For the "débris" in question bring Mme de Tourvel back again to the other women in Valmont's life, those whom he seduced and abandoned: "De ce moment, elles ont tout perdu, jusqu'à l'estime de celui à qui elles ont tout sacrifié" (118). In sacrificing themselves to a man women lose everything. The thought of this terrifying sacrifice precipitates a frenzy of imperatives: "Laissez-moi, ne me voyez plus; ne m'écrivez plus, je vous en prie;

je l'exige. Cette Lettre est la dernière que vous recevrez de moi"
(118). Her supplication, however, undercuts her imperiousness and
generates her next letter.

She now writes to justify her attitude and to propose a solution to
the dilemma: friendship. This would neutralize the sexual component of their relationship: "En vous offrant mon amitié, Monsieur, je
vous donne tout ce qui est à moi, tout ce dont je puis disposer. Que
pouvez-vous désirer d'avantage?" (139). In this logic, anything else
would not be part of herself or not hers to give—thus removing her
sexuality from the realm of exchange. Nonetheless, Valmont reads
this letter as a "projet de capitulation" and resents the facility with
which she maintains her good conscience. He is, indeed, after something else: "Mon projet, au contraire, est qu'elle sente, qu'elle sente
bien la valeur et l'étendue de chacun des sacrifices qu'elle me fera
. . . de faire expirer sa vertu dans une lente agonie; de la fixer sans
cesse sur ce désolant spectacle; et de ne lui accorder le bonheur de
m'avoir dans ses bras, qu'après l'avoir forcée à n'en plus dissimuler le
désir" (143). From the beginning, Valmont expressed the determination to make Mme de Tourvel's defeat a conscious one on her part, a
painful realization. This *spectacle* of virtue immolated to passion, this
agon, is Valmont's version of the drama Mme de Tourvel had fantasized earlier. An important refinement to the simple *victim/
victimizer* polarization, however, is introduced here; the medi-
ating participation of the victim. It is not enough for Mme de
Tourvel to witness passively the sacrifice of her virtue, she must be
moved to the conscious *articulation* of her own desire.

In Mme de Tourvel's next letters that desire is admitted, although
the resolve to control it does not change: "Vous le voyez, je vous dis
tout, je crains moins d'avouer ma faiblesse, que d'y succomber: mais
cet empire que j'ai perdu sur mes sentiments, je le conserverai sur
mes actions; oui, je le conserverai, j'y suis résolue; fût-ce aux dépens
de ma vie" (206). Words may have lost their deadliness and the feelings they represent become admissible, but the resistance is only
displaced. The struggle is still a matter of life and death. And Mme
de Tourvel, like Julie, having confessed to weakness, turns to her tor-
mentor for help: "Alors, respirant par vos bienfaits, je chérirai mon
existence, et je dirai dans la joie de mon coeur: 'Ce calme que je res-

sens, je le dois à mon ami' " (207). Mme de Tourvel thus puts her
fate clearly in Valmont's hands, granting him power of life and
death—but withholding, nevertheless, access to her *person*: "Mais
devenir coupable! . . . non, mon ami, non, plutôt mourir mille
fois" (207). Life, then, is equivalent to innocent serenity; sexual col-
laboration emerges as the mean term: a fate different from, but worse
than death.

Mme de Tourvel and Julie are both attracted to a concept of love
purified and desexualized by the exercise of virtue. They are stimulated by the challenge of sublimating their own feelings. At the same
time, reluctantly assimilating the sexual imperative into their own
system, their resistance takes the form of an attack on the life of passions as incarnated by men. The real victory sought is to force the
lover to accept voluntarily what essentially amounts to a castration in
the name of love: love untainted by desire, mediated by platonic
friendship or Christian devotion—love, in a word, that women can
control.

Having lost control over her feelings, Mme de Tourvel now feels
free to use the forbidden words, not in her correspondence with Valmont, for she is still engaged in a linguistic struggle with him, but
with Mme de Rosemonde: "Que vous dirai-je enfin? j'aime, oui,
j'aime éperdument" (238). There are no more letters to Mme de
Volanges, the voice of reason and duty. From this point on, the older
woman, Valmont's aunt, becomes her sole confidante. By her confession Mme de Tourvel seeks to transform Mme de Rosemonde into
a surrogate mother: "Regardez-moi comme votre enfant. Ayez pour
moi les bontés maternelles; je les implore" (237). Promising to tell
her "mother" everything, Mme de Tourvel hopes to obtain what
Julie is given by Claire—another, better self to protect her against
danger: "Votre vertu remplacera la mienne . . . je chérirai en vous
l'indulgente amie, confidente de ma faiblesse, j'y honorerai encore
l'Ange tutélaire qui me sauvera de la honte" (239). By thus becoming
the prodigal daughter, she can remain integrated within society and
at the same time unburden herself without fear of condemnation.

Reconstructing the history of her passion in her letter of revelation
and explanation, Mme de Tourvel laments especially the very security that allowed her to experiment with love. As Julie discovered,

contemplation of "ce dangereux spectacle" is in itself participation. Caught despite herself in the trap of fatal love, Mme de Tourvel struggles to find a way out through the exertion of her will, but Valmont has other plans for her. Having followed the evolution of her state of mind by reading her uninhibited letters to Mme de Rosemonde, he has now only to act on what he knows: "Je n'ai absolument besoin, pour réussir, que de me rapprocher d'elle, et mes moyens sont trouvés" (276). He will play to her original fantasy of the reformed libertine, saved by love. The pretext for his visit is to return her letters, the very letters that recorded the traces of a love she wanted to destroy. Mme de Tourvel, taking the scenario to its ultimate extrapolation, imagines that Valmont, newly converted, will come to reject her as an obstacle to his redemption. He will save her despite herself.

Mme de Tourvel has already prepared her own penitence: "Je m'imposerai la honte de les relire chaque jour, jusqu'à ce que mes larmes en aient effacé les dernières traces; et les siennes, je les brûlerai comme infectées du poison dangereux qui a corrompu mon âme" (294). The tears which first revealed her unhappiness and vulnerability and then stained Valmont's Dijon letter (thus giving him the proof he needed to persevere) will now erase the materialization of her weakness—the words of her corruption. Mme de Tourvel will also burn Valmont's letters—the carrier of the disease—to prevent further contamination. Indeed, for both Julie and Mme de Tourvel, flight from the danger of male sexuality is not enough. Their own *response* to the sexual imperative must be transformed through sacrifice, at whatever cost. The resolution of the passion that she anticipates here, however, the *renunciation* of desire, will be achieved through its very opposite: surrender.

The very next letter of the correspondence opens with Valmont's announcement of victory: "La voilà donc vaincue, cette femme superbe qui avait osé croire qu'elle pourrait me résister!" (296). Predictably, the description of Mme de Tourvel's fall evokes the battleground:[7] "A ce dernier mot, elle se précipita ou plutôt tomba évanouie entre mes bras . . . je la conduisais, ou la portais vers le lieu précédemment désigné pour le champ de ma gloire; et en effet elle ne revint à elle que soumise et déjà livrée à son heureux vainqueur" (302). Mme de Tourvel yields only after a morally and physically debilitating crisis. In a pattern paradoxically reminiscent of Saint-Preux's seduction of Julie, it is the threat of abandonment following death-wish murmurings that provides the key to the ultimate victory. In Valmont's account of the salient details, the utter helplessness of his prize(d) victim is underscored by the choice of verbs itself: Mme de Tourvel is carried, not led, to the prearranged site of her defeat and Valmont's glorification. When she recovers from her swoon, she has already been delivered to her conqueror. The object of desire is quite literally an object. But both Julie and Mme de Tourvel, in the face of the *fait accompli,* themselves choose to reenact the "crime" so long avoided. This is a conscious decision to assure the happiness of their lovers and, curiously, to justify the transgression by voluntary self-sacrifice: " 'Je ne puis plus supporter mon existence, qu'autant qu'elle servira à vous rendre heureux. Je m'y consacre tout entière: dès ce moment je me donne à vous, et vous n'éprouverez de ma part ni refus, ni regrets' " (303). For Mme de Tourvel, the denial of original values is complete and generates transformation, the creation of a new and positive self—a joyous martyrdom. For Julie, however, sacrifice—acceptance of sexuality—generates a negative self which she will resacrifice to a higher value: marriage.

Furthermore, Mme de Tourvel accepts and demonstrates her desire: "L'ivresse fut complète et réciproque" (304), reports Valmont. Although his version may be suspect as wish fulfillment, his recognition (within the same sentence) of a unique reaction on his part—"et pour la première fois, la mienne survécut au plaisir"—lends credence to his claim of mutuality. Mme de Tourvel confirms her participation in the language of *l'amour-passion:* "C'est pour lui que je me suis perdue," she explains to Mme de Rosemonde, "il est devenu le centre unique de mes pensées, de mes sentiments, de mes actions" (309). This rare synthesis is not lost on Valmont, who later will comment on Mme de Tourvel's lovemaking in their subsequent encounters. He describes seeing her "sortir du plaisir tout éplorée, et le moment d'après retrouver la volupté dans un mot qui répondait à son âme" (320). This *involuntary* attachment to pleasure—that very pleasure Merteuil had deemed her incapable of—marks Mme de Tourvel

as a sexual being and distinguishes her representation from Julie's—
for Julie, the erotic will find complete expression only in death.

The potentially threatening implications of such an unconditional
commitment to love are clear to the older, more experienced Mme
de Rosemonde. As she writes in her letter of "condolence": "Les
hommes savent-ils apprécier la femme qu'ils possèdent?" (313). The
lesson of her experience is that love is necessarily a disappointment to
women because of a fundamental difference that can never be overcome: "L'homme jouit du bonheur qu'il ressent, et la femme de celui
qu'elle procure. . . . Le plaisir de l'un est de satisfaire des désirs,
celui de l'autre est surtout de les faire naître" (313). Mme de Tourvel
refuses this logic of contraries which guarantees unhappiness for
women. She asserts the proof of her own happiness and Valmont's
difference from other men. Her conviction is based upon her *secret*
understanding of Valmont: "Ah! si vous le connaissiez comme moi!
je l'aime avec idolâtrie, et bien moins encore qu'il ne le mérite"
(317). Through her Valmont has known true love ("le véritable
amour") and has been transformed, his previous expressions of masculinity annulled. Mme de Tourvel further resists her "mother's"
view of love as social incompatibility by invoking a higher destiny:
"Qui sait si nous n'étions pas nés l'un pour l'autre! si ce bonheur ne
m'était pas réservé, d'être nécessaire au sien! Ah! si c'est une illusion,
que je meure donc avant qu'elle finisse" (318). Less fortunate than
Julie, as we will see, the end of illusion will not be perfectly
synchronic with death.

Valmont's first betrayal of Mme de Tourvel—appearing in public
with a *fille*—occurs predictably at the height of Mme de Tourvel's
optimism. In fact, it necessarily occurs here since, in the dynamics of
literary passion, extreme happiness implicitly posits the polar term of
despair. In the face of this outrage to her self-respect, Mme de Tourvel duplicates her original response: she writes to ask for the return of
her letters. The heart of her anger again is Valmont's failure to distinguish "la femme faible de la femme dépravée" (327); she will not be
treated like other (i.e., sexually available) women. When Valmont
provides an explanation (Mme de Tourvel's misinterpretation) and reaffirms his devotion, Mme de Tourvel agrees to begin again. Moreover, in her determination to maintain the connection, she finds a

way to reconvert her suffering into positive terms: "Ou ma félicité est plus grande, ou j'en sens mieux le prix depuis que j'ai craint de l'avoir perdue: mais ce que je puis vous dire, c'est que, si je me sentais la force de supporter encore des chagrins aussi cruels que ceux que je viens d'éprouver je ne croirais pas en acheter trop cher le surcroît de bonheur que j'ai goûté depuis" (333). By embracing as *necessary* the connection between love and suffering, Mme de Tourvel willingly assumes her martyrdom. The question that remains is whether she has the strength to continue paying the price for her rejection of received values, and the tenets of maternal discourse.

The compensation implicit in Mme de Tourvel's evaluation of the economy of fatal love is reciprocity. Thus, when Valmont, succumbing to the demands made upon his ego by Merteuil, sends Mme de Tourvel the "ce n'est pas ma faute" letter Merteuil has transcribed for him, Mme de Tourvel necessarily receives a mortal blow: "Le voile est déchiré, Madame, sur lequel était peinte l'illusion de mon bonheur. La funeste vérité m'éclaire, et ne me laisse voir qu'une mort assurée et prochaine, dont la route m'est tracée entre la honte et le remords. Je la suivrai . . . je chérirai mes tourments s'ils abrègent mon existence" (340). Whereas for Julie, once the veil of error is removed and the truth is revealed, it is to a realm of light and virtue that she hopes to ascend, for Mme de Tourvel the truth illuminates the path of an ignominious death. Having abandoned everything to follow Valmont, there is essentially nothing left but the catastrophic consequences of lost illusions. She remains attached, however, to her suffering because it affirms the connection with death.

Like Clarissa, whose story she had read along with *Pensées chrétiennes* (255), Mme de Tourvel's humiliation depletes her and what she requests of her friend and confidante is to be allowed to disappear: "Exaucez ma dernière prière; c'est de me laisser à mon sort, de m'oublier entièrement, de ne plus me compter sur la terre" (340). Since she can no longer be what she was, she would rather be nothing: "Rien ne peut plus me convenir, que la nuit profonde où je vais ensevelir ma honte. J'y pleurerai mes fautes, si je puis pleurer encore! car, depuis hier, je n'ai pas versé une larme. Mon coeur flétri n'en fournit plus" (340). Since tears, beyond being the ultimate objective correlative of feminine misery, are also strategic weapons, the *end* of tears signals the end of the struggle: tears cease when there is nothing more to be gained. This is Mme de Tourvel's response to the irrefutable proof of Valmont's betrayal. The comparable moment for Clarissa is her realization that Lovelace has brought about her worst fantasy; he has destroyed her virginity, the place of her pride. Clarissa can weep no more, for her *head* is gone.

For Mme de Tourvel, the damage has been done to her heart. What had sustained her in playing the dangerous game was Valmont's ostensible respect for her heart; what had sustained Clarissa was Lovelace's apparent respect for her head. In both cases, the synecdoche is potent since both Clarissa and Mme de Tourvel respond to the local assault as totality. Clarissa longs to be shut away in a private bedlam; Mme de Tourvel seeks the protection of darkness. And just as Clarissa falls ill, victim to a disease to which there is no remedy (except the will to live), and transforms the room in which she has taken refuge into a mortuary chamber, Mme de Tourvel, stricken with a mysterious fever, installs herself in her former room in the convent: "Ce fut alors qu'elle déclara qu'elle revenait s'établir dans cette chambre, que, disait-elle, elle n'aurait jamais dû quitter; et qu'elle ajouta qu'elle n'en sortirait *qu'à la mort*; ce fut son expression" (347–48). Mme de Tourvel returns to the convent—the official locus of adolescent purity. This is the place she *ought never have left*. For both heroines the odyssey of displacement and desire ends with an attempt to effect a final homecoming through death.

Mme de Volanges reports on Mme de Tourvel's confession to her: "Enfin, en me parlant de la façon cruelle dont elle avait été sacrifiée, elle ajouta: 'Je me croyais bien sûre d'en mourir, et j'en avais le courage; mais de survivre à mon malheur et à ma honte, c'est ce qui m'est impossible' " (353). If, then, immolation of virtue ends in death, it is compensated by the consequences of *l'amour-passion* in which death retroactively redeems the sacrifice. Surviving would suggest the triviality of the illicit. (Thus Clarissa, offered the possibility of life in an American colony for a few years, waiting for the scandal to pass, is unmoved. That is a solution for Moll.) To live with misery and shame is incompatible with the angelic disposition; there can be no earthly consolation.

Before she dies, Mme de Tourvel receives a last letter from Valmont (which the reader does not see) to which she replies, dictating the letter to her chambermaid. In her delirious last letter (indeed, Mme de Volanges fears that la Présidente has suffered "une vraie aliénation d'esprit" [347], just as Lovelace suspects that Clarissa's "intellects are irreparably hurt") she alternates as did Clarissa after the rape, between condemning herself and excoriating the seducer. But where Clarissa addressed separate letters to the various people who might be concerned with her fate, Mme de Tourvel's letter is addressed to no one ("La Présidente de Tourvel A . . ." [372]) and the addressee emerges variously as Valmont, her husband, her friends, and herself. The letter is never delivered, for Mme de Volanges decides that "l'écrit . . . ne s'adresse à personne pour s'adresser à trop de monde" (372), saving face for her friend who seems to have given up on her reputation. The reader can only surmise that the contents of Valmont's last letter, following his pattern of betrayal and self-justification, are a redeclaration of love, and a seductive reminder of their past happiness; for it is precisely this memory that torments her: "En me laissant mes douleurs, ôte-moi le cruel souvenir des biens que j'ai perdus. Quand tu me les as ravis, n'en retrace plus à mes yeux la désolante image" (372–73). As with Julie, suffering is reactivated by the evocation of the past, and nostalgia is converted to guilt: "J'étais innocente et tranquille: c'est pour t'avoir vu que j'ai perdu le repos; c'est en t'écoutant que je suis devenue criminelle" (373). The history of the past, then, is the story of the *sentiment involontaire*; love's fatal power to destroy exemplary femininity and to create, in its place, an outlaw: a desiring self.

Having declared herself a criminal, Mme de Tourvel dramatizes her fate as a pariah: "La pitié s'arrête sur les bords de l'abîme où le criminel se plonge. Les remords le déchirent, et ses cris ne sont pas entendus!" (373). Beyond the pale, the social contract is broken and communication is annulled. Once this vision of hell is conjured up, the Présidente calls upon her husband to punish her: "Que fais-tu loin de moi? Viens punir une femme infidèle. Que je souffre enfin des tourments mérités" (373). By evoking her husband and *naming* her crime, Mme de Tourvel focuses on the betrayal *she* has perpetrated: "Que cette Lettre au moins t'apprenne mon repentir. Le ciel a pris ta cause; il te venge d'une injure que tu as ignorée" (373). The letter, therefore, to the extent that it is addressed to her husband, is to be taken both as a confession and a gesture of repentance. But by introducing God as agent in her inculpation, she necessarily returns to her exculpation: "Impitoyable dans sa vengeance, il m'a livrée à celui-là même qui m'a perdue. C'est à la fois, pour lui et par lui que je souffre. Je veux le fuir, en vain, il me suit; il est là; il m'obsède sans cesse" (373). Love, then, is not only an involuntary feeling but part of a divine plan. Providence's prey, like Julie, Mme de Tourvel's fate is overdetermined.

At the end of her letter, the leitmotif of persecution reappears, the return to "vous" and the crisis of the word: "Pourquoi me persécutez-vous? que pouvez-vous encore avoir à me dire? ne m'avez-vous pas mise dans l'impossibilité de vous écouter, comme de vous répondre? N'attendez plus rien de moi. Adieu, Monsieur" (374). Before reaching this point, Mme de Tourvel has evoked the Valmont of her dreams ("Oh! mon aimable ami! reçois-moi dans tes bras; cache-moi dans ton sein" [373]) and of her nightmares ("Laisse-moi: je frémis! Dieu! c'est ce monstre encore!" [374]), the "pour lui" and the "par lui." This alternation in Mme de Tourvel's delirium between a positive and negative vision of her connection to Valmont in fact *summarizes* their history: a case of mistaken identity and miscast roles. Having exhausted the permutations of pleasure and pain, she returns to the familiar farewell of the earlier letters. Her last words reinscribe the theme of the impossible communication that characterized the beginnings of their correspondence. Nonetheless, her final effort is for him: having learned of Valmont's death ("Par une fatalité attachée à son sort" [378]), she comes to life long enough to beg for his forgiveness (" 'Dieu tout-puissant . . . je me soumets à ta justice; mais pardonne à Valmont' " [379]), and to see her confessor. Like Clarissa at her last moments, "celle que tout le monde pleurait fut la seule qui ne se pleura point" (380).

Mme de Volanges, whose role it has been to recount her friend's last moments, does not content herself with mere reporting; she also points the moral of the tale:

Tant de vertus, de qualités louables et d'agréments; un caractère si doux et si facile; un mari qu'elle aimait, et dont elle était adorée; une société où elle se plaisait, et dont elle faisait les délices; de la figure, de la jeunesse, de la fortune; tant d'advantages réunis, ont donc été perdus par une seule imprudence! (380).

In a single sentence we are given an abridged version of a tragic feminine destiny. A woman who was and had everything is left with nothing; and through a single mistake: "une seule imprudence." (Cécile too, though less movingly perhaps, is no less dispossessed through, as her mother puts it, "une seule liaison dangereuse" [399].) In the letter that closes the volume, Mme de Volanges's anguished reflections on the catastrophic dénouement of which she is the helpless witness constitute not so much a solution to such awesome causality as rhetorical questions: "Quelle femme ne fuirait pas au premier propos d'un séducteur? Quelle mère pourrait, sans trembler, voir une autre personne qu'elle parler à sa fille?" (399). This insistence upon the dangers inherent in *words* recapitulates as we have seen the Présidente's own reading of the events that led to her fall: "C'est en t'écoutant que je suis devenue criminelle" (373). That the first word, the first letter should lead inexorably to the first step, the *faux pas* and descent into the abyss—despite the most heroic measures of resistance—is the premise of the dysphoric masculine plot has been abundantly, even redundantly clear. And although this brutal and curiously *magical* scenario—a foregone conclusion from (before) the outset of the novel—is deemed by the publisher of the *Liaisons* as implausible "*aujourd'hui*," it is nonetheless plausible enough for the eighteenth century. For while it is true that *today*, as Elizabeth Hardwick has put the matter, "the old plot is dead, fallen into obsolescence," because "you cannot seduce anyone when innocence is not a value,"[8] in 1782 the plot, if already familiar, was still up to date.

But if the valorization of innocence is what underlies the potency of the "old plot," and gives it meaning, by the same token that meaning is produced in the eighteenth-century novel only when the innocence at stake is female and threatened. What is one to make of this plot to undo feminine virtue beyond observing its recurrence and its literariness? Paradoxically, it would seem to be a working out of an unsaid ambivalence on the part of male writers toward the very existence of female desire, and an unsayable anxiety about its power.

Chastity, we have seen, in the discourse of the professional seducer, is thought to be a cover-up, the surface structure of repressed desire: one has only to find the proper key and this socially disguised sexual energy will be released. This unconvincing artifact is much more than a cause for skepticism, it presents a fundamental challenge to the truth of sexual difference.[9] To seduce a woman who would deny her sexual self is to prove in some irrefutable way that she is neither what she says she is, nor fundamentally other: "A woman's chastity," a reader of the *Liaisons* has observed, "is an inadmissible and empty presumption in the eyes of men. Thus possession has more than one meaning: it forces woman to acknowledge her own desire and therefore her subordination to a shared carnality."[10] But to prove the existence of female sexual susceptibility, vulnerability really, is not only a desire to unveil that truth. Sexual possession is a gesture of exorcism and mastery in this fictional universe whereby "a man frees himself of woman's *power*: the power to bind and dominate that derived from *his* desire for her."[11] In this sense, masculine possession can be read as a gesture performed in order to recover a lost *self*-possession; and we might also say that the seducers are as terrified of sex as their victims. Valmont and Lovelace before him are authorized to find out, at some expense, the "truth" of the Prude and of the Exemplar. In the end they learn that sexual difference is not written in the terms they had originally imagined—Clarissa can be raped, but not subdued; Tourvel subdued and still desired—but the discovery comes too late to change the *dénouement* of their plots.[12]

Chapter Nine

THE NEGATIVE HEROINE

Les Liaisons Dangereuses

> *Lieu d'occultation ou de valorisation, la femme sera un pseudo-centre, un centre latent ou explicite, celui qu'on expose ostensiblement ou bien qu'on camoufle avec précaution pudique, le centre présent ou absent du discours romanesque (psychologique) moderne, dans lequel l'homme cherche l'homme et s'y divinise, ou bien la femme veut se faire homme.*
> —Julia Kristeva, *Le Texte du roman*

In her autobiographical letter to Valmont, Mme de Merteuil reflects upon her entrance into the world as a young lady, and comments on her good fortune in having avoided what will prove to be the fate of Cécile, the fifteen-year-old "Héroïne" of the "nouveau Roman" the Marquise is "writing" with the Vicomte: "peut-être une seule occasion m'eût perdue." [1] Although she bypassed that trajectory of innocence lost, she is nonetheless ruined by a mistake. Not her famous "blunder"—declaring war on Valmont, seeming to forget that he can ruin her—but a faux pas that is overdetermined and literary. She forgets that her plot is only part of a master plot not of her own writing, that she is a heroine—a woman with a taste for letters—and not an author after all. She can write her own script, but only to a point; and at that point she stops circulating meaning (regulating the flow of desire) to be circulated, and recirculated. Laclos punishes this witty scribe by publishing her letters. The history of her private life and not the fiction she was planning to write, Valmont's *Memoirs:* "Oui . . . vos Mémoires, car je veux qu'ils soient imprimés un jour, et je me charge de les écrire" (13). The memoirs she would have written for her lover in the end write her; no longer her own "ouvrage" as she styled herself, but the pretext of M.C. . . . . . De L. . . 's "Ouvrage." Merteuil fails to understand that she is a heroine and not an author because despite her ability to exploit the laws of difference, she fails to take their measure. Or rather, because Laclos, in his "feminism," could go so far and no farther.[2] The Marquise brings her punishment upon herself. The locatable crime for which she is punished, if we take Prévan's rehabilitation as the index of heroism in the world of the *Liaisons*,[3] is usurping the masculine prerogative: to make advances. But more generally, she is banished and silenced for undervaluing the privileged signifiers of eighteenth-century fiction and sociality. She attempts to be a male hero—a desiring subject— only to be recast as a negative heroine; in the end, an object of desire no longer, she is betrayed without being seduced.

Merteuil then has a heroine's destiny, despite her egregious villainies, and despite herself. A destiny equal to the terms of her erotic experience, but not a destiny shaped by the dialectic of *l'amour-passion* or by the negotiation of her favors for financial gain. A trajectory of paradoxical pathos that begins with a cajoling solicitation, "Revenez, mon cher Vicomte, revenez" (13), and ends—in her own words— with an abrupt "Adieu" (371). In that space of representation, Merteuil, the only heroine in these novels neither outclassed nor declassed by her lover—they are social equals—enjoys a destiny of possibility underwritten by financial independence and widowhood that is systematically undermined by the strictures of feminine representation. No less than Mme de Tourvel, Mme de Merteuil goes from all in this world to nothing, sacrificed to a masculine idea(l).

The *donnée* of Merteuil's new novel is relegated to an editorial footnote. It would appear to be an *hapax*: the unique occasion upon which she was the victim of an episode of seduction and betrayal. This rejection, however, like the one perpetrated by Lovelace's "quality jilt," constitutes the motive for Merteuil's local revenge and inaugurates the first sequence of her plot: the "forming" of her betrayer's bride-to-be, Cécile. The Marquise's (inter)actions fall into four major configurations: the seduction of Cécile through Valmont, the defeat of the Présidente again through Valmont, the ruin of Prévan to prove herself to Valmont, and the seduction of Danceny to provoke Valmont. Each involves Valmont and the exercise of sexuality, but it is only in the last two that Merteuil performs directly. The Prévan adventure best demonstrates the sense of her struggle with Valmont. As Valmont reads the text, Prévan, by virtue of his extravagant past, is too dangerous for even Merteuil: "Voilà l'histoire de Prévan; c'est à vous de voir si vous voulez ajouter à sa gloire, et vous atteler à son char de triomphe" (170). The Marquise, however, is stimulated not only by the difficulty and the danger of the challenge per se, but by Valmont's denigration of her combat capabilities: "Ah! mon pauvre Valmont, quelle distance il y a encore de vous à moi! Non, tout l'orgueil de votre sexe ne suffirait pas pour remplir l'intervalle qui nous sépare. Parce que vous ne pourriez exécuter mes projets, vous les jugez impossibles!" (173). Taking the measure of their generic difference, Merteuil rejects the very basis of comparison: "Pour vous autres hommes, les défaites ne sont que des succès de moins. Dans cette partie si inégale, notre fortune est de ne pas perdre, et votre malheur de ne pas gagner" (174). His victories derive tautologically from the fact of his maleness, hers from the subversion of phallocentric truth.

In the Prévan encounter, then, Merteuil sees herself engaged in fighting not so much a private battle as the definitive war between the sexes—". . . née pour venger mon sexe et maîtriser le vôtre" (175)—and she takes this opportunity to remind Valmont of the *history* of her preparedness. In order to win she has devised personal methods of warfare and principles of behavior which lead to her claim of originality: "Je suis mon ouvrage" (176).[4] Follows the fable of her autopygmalionism, a recapitulation of the maxims of the feminine condition. Her entrance into the world corresponds to a period of institutionalized passivity. "Vouée par état au silence et à l'inaction" (176), Merteuil, however, turns silence to good account: if she cannot participate verbally, she can interpret. Intelligence and curiosity aid her to break the codes, to uncover the important and hidden message, to decipher, in a word, the subtext of desire. Although stimulated by the mystery of sexual pleasure and impatient to complete her understanding, Merteuil fortuitously avoids the trap of precocious exploration: "Je ne sais où ce désir m'aurait conduite; et alors dénuée d'expérience, peut-être une seule occasion m'eût perdue: heureusement pour moi, ma mère m'annonça peu de jours après que j'allais me marier; sur-le-champ la certitude de savoir éteignit ma curiosité, et j'arrivai vierge entre les bras de M. de Merteuil" (177). Having been preserved in chaste conventionality, and having intuited the dangers of showing signs of pleasure, Merteuil learns to manipulate her husband by a socially impeccable feminine unresponsiveness. Widowhood, however, soon frees her from conjugal submission and she reenters the world of dangerous relations wiser than her years.

Beyond social independence, however, Merteuil would be free from the *female* condition which means being a prisoner of sex, and blind to the dynamics of love and sex: "Je m'assurai que l'amour que l'on nous vante comme la cause de nos plaisirs, n'en est au plus que le prétexte" (178). Despite Merteuil's "virile" stance (she is, for example, the only woman in these novels to ascribe to herself the aggressive lexicon of the battlefield that normally belongs to the seducer), her strategy, however martial, is defensive. Thus: "Mon premier soin fut d'acquérir le renom d'invincible" (180). The precaution is necessary in a culture where the double standard prevails, and a woman cannot afford the luxury of being revealed publicly as a sexual being.[5] Merteuil's erotic maneuvers, moreover, are all protected by some form of preventive blackmail: "Nouvelle Dalila, j'ai toujours, comme elle, employé ma puissance à surprendre ce secret important" (181). Her real strength, then, belongs to archetypal *feminine* behavior: psychological penetration of private vulnerability.

Valmont, she explains to him, attracted her as a worthy enemy: "Séduite par votre réputation, il me semblait que vous manquiez à ma gloire; je brûlais de vous combattre corps à corps" (181). Valmont is publicly sexual, a conqueror of women, and as such, a valid measure of her own prowess. Nonetheless, however tempted she might have been to give in to her desire, "C'est le seul de mes goûts qui ait jamais pris un moment d'empire sur moi" (181), she remains aware of the risk involved and treats Valmont as she does all the others: withholding her feelings. (It is only after the fact that she can tell him how much power he in fact had.) Thus, as Merteuil sees it, Valmont is now asking her to abandon her policy at the height of her career, to question the solidity of her acquired power. To suggest, "qu'après m'être autant élevée au-dessus des autres femmes par mes travaux pénibles, je consente à ramper comme elles. . . ." (182) is to imply that she is nothing but a woman.

Merteuil's destiny, like Manon's, is the obverse of the beleaguered heroine's. The bottom line is a contest of wills; the stakes, not virginity but another integrity: the *self* inviolate. Merteuil would have Prévan despite Valmont; Manon, G . . . M . . . (father and son) despite Des Grieux: "Il faut vaincre ou périr. Quant à Prévan, je veux l'avoir et je l'aurai; il veut le dire, et il ne le dira pas: en deux mots, voilà notre Roman. Adieu" (182). By the law of the excluded middle that regulates their fiction, there is no more to be said. Indeed, Merteuil writes to recount her adventure with Prévan before Valmont can reply: "Ecoutez, et ne me confondez plus avec les autres femmes" (190). And she rests her case. Her triumph is the story of a seduction which proceeds by canonical stages. The familiar pattern is ironized by the self-consciousness that informs it: "Vous jugez bien que mes timides regards n'osaient chercher les yeux de mon vainqueur: mais dirigés vers lui d'une manière plus humble, ils m'apprirent bientôt que j'obtenais l'effet que je voulais produire" (193). Valmont is invited to admire the proficiency of her technique and the entire narrative, in fact, functions as an explicit demonstration of the principles outlined in her famous letter of self-analysis.

Like Valmont, Prévan is more than a specific man, he is the representative of a type: "Qu'il est commode d'avoir affaire à vous autres *gens à principes!* . . . votre marche réglée se devine si facilement! L'arrivée, le maintien, le ton, les discours, je savais tout dès la veille. Je ne vous rendrai donc pas notre conversation que vous suppléerez aisément" (193). Being an actor of the same scope, Valmont is expected to know the script: there are no surprises, only refinements. Merteuil, for her part, acts out the traditional feminine role: "Voulant frapper le coup décisif, j'appelai les larmes à mon secours. Ce fut exactement le *Zaïre, vous pleurez.* Cet empire qu'il se crut sur moi, et l'espoir qu'il en conçut de me perdre à son gré, lui tinrent lieu de tout l'amour d'Orosmane" (194). The rhetoric of tears motivates the quotation, and a second text comes to corroborate the first. Each subsequent transition is marked by a cliché of tragic register: "Le jour fatal arrive, ce jour où je devais perdre ma vertu et ma réputation. . . . Je m'acheminais ainsi à ma perte" (196–97). Merteuil's feeling for a scene, for the language of the drama she is playing out, carries the parody to its ultimate conclusion. Valmont, *voyeur*, is called to witness her "defeat": "Me voyez-vous, Vicomte, dans ma toilette légère, marchant d'un pas timide et circonspect, et d'une main mal assurée ouvrir la porte à mon vainqueur? Il m'aperçut, l'éclair n'est pas plus prompt. Que vous dirais-je? je fus vaincue, tout à fait vaincue, avant d'avoir pu dire un mot pour l'arrêter ou me défendre" (197). Like Moll, she lowers the veil of modesty when it comes to the final favor, the better to underline her surrender: "tout à fait vaincue." The scene is brought to an end by the prearranged *flagrante delicto*, and the tableau of virtue wronged: "Là, prenant mon ton de Reine, et élevant la voix: 'Sortez, Monsieur, continuai-je, et ne reparaissez jamais devant moi' " (197).

Having successfully demolished Prévan, the Marquise now prepares to appropriate Danceny. Her purpose is threefold: to compromise his relationship with Cécile, to antagonize Valmont and to replace a boring lover (Belleroche). She is, moreover, ready to undertake Danceny's sentimental education. (Merteuil's final sexual experiment will be a classic one: the initiation of an innocent young man.) Valmont rises to the challenge: "Je vous le dis sérieusement, je désapprouve ce choix, et quelque secret qu'il restât, il vous humilierait au moins à mes yeux et dans votre conscience" (276). Whereas in the Prévan adventure, Valmont feared—or so he claimed—the humiliation of inevitable and *public* embarrassment for Merteuil, here his concern is *private* and personal. Superimposing his first prohibition on the second, underscores not only the possessive aspect of his friendship but its premises: Merteuil's *libertinage* is acceptable only if the objects of her desire do not threaten his erotic prerogatives. Indeed, he resents finding another—quite literally—in the place he planned to occupy: "Laissez là Danceny, et préparez-vous à retrouver, et à me rendre les délicieux plaisirs de notre première liaison" (278). Valmont, confident of imminent success with Mme de Tourvel, is planning his victorious return. Not receiving a reply, he restates his case: "Souvenez-vous cependant que le nouvel Amant ne veut rien perdre des anciens droits de l'ami. Adieu, comme autrefois

. . . *Oui, adieu, mon Ange! Je t'envoie tous les baisers de l'amour"*
(304).

It is Valmont's complacency in returning to Merteuil, his assumption of an emotional continuum, that provokes in Merteuil the anger
which in turn determines the concluding phase of the novel. Not
surprisingly, Merteuil resents Valmont's nostalgia: "*Adieu, comme
autrefois,* dites-vous? Mais autrefois, ce me semble, vous faisiez un
peu plus de cas de moi; vous ne m'aviez pas destinée tout à fait aux
troisièmes Rôles; et surtout vous vouliez bien attendre que j'eusse dit
oui, avant d'être sûr de mon consentement" (308). Valmont at this
point chooses to reply to her unspoken hurt, rather than to her anger:
"Je n'imagine pas que vous ayez pu penser sérieusement, qu'il existât
une femme dans le monde, qui me parût préférable à vous . . ."
(311). He reaffirms her position at the top of the feminine pyramid
and reiterates his recognition of her empire: "Dites seulement un
mot, et vous verrez si tous les charmes et tous les attachements
me retiendront ici, non pas un jour, mais une minute. Je volerai à
vos pieds et dans vos bras, et je vous prouverai, mille fois et de mille
manières, que vous êtes, que vous serez toujours, la véritable souveraine de mon coeur" (312). Valmont couches his response in the
hyperbolic language of gallant passion that corresponds to a so clearly
coded lovers' quarrel. And despite its rhetorical flourish, his declaration of love and servitude serves to placate Merteuil temporarily as
the change in tone of the letters indicates. Now that she "has" him
again, she can return to the sophisticated banter of the earlier letters:
"Causons de bonne amitié" (315).

Merteuil takes a disabused look at the relationship: while she is
willing to spend a night with him as his *due* ("Je ne vous refuse pas le
prix convenu entre nous" [315]), she maintains that a renewal of
their liaison on the old terms would be doomed to failure. And
describes the situation in a tone exempt from irony:

Dans le temps où nous nous aimions car je crois que c'était de l'amour, j'étais
heureuse; et vous, Vicomte! . . . Mais pourquoi s'occuper encore d'un bonheur qui
ne peut revenir? Non, quoi que vous en disiez, c'est un retour impossible. D'abord
j'exigerais des sacrifices que sûrement vous ne pourriez ou ne voudriez pas me faire,
et qu'il se peut bien que je ne mérite pas; et puis, *comment vous fixer?* (316; italics
mine).

There is a certain poignancy to this assessment which is absent from all of Merteuil's other analyses. If one compares this admission of love—in the past tense—with the statement of the autobiographical letter, in which she described her feelings as "goût," the shift becomes clear. How different is this in spirit from Mme de Tourvel's reflection:

Je n'ai pas la vanité qu'on reproche à mon sexe; j'ai encore moins cette fausse modestie qui n'est qu'un raffinement de l'orgueil; et c'est de bien bonne foi que je vous dis ici, que je me connais bien peu de moyens de plaire: je les aurais tous, que je ne les croirais pas *suffisants pour vous fixer* (106; italics mine).

The Présidente speaks from weakness and with pathos, the Marquise from strength and with a certain melancholy; but both feel threatened in their femininity by Valmont's inconstancy.

The Marquise, however, unlike her rival, has too much experience and too many defenses to ignore what she knows. After completing a diagnosis of Valmont's last letter, she concludes that he is in love: "Ou ce sont là, Vicomte, des symptômes assurés de l'amour, ou il faut renoncer à en trouver aucun" (322). He can no longer claim to dominate his feelings, and as a result cannot perform in the heady mode that must characterize their relationship: "votre coeur abuse votre esprit" (322). She explains nevertheless the nature of the sacrifices she would require: "J'exigerais donc, voyez la cruauté! que cette rare, cette étonnante Madame de Tourvel ne fût plus pour vous qu'une femme ordinaire, une femme telle qu'elle est seulement" (323). But decrystallization would not be enough: "Je serais capricieuse. . . . Je vous demanderais . . . de continuer ce pénible service [making love to Cécile] . . . jusqu'à nouvel ordre de ma part; soit que j'aimasse à abuser ainsi de mon empire; soit que plus indulgente ou plus juste, il me suffit de disposer de vos sentiments, sans vouloir contrarier vos plaisirs. Quoi qu'il en soit, je voudrais être obéie; et mes ordres seraient bien rigoureux!" (323). Both demands, if complied with, would reinstate Merteuil as the lady in the courtly love game they play, for she would then control the activities of her knight, and the expression of his feelings would be organized uniquely to serve her needs. Desacralizing Mme de Tourvel reestablishes the Marquise as the "véritable souveraine de [son] coeur;"

dallying with Cécile provides the diversion indispensable to the fable and protects Merteuil's ascendence. Such courtly compliance, however, is contractual: "Il est vrai qu'alors je me croirais obligée de vous remercier; que sait-on? peut-être même de vous récompenser" (323). Valmont's sacrifices would require their counterpart; and reciprocation would lock her into a situation she has already evaluated as too dangerous for her: "Croyez-moi ne soyons qu'amis, et restons-en là. Sachez-moi gré seulement de mon courage à me défendre: oui, de mon courage; car il en faut quelquefois, même pour ne pas prendre un parti qu'on sent être mauvais" (323). Merteuil, who generally attacks in order to protect herself, here demurs, seeking protection in the more "feminine" mode; momentarily she joins Mme de Tourvel, who would substitute the safety of friendship for the disappointments of love. The Marquise then withdraws the fiction of their future by reminding Valmont that the script she has sketched out is only "un simple récit d'un projet impossible" (324). She would have instead the legitimacy of nonconsummated courtly love.

After this lapse of confessional warmth, Merteuil returns to the battlefield of vituperative mockery that informs her exchanges with Valmont. By comparing him to a sultan whose favorite is Mme de Tourvel, she defines the aspect of his behavior that makes the idea of renewing their contract unacceptable: "Ma comparaison me paraît d'autant plus juste, que, comme lui, jamais vous n'êtes ni l'Amant ni l'ami d'une femme; mais toujours son tyran ou son esclave" (337). Thus, not only does Merteuil refuse Valmont's tyranny, but she refuses to accept him as her rival's slave. Valmont's reluctance to accede to her vision leads her to put him to the test. She provides him with the means to prove his loyalty, and to act on what he claims his preference to be: a letter of rupture to be sent to Mme de Tourvel. Once the letter has been "forwarded," Merteuil's destiny is sealed. She has taken authorship too far. The maxim of female vindictiveness— "quand une femme frappe dans le coeur d'une autre . . . la blessure est incurable" (344)—generates a certain narrative logic: the woman in the eighteenth-century text who destroys exemplary femininity must pay with her own body. No less than Mrs. Sinclair who "breaks" Clarissa for Lovelace, Mme de Merteuil will be mutilated for having found Tourvel's "endroit sensible."[6] By this phallic usurpation, the Marquise signs her own defeat.

It is, I think, this letter and not her subsequent decision to choose war rather than accept the terms of Valmont's peace offering that engenders the final disasters. Merteuil, by outmanning her partner, forces the author to revirilize his hero—as though it were not after all "sa faute"—and to restore masculine privilege. Indeed, before he dies, in a parting gesture of male solidarity, Valmont puts into Danceny's hands the proof of Merteuil's machinations and it is this posthumous weapon that wins the war.[7] By embracing his rival, moreover, Valmont not only wounds Merteuil but disassociates himself from their *liaison*; for he thus chooses as his ultimate alignment the public male bond rather than the private couple.

Of all the letters put into circulation, two are singled out for particular attention: "L'une où elle fait l'histoire entière de sa vie et de ses principes, et qu'on dit le comble de l'horreur; l'autre, qui justifie entièrement M. de Prévan . . . par la preuve qui s'y trouve qu'il n'a fait au contraire que céder aux avances les plus marquées de Madame de Merteuil et que le rendez-vous était convenu avec elle" (384). Thus, as Mme de Volanges reports the reaction of society, the heart of the scandal arises from Merteuil's flagrant violation of the codes of masculine and feminine behavior: she has beaten Prévan at his game, and with his rules. For what was Prévan's reputation based upon if not the very subterfuge and humiliation with which Merteuil is reproached? By usurping the male prerogative of *attack* Merteuil becomes guilty of female depravity. Women can only lose if they defy the founding grammatical declension which assures their *difference* from men.[8]

In making the letters public, Danceny sought not only to justify himself, Valmont, and Prévan, but to expose Merteuil in the name of the general good:[9] "J'ai cru de plus, que c'était rendre service à la société, que de démasquer une femme aussi réellement dangereuse que l'est Madame de Merteuil, et qui, comme vous pouvez le voir, est la seule, la véritable cause de tout ce qui s'est passé entre M. de Valmont et moi" (387). Thus, in a unique moment of "manly" action, Danceny sets up the mechanism that inexorably undoes Merteuil. By making public private letters, he destroys her status in the world. Merteuil's social disgrace occurs at the theater which is the place *par excellence* where reputations are made and unmade. The humiliation first takes the form of public rejection. When Merteuil goes to sit down, the women rise up in concert to leave her alone. But it is the action of the *men* that confirms her as pariah: "Ce mouvement marqué d'indignation générale fut applaudi de tous les hommes, et fit redoubler les murmures, qui, dit-on, allèrent jusqu'aux huées" (395). The élite of the theater functions as a social microcosm; the reaction is collective and generalized; the "dit-on" inscribes the anonymity of the public voice. Merteuil's performance—in reality a simple appearance on the scene—is unanimously panned. The hostility of the reception is underscored by the contrast with Prévan's canonization: "Dès qu'on l'aperçut, tout le monde, hommes et femmes, l'entoura et l'applaudit; et il se trouva, pour ainsi dire, porté devant Madame de Merteuil, par le public qui faisait cercle autour d'eux" (395). Thus Prévan and Merteuil are placed face to face in precisely the opposite position to their last encounter; this time, with violent symmetry, it is Merteuil who is publicly condemned.

Merteuil returns to the privacy of her home only to be struck down with smallpox. Her punishment, however, is not to die but to endure in her new state. The transformation is, in fact, seen as such by Merteuil's circle: "Le Marquis de*** . . . disait hier, en parlant d'elle, que la maladie l'avait retournée, et qu'à présent son âme était sur sa figure. Malheureusement tout le monde trouva que l'expression était juste" (398). Society then closes ranks against Merteuil, naming her now that the horror of her essence can be *seen*. In her illness, Merteuil, in accordance with the period's favorite mutilation, loses an eye; but that loss is compounded by another: her lawsuit, "elle l'a perdu tout d'une voix." She is stripped of her social security, and again the decision is unanimous. Of her servants, "aucun d'eux n'a voulu la suivre" (398), and so Merteuil is left in spiritual quarantine. In leaving the country she leaves bankruptcy behind; the family then proceeds to restore order.[10] The editor, in a note to the reader, explains that he is not in a position to "faire connaître les sinistres événements qui ont comblé les malheurs ou achevé la punition de Madame de Merteuil" (399). Further information is not required: Merteuil disgraced, disfigured, dispossessed, and displaced has completed the circuit of her representation; textual saturation is reached when every positive term has been converted to a negative one.

In the end, the *Liaisons* would seem to be a novel built from a single sentence; and a sentence derived tautologically from an etiology of gender. Both Mme de Tourvel and Mme de Merteuil might be said to be ruined through a single mistake. In both cases, of course, the mistake is iterative, and persistently reinscribed. (Mme de Tourvel, after all, "listened" to Valmont more than once.) The mistake the two women make—like all tragic heroines—is to believe that they are different from other women and that because they are different, they will be exceptions to the rules of a (fictional) feminine destiny. Mme de Merteuil takes the notion of originality to the outer limits of what is meant by femininity in the eighteenth century. Although I would not go as far as does Aram Vartanian in diagnosing her behavior as a case of "radical hermaphroditism," his sense that "she is an embodiment of the thought, both perversely fascinating and obsessively disturbing, that the distinction of the sexes might not, after all, be real or necessary,"[11] is to the point. Her refusal to be contained by the rules of a universe which would define her in a simple binary relation according to which the feminine term is always generated by opposition and is never itself generative, to be contained by the laws of the couple, however libertine—laws themselves structured according to the prerogatives of masculine desire—violates the syntax of the eighteenth-century sociolect and so retribution must ensue.

The punishment, moreover, fits the crime. Mme de Merteuil is castrated, not the men. Over and above the stripping away of her powers and the charms of her femininity, she is marked symbolically (and perhaps onomastically) with a single "oeil," the sign of her partial blindness, her partial knowledge. She failed to understand the limits of her sex, and that failure is literally and literarily intolerable. The end of the novel functions as a return to order, a reminder of the dangers of ignoring difference. As Vartanian has seen: "In the *dénouement* that follows the proper role of each sex is re-affirmed with a vengeance. . . . The Marquise de Merteuil is reduced to the most pathetic fate that can befall the 'weaker sex.' "[12]

In the final analysis, then, the *Liaisons* has three female victims, not two. Mme de Merteuil, for all her worldliness, is not protected from the fate of the innocent Présidente, or the innocent Cécile. Merteuil's "error" in provoking a war with Valmont is not tactical.

Her error was to have imagined all along that her brand of heroine-ism exempted her from the fictional rules of erotic experience. She is punished too—and perhaps first of all—for believing her own phallic discovery that "l'amour que l'on nous vante comme la cause de nos plaisirs, n'en est au plus que le prétexte" (178)—and that she could write about it with impunity. Although Valmont learns the inadequacy of that maxim as well, and too late, he exits with a certain style, and the author's sympathy. Only Merteuil is humiliated for her misprision. The wittiest "woman" writer of eighteenth-century letters tried to "se faire homme," and would up like Polyphemus: unmanned.

Epilogue

The plots of these feminocentric fictions are of course neither female in impulse or origin, nor feminist in spirit. In the final analysis, moreover, despite their titles and their feminine "I," it is not altogether clear to me that these novels are about or for women at all.[1] At best one might say of their authors (some of them at least), as Carolyn Heilbrun writes of Richardson, that they "perceived imaginatively the terrible danger inherent in [the] segregation of sexual impulse, and prophesied the danger to society in denying women a channel for their energy."[2] They are indeed aware of the perils of erotic polarization in their practice of the sociolect that writes woman as an identity derived from her status as a daughter, and, implicitly, as a wife; as a sign, then, in the signifying chain which does not so much produce meaning as allow meaning to be produced around it.[3] The daughter must be exchanged but she must also remain *in her place*. The daughter must marry but she must remain within the family, chaste and willing to circulate, but only and necessarily in accordance with the law of the father. At the mid-century the stakes of violating that law are clearest with Richardson and Rousseau. Once outside the father's house, Clarissa is raped; and dies still waiting for her father's forgiveness. Rousseau, rewriting, keeps Julie at home. But if Julie gives herself to her lover inside the father's house, it is only to take herself back in the name of the father, and give herself again in the deferred security of the grave. The middle-class dream of the family hesitates between the gates of ivory and the gates of horn: a dilemma born of an old fantasy and a new reality; the nostalgia for authority and order confronted with a more modern sense of equity for the demands of individual selfhood.

The dream of an impeccable private life does not come true when the daughters resist the paternal injunction and take up their pens. The transmission of the daughter from the father to the paternally designated husband breaks down when the daughters exchange letters with their lovers. And the exchange of letters becomes the novel; the epistolary novel embodies the dysfunction and the dysphoria of the new. The feminocentric novel in letters—*Clarissa, La Nouvelle Héloïse, Les Liaisons dangereuses*—is the locus of an exchange of desires unauthorized by the fathers; unauthorized precisely by the morality—however conventional or ambiguous—of the authorial preface. The correspondence is the scene of polarized desires, of warring sexual strategies. The rhetoric of the masculine letter is designed to persuade and seduce; the feminine, to dissuade and resist. And the ideology that underwrites the intersection of the two rhetorics is what has been in question in these pages. Rousseau writes in his preface that no chaste girl has ever read a novel; all is lost were she to read a single page of his. One could also say that all is lost once a chaste girl reads a letter; but once she does, and because she answers, her loss *becomes* the novel as the novel records the traces of her passage into desire and death. Why that reluctant inscription should be so prized in and as literature—think of Lovelace's jubilation when he imagines he has deciphered the proof of Clarissa's love for him *in writing*—is not so easily understood. It seems to me, however, that the text of feminine surrender must be seen as at least a double fiction: a masculine representation of female desire produced ultimately for an audience not of women readers, but of men. The victory sought on paper, I think, is auto-referential: a self-congratulatory and self-addressed performance destined to be celebrated by other men; an anxious simulation of alterity that would rewrite otherness as sameness. The feminocentric text made one of the great traditions of the novel possible: women are its predominant signifiers, but they are also its pretext.

But I have been speaking here primarily of the tragic plot told in letters. What of the comedic plots of female *Bildung* told in retrospection, the story of a successful female life: the well-negotiated entrance into the world, and the mastery of its terms? Moll, Marianne, and Fanny play the games of innocence and worldliness as women and win. These daughters too are subject to the laws of exchange, they too are bound to the propriety of circulation. But the trajectory of the orphan-heroines operates a swerve from the paternal orbit. They pursue instead the security of self-possession through a series of female alliances: through, in particular, the agency of a maternal figure. Female "independence" in the eighteenth-century imagination would seem to require a devalorization of paternal authority and the matrimonial bond. Nevertheless, as the heroines find their *place* in the world, they all do marry; and in that sense the challenge to the conventions of the feminine condition, if challenge there is, is finally attenuated. The fiction of the novel's heterosexual contract is maintained in the blanks of affiliation, the anonymity of the ***.

Still, unlike the ostensibly more fortunate (and letter-writing) daughters of the middle classes, these memorializing orphans, particularly Moll and Marianne, are granted destinies of relative autonomy in a feminocentric universe. The specifically sexual perils of the world prove to be less determinative of female selfhood than its social strictures. I leave to others the status of Defoe's feminism. It seems fair to say, however, that *Moll Flanders*, despite a certain biological extravagance, is convincingly feminocentric. The same could be said, though for different reasons, of *La Vie de Marianne*.[4] To the extent that the feminine—understood as a conventionally assigned and culturally overdetermined attention to the intricacies of sociality and its plots—is at the heart of his novel, Marivaux is another plausible "female impersonator."[5] It is perhaps because both heroines, though so obviously different from each other in class and style, ultimately *devalue* the erotic as the core of their identity, that their texts seem more than an acting out of masculine anxiety about the self in an unheroic world. It is Pamela, however, the heroine who maintains her innocence and is rewarded for her exemplary filiality by marriage, who becomes the incarnation of the feminine ideal in the eighteenth century (and after), and not Moll or Marianne or Fanny.

If the feminocentric eighteenth-century novel can be shown to end at some chronological and literarily historical point, it ends in France with Sade, and in England with Jane Austen. This unlikely pair in radically different ways establishes the outer limits and the culmination of the century's concern with the forms of a certain private life, with a self imagined in the bedroom and at home. In the figures of Justine and Juliette, the heroine's text, read as the sexual performance of a female self, is stretched to the limits of credibility. Justine's trials, the misfortunes of the virtuous orphan, take the dysphoric scenario to its ultimate fictional possibility and impossibility:

the plot of negative capacity infinitely reiterated. Her sister Juliette, who converts impoverishment into prosperity, and as everyone knows reaps the rewards of vice at the cost of virtue, takes the euphoric trajectory to the breaking point of the novel. With Elizabeth Bennet, however, the favorite and favored daughter of the middle classes is finally granted the rewards of virtue, the promised land of the eighteenth-century English novel is hers: social ascent comes as recompense not for her chastity (which is taken for granted) but for an integrity of character and feminine intelligence, not to say wit. Mr. Darcy may try her patience, but his courtship is not a trial designed to break her spirit. For better or for worse, with Austen and Sade, the fiction of the eighteenth-century novel attains total transparency.

Thus Justine, who prizes her virginity with the passion for synecdoche that animates Clarissa, dies soiled and mutilated just when she thinks her troubles are over. The lightning bolt that strikes her when amelioration, implausibly and by her own account, seems to end her cycle of suffering—" 'Je ne suis pas née pour tant de félicités. . . . Il est impossible qu'elles soient longues' "—not only kills her (the least of it), but degrades her feminine charms: effacing her bosom, her face, in its trajectory from her heart to her "ventre" (a penultimate euphemism). In the end, the author perversely refuses Justine her proper Christian name, and she exits as Thérèse from the fiction of victimage she could barely say. Delivered miraculously from human *"foutre"* only to be condemned by divine *"foudre,"* Justine's martyrdom is never rewarded. Despite her saintly heart, she neither is saved from circulation by marriage like Fanny, nor allowed to choose her death like Clarissa. She is impaled by a stroke of the pen ("les crayons, peut-être un peu forts") of an author who learned, by his own account, the secrets of the human heart from Richardson.

Following in the footsteps of her aristocratic predecessor the Marquise de Merteuil, but radicalizing the path as she advances, Juliette exploits sexual experience until she becomes, ostensibly, her own master. The ultimate female libertine, in this fantasmatic *Bildung,* Juliette is the incarnation of that basic Sadian trope: *reversal.* Her apprenticeship teaches her to be a phallocrat: like a man, a "femme-alibi." But the place in which the *borrowed* power of the feminine can be seen most clearly to be just that, a *temporary ascription* of the

"I" of narration, is not so much in the sexual "phallacy" of the content, as in the status of the "I" itself. Here Sade merely continues the eighteenth-century model of female impersonation: he lends Juliette his name for the time it takes to tell the "interesting" parts of her story. The tenure of her enunciation, however, does not include the last word. Closure and the posterity of the text do not belong to the heroines of male fantasy: Juliette, no less than Justine, and no less, of course, than Merteuil, is finally preempted by authorial privilege. She *testifies* simply to the power not of the female imagination, but to the power of the female in the male imagination. To the extent that she is a heroine, she is *that which* allows men to write, to and of each other.

Having conjured up in closing these two sisters who by their exaggerated outlines mark the end of a certain feminocentric novel in France (at bottom all variants of philosophy in the bedroom), and having paired Sade's heroines with Austen's, I find myself vulnerable on two accounts. If Sade lays bare—by sheer hyperbole at the very least—the structure of the feminine "sentence," why have I not included his novels in this study as the *dénouement* of my plot? And why, if this syntax is a masculine construct, did I not contrast it with novels written by women? Despite the obvious generic or topical bonds—first-person memoirs framed by moralizing prefatory statements, erotic education thematized as social initiation, destiny as sexual experience, etc.—I did not include Sade's novels because they throw the social contract of the genre into question. It is of course possible to read Sadian fiction as though it were nothing more than a perverse variant of the eighteenth-century text,[6] but in the final analysis, it escapes; setting itself apart by the excess of its content. A content of rupture that finds its most articulate *form* of expression in the *120 Journées de Sodome*, where we witness the defeat of plot by the logic of permutation. Unlike Cleland's titillating storytellers who find their place within a soft-core eroticism recontainable by novelistic convention, Sade's *historiennes* undo the grammar of the eighteenth-century novel.

The absence of women novelists poses a more complicated problem. I could have generalized following the example of a Pierre Fauchery—"in the eighteenth century, the myths of a feminine destiny as created by men are for the most part adopted as is by the women novelists"[7]—and been generally right. Or I could have written a different book. For while it is true that the heroine's text in the novels of eighteenth-century women writers seems to reinscribe the male scenarios of woman's fragile fate, the novels present variations on the theme that are interesting not so much as counter*plots* but counter*weights*: courtship, seduction and betrayal, disparity of social conditions, all the stock-in-trade patterns of the standard eighteenth-century narrative are there to be read, but they add up differently. Mme Riccoboni's Fanni Butlerd and Mme de Tencin's Adélaïde de Comminges, to cite two of the better-known French heroines, rise to the occasion, as it were, rather than succumb to it: the one writes to her "quality jilt" as Lovelace would say, and by going public unwrites the contract that bids women to suffer their shame in silence (or in pathos, like the Portuguese nun); the other chooses the marriage that must separate her from her star-crossed lover rather than passively embrace the parental decree *à la* Julie. On the other side of the Channel, whether pre-Richardsonian like Mrs. Haywood's Melliora in *Love in Excess* (1719), or post-, like Fanny Burney's Evelina in *The History of a Young Lady's Entrance into the World* (1778), the English heroine of feminocentric fiction stars, for the most part, in scenarios of persecuted innocence. But if the women novelists reinscribe, or rather *produce* "conventional" plots of vulnerable female virtue tried by the relentless assults of male aggression in an insistently hostile world,[8] they do not unambiguously subscribe to the masochistic implications of their plots. Nor are the rewards of marriage which ultimately compensate Melliora, Evelina and their sisters (or the alternatively blissful deaths of countless others) the whole-hearted embraces of the happy end critics have traditionally taken them to be. The heroine's text in novels by the English women writers of the period is at least ambivalent about the conventions and the morality of society and fiction as they govern the possibilities of living and rendering a female life.[9]

These inflections of the genre, a matter of emphasis and insistence, are not, however, epiphenomena to be accounted for by counterpoint: a gesture ultimately of subordination; the obligatory chapter on the "woman novelist." The status and specificity of women's feminocentric writing are indeed the missing chapter of this book, but I was not ready to write it. I regret what must appear to be my complicity in reading the eighteenth-century novel as though it were born of men. But the urgency that animated me when I began these essays many years ago was of another order: it was to confront the phenomenon, on its own terms, of a feminocentric fiction created by male authors; to accept, then, in a first stage, the givens of literary history and its process of elimination. To accept the absence of women writers, but to interrogate the presence of women in and as representation. The second stage belongs to what I like to think of as the new literary history being produced today by feminist scholarship; and it should be a book of its own. However, we would do well to remember that in the eighteenth century women writers were not the marginal figures they have become in the annals of literary history. They were active participants in the production and dissemination of the novel: they were not only its readers, they wrote best sellers.

But if the majority of the women novelists of the period in England and in France have been relegated to critical oblivion, there is, we know, one survivor: Jane Austen. With Austen, feminocentrism as the organizing focus and energy of the novel is no longer a pretext, but the text itself. The center of her universe is a crowded and a full space. The vicissitudes of the quotidian, courtship, the desire for the happy end, the fate, in particular, of the marriageable daughter, become not opportunities for playing with the anxieties of a *male* self—the fathers, the sons, and the place of masculine desire and heroic action in mercantile or libertine society, as is the case for the "female impersonators"—but the occasion for exploring, with wit and irony, the possibilities of feminine mastery in a world circumscribed by income and the intersubjective. With Austen, the narrowness of private life becomes a widening, precisely, of the realm of the interesting. Feminocentrism becomes what it had pretended to be but rarely was in its masculine location: an unsentimental confrontation of the self in its irreducible dailiness and the trivial excitement of the details of representable experience; the cost of love, of marriage, of property, and the specifics of that worldly intersection. Though they are clearly limited by the conventions of plot and society which move them inexorably toward the *telos* of marriage, Austen's heroines, unlike Richardson's, thrive in that space. There is power to be read in their experience of limits: Anne Elliot after Elizabeth Bennet chooses with a certain freedom the man and the manner of the happy end.[10]

But the proper question of an epilogue to this study should perhaps ask what happens to the heroine's text as we leave the eighteenth century.[11] The two major women writers in France, Mme de Staël and George Sand, produce feminocentric fictions which continue the legacy of the French eighteenth-century women novelists while participating respectively in the pre-Romantic and Romantic-Realist modes of the nineteenth-century novel. With *Corinne*, Mme de Staël creates a radically new type, the woman of genius, a poet and performer. Though she suffers ultimately the fate of the eighteenth-century exceptional heroine—she is not made for this world and she dies—Corinne is the first *artist*-heroine. George Sand's heroines in their multiple guises also protest against the standard female destiny, but unlike Corinne, their heroine-ism, for the most part, is subsumed by Romantic paradigms. After Austen, however, the great women novelists of nineteenth-century England make the heroine's text their own; and the implications of that possession can only be touched upon here. The heroines of Charlotte and Emily Brontë, and of George Eliot, contest the limits of woman's proper place and the universality of the maxims which determine the plausibility and the possibility of a woman's destiny. If Maggie Tulliver drowns in a flood that carries her definitively away from a happy end she has already refused, so does M. Paul Emmanuel, the fiancé of Lucy Snowe's dreams; and Grandcourt, the husband of Gwendolen Harleth's nightmares. These heroines at least are allowed to *imagine* life elsewhere and otherwise, life outside the polarities of the eighteenth-century model. To some extent, obviously, the greater complexity of these heroines' destinies is a historical phenomenon. As the novel of female and male authors moves away from epistolary and memorial forms, out of the writing closet to a desk and a pen acknowledged as *public* instruments of fiction, it moves into more complicated spaces: a world of professions where fortunes are made and lost; a world mapped as a topography of cities and landscapes; and affected by historical event. The drawing room remains, and the bedroom, but the protagonists of the nineteenth-century novel, male and female, explore other scenes and function in a society complicated by heterogeneity. This is not to suggest, however, that the heroine's text of the nineteenth-century novel completely revises the rules of the game for its female protagonists, that the stereotypes of literary femininity disappear: Mme de Tourvel and Julie live on in the angelic, "natural" women of Stendhal's Mme de Rênal and Balzac's Mme de Mortsauf; Marianne's social-climbing "feminine" wiles reappear in Thackeray's charming orphan Becky Sharp; Manon's eternal femininity returns in Zola's Nana. And the cruel boudoir games of innocence and worldliness played in the *Liaisons* shift to the parlor in James. There are of course new figures and configurations: the adulterous (or tempted) wife, the good and bad mother, the old maid and the "older woman," compete for attention with the ingénue as the interesting feminine moment is moved ahead a few years. But the ideological underpinnings of the old plot have not been threatened seriously: experience for women characters is still primarily tied to the erotic and the familial. The sexual faux pas is still a fatal step. There is perhaps no greater testimony to the persistence of that eighteenth-century law of consequence than Hardy's *Tess of the d'Urbervilles*, where the "confused surrender" of a sixteen-year-old "Pure Woman" leads to every possible psychological and social catastrophe, and finally to death by hanging.

It would be comforting for a feminist critic to say that the literature of the twentieth century in its feminocentric novels has rewritten the fictions of the eighteenth century; that the heroine's text is dead; that women's experience has been redefined in literature and the shape of a female life radically redesigned. It would not, however, be true. There have been attempts on the part of women writers to pose the social facts of female and feminine differently in fiction, to imagine other plots; and feminist scholarship has begun to take the measure of that difference. But on the whole, literary femininity in the traditional novel remains faithful to commonplaces of a familiar inscription: and female *Bildung* tends to get stuck in the bedroom. This observation is not meant as a condemnation. Because the novel, more than any other form of art, is forced by the contract of the genre to negotiate with social realities in order to remain legible, its plots are largely overdetermined by the commonplaces of the culture. Until the culture invents new plots for women, we will continue to read the heroine's text. Or we could stop reading novels.

Notes

References to primary sources are indicated by parenthetical numbers in the text. All translations of critical material are mine unless otherwise noted. For complete bibliographical information on works referred to here, see "Works Cited."

Preface

1. The argument for the crucial role of women in the evolution of the novel in France, and the feminocentrism of its major fictions in the eighteenth century, is best made by Georges May in *Le Dilemme du roman au XVIIIᵉ siècle* (see especially, "Féminisme et roman," pp. 204–05); and for the importance of a female readership in England by Ian Watt in *The Rise of the Novel*, especially pp. 43–49 and 151–54. The central place of "woman" in the European novels of the eighteenth century has been amply documented by Pierre Fauchery throughout his *La Destinée féminine*.

2. I am indebted to A. J. Greimas for this terminology, which I have adopted and adapted for my own use. The opposition he posits—" 'euphorie' vs. 'dysphorie' "—corresponds to positive and negative axiological categories within a given semantic universe. See his *Sémantique structurale*, p. 226 ff.

3. My own definitions of "heroine-ism" will emerge in these pages. But I would like to indicate here two current though different uses of the term: "heroinism," in the late Ellen Moers's *Literary Women* (see especially pp. 121–24 and 113–242); and "heroine-ism," in Diana Trilling's "The Liberated Heroine," especially p. 504.

1: A Harlot's Progress: I

1. I follow G. A. Starr's edition of the novel, *The Fortunes and Misfortunes of the Famous Moll Flanders*.

2. In a recent article, "Moll Flanders: 'A Woman on her own Account,' " pp. 101–17, Miriam Lerenbaum reviews the "debate," and in particular takes Ian Watt to task for his ostensibly personal claim—as cited—that " 'the essence of [Moll's] character and actions is, to one reader at least, essentially masculine . . . [and that] it is at least certain that Moll accepts none of the disabilities of her sex . . .' " (p. 101). She offers instead an interesting biological (even psychogenic) and social reading of Moll's destiny which intersects my own at several important points.

3. Commenting on the French eighteenth-century novel, Philip Stewart observes: "The typical narrator begins his real story, not at birth, but at the time he became a socially functioning individual. . . . Usually the main narrative begins around age sixteen or, in exceptionally precocious cases, in early adolescence." "The Child Comes of Age," pp. 134–35. The English novel generally conforms to this rule.

4. It seems unnecessary to rehearse this argument in detail here since it has been so well articulated elsewhere. See, in particular, for the French eighteenth-century novel, Peter Brooks's *The Novel of Worldliness* and English Showalter, Jr.'s *The Evolution of the French Novel 1641–1782*, especially pp. 262–347, which focus specifically on the relations between the individual and society. That theme can also be said to constitute the underlying preoccupation of Ian Watt's *The Rise of the Novel*. One might consult as well Patricia Meyer Spacks's *Imagining a Self*, especially her first chapter, "Identity in Fiction and in Fact," pp. 1–27.

5. Peter Brooks, for example, demonstrates convincingly the erotic stakes of socialization in his astute reading of eighteenth-century fiction, *The Novel of Worldliness*.

6. For an overview of this and other female patterns in the eighteenth-century novel, the reader should consult Pierre Fauchery's *La Destinée féminine dans le roman européen du dix-huitième siècle*. (I have indicated my attitude toward Fauchery's "text" in a review article, "The Exquisite Cadavers." Important too, though less general, is John Richetti's analysis of the trials of female innocence in his *Popular Fiction before Richardson*.

7. The power of this ambition, however unrealistic, is crucial to the shaping of Moll's narrative: "Moll's fantasy is of authentic independence through labour, an apparently rare possibility for very young children who were engaged in spinning yarn for the manufacture of woolens. What Moll will have to learn to do in the course of her narrative is to relinquish this middle-class dream of honest and self-sufficient survival." John Richetti in his chapter on *Moll Flanders*, "The Dialectic of Power" in *Defoe's Narratives*, p. 99. After briefly reviewing the irony controversy which has colored, not to say overdetermined, the various interpretations of *Moll Flanders*, Richetti proposes a Hegelian grid for the novel, and, I think, successfully eliminates the vexed and tired problem of "psychological inconsistency" in Moll (the ironists' trump card): "[N]ovelistic character is primarily a means towards a larger structural end rather than an end in itself. That notorious contradiction the character of Moll Flanders embodies is the most visible expression of the structure of the novel. Her narrative self is a means of enacting for us independence of the 'other,' that is, of society, history, and circumstance in general" (p. 96). My analysis parallels Richetti's—and more often than I might wish—with this important distinction: the self he tracks is, at heart, beyond gender.

8. Clued or cued, the reader can proceed to supply the missing and anticipated pieces of the textual puzzle: "Genre functions like a code common to the emitter and the receiver, which restricts and predetermines the latter's expectations by establishing lines of least resistance (total predictability)." Philippe Hamon, "Pour un statut sémiologique du personnage," p. 158. To decode appropriately, of course, the reader must possess, as Hamon puts it, the " 'grammar' of the genre." In his "Système d'un genre descriptif," Michael Riffaterre also defines genre in terms of reader response: "It is a phantom form which only exists as a whole in the reader's mind; indeed, it is only a standard of measurement against which he tests the actual works. In short, a structure of which the texts are variants" (p. 16).

9. "A genre . . . has a grammar and this grammar merely develops a very limited number of matrix sentences. The Gothic novel, for example, is built upon the expansion of sentences linking innocence and a threat to that innocence, and linking the threat and the past, with the corollary that the past is secret." Michael Riffaterre, "On Deciphering Mallarmé," p. 80.

10. "Narrative cliché is a fixed structural model which stands out against the structural freedom of 'normal' narrative and can be identified as an autonomous unity within the fiction to which it belongs." Laurent Jenny, "Structure et fonctions du cliché" (p. 504).

11. The label and the elaboration of the pattern are Laurent Jenny's as cited above. I have modified his model for my purposes.

12. "Moll stated the fact bluntly, but fact it was. A woman's sex function was her dowry if she had no cash; the market was frankly open, and she might take it to the Exchange, which was marriage, or play it on the Curb, which was prostitution. What price chastity?" G. B. Needham and R. P. Utter, *Pamela's Daughters*, p. 31.

13. This split between commentary and event has been read as an example of the "literature of casuistry": "We are asked to distinguish between act and agent—between what Moll does and what she essentially is: without minimizing her culpability, the narrative seeks to deflect our severity from the doer to the deed, and to retain sympathy for the erring heroine." George A. Starr, *Defoe and Casuistry*, p. 112. Richetti speaks of the self and its fictional contexts: "Moll pretends to be a novelistic character who is subject to compulsions of development within the conditions of her environment, so that her story may deliver the pattern of an indestructible and elastic self." *Defoe's Narratives*, p. 119. Both analyses, however, undervalue the content of the rhetorical strategies at work in Moll's auto-representation: the persistent *reference* to an abstract model of specifically female behavior.

14. I should perhaps comment here that when I speak of degradation, I am not referring to some form of psychosexual perversion, but to a purely narrative phenomenon. I am referring, in fact, to the early work of Claude Bremond. In Bremond's scheme all narrated events of human projects can be classified within two types of sequences: amelioration and/or degradation. As these labels suggest by their very names, a pattern of amelioration demonstrates the successful and desired fulfillment of a given project; degradation, its countertext. The sequences of amelioration and degradation are further classifiable into specific patterns. See "La logique des possibles narratifs," in that watershed issue of structuralist analysis, *Communications* (1966), no. 8.

15. The importance of these surrogate mothers has been observed. Starr comments in his introduction to the novel: "Moll is less intimate with any of the men in her adult life than with this series of maternal figures. It is as if she were intent on demonstrating that she would have been an ideal daughter had she had a proper mother" (p. x). "Moll's career," Richetti writes, "is, on the surface, a series of relationships with men, but those relationships are usually subordinate to a powerful and instrumental alliance with a female conspirator. . . . Women thus 'organized' are . . . an authentic group manipulating the inauthentic relationships ordinary society offers." *Defoe's Narratives*, pp. 110–11. Moll's successful female bonding is indeed key to the shape of her quest for security and identity and as such might also be seen as a muted challenge to the paternal metaphor, as a male fantasy—acted out through the fiction of the female—of independence from the law of the fathers.

16. If Moll is often a wife, or at least partner in a couple, her evolution is also determined by maternity. Moll may not nurture her children, but she continues to bear them until biology intervenes. Moll's many children serve less to present Moll as a parent than to underline the specificity of a female quest for social and economic security. The sequences of marriages and births intercept in a dialectic of contradiction that is resolved only at the end. The children on the whole function as obstacles to the successful realization of Moll's original project. It is nonetheless the family principle that ultimately assures success. On Moll's maternal dilemma and contemporary social attitudes toward the abandoning of children, see Lerenbaum's subsection "Moll as Mother," in "Moll Flanders," pp. 106–11.

17. Lerenbaum is the only critic to my knowledge who connects as I do Moll's "change of life" to her change of "career." Although I am not entirely comfortable with her psychosexual interpretation, i.e., that Moll finds in crime "compensation for the loss of her roles as wife and mother" (p. 115), there is no doubt that Moll's narrative registers a biological causality and a gyn-economy. She must find another way of filling her "Purse," as it were.

18. The alibi of necessity which frames the crime narrative may well be as disingenuous as the alibi of ignorance in the initial seduction sequence, but how else is Moll (the narrator) to seduce the reader? And seduce the reader she must if she is to be "forgiven." I do not, as will become immediately clear, discuss Moll's career as a criminal, agreeing here with Lerenbaum that "the particular details of Moll's criminal career are not especially relevant to the question of her femininity" (p. 115).

19. In the same way, Manon, after her incarceration, wishes only to die faced with the prospect of her own miserable life, but when brought to the realization that Des Grieux has suffered on her account, accepts to live and struggle in a *new* way: "Mais vous ne sauriez croire combien je suis changée. Mes larmes, que vous avez vues couler si souvent depuis notre départ de France, n'ont pas eu une seule fois mes malheurs pour objet." For Manon, Des Grieux's attachment to her despite the suffering he has incurred at her hands provides her with a sense of self-worth which in turn allows her to revise her negative assumptions—revision in turn necessary to the rhetoric of regeneration.

20. Starr observes: "Hitherto frustrated in the search for an ideal mother, Moll seizes on an alternative possibility, and the reunion with her son Humphry serves as a testimonial that she herself, favoured with a proper child, would make an ideal mother" (pp. x–xi). As should be clear, I do not take Moll's maternal strivings as psychological *truth*, but as the ideological underpinnings of plot.

21. Mark Schorer, introduction to the Modern Library edition of the novel (New York, 1950), p. xiii. I should mention that Schorer, counting up Moll's husbands, lovers, children, etc., takes the "myth" as a statistical "absurdity" and a "vast joke." I need not detail my dissent.

22. Watt, *The Rise of the Novel*, p. 105.

23. Richetti, *Defoe's Narratives*, p. 100.

24. Watt, *The Rise of the Novel*, pp. 104–05.

25. Ibid., p. 105.

26. Leo Braudy, in "Daniel Defoe," pp. 76–97, takes up the matter of Moll's " 'real name.' " Commenting on the problem of the name in Defoe's work, he writes: "A name you are born with can relate you to a past history, especially to a genealogy; a name you choose yourself can help you to disengage yourself from your past and family" (88). Moll never reveals her "true name," but she no less assumes, in her text, her connections to the facts and fictions of her past, and by the same token, of her family.

2: *The Virtuous Orphan*

1. In *The Novel of Worldliness*, Peter Brooks explains the fact of this truncated biography in terms of Marivaux's special interest in Marianne's initiation into the world of Parisian life (p. 96). Although I do not agree, as I will suggest in these pages, that Marianne's self and sociality as they are bound to the world are Marivaux's only concern in this novel, it is indeed true that Marivaux's text—unlike Balzac's, as Brooks points out, and unlike Defoe's, as I have tried to show—is not the *ego contra mundum*.

2. Brooks (p. 96) cites Leo Spitzer's well-known distinction between a "roman d'éducation" and a "roman d'explicitation," and with Spitzer prefers the latter. My feeling is that while *Marianne* on one level merely renders explicit what from the beginning is implicit, i.e., the heroine's *aptitude* for the world, the novel is also an apprenticeship, and as such is the vehicle of a *movement* to mastery.

3. As Trilling describes him: "He need not come from the provinces in literal fact, his social class may constitute his province. But a provincial birth and rearing suggest the simplicity and the high hopes he begins with—he starts with a great demand upon life and a great wonder about its complexity and promise. He may be of a good family but he must be poor. He is intelligent, or at least aware, but not at all shrewd in worldly matters." "The Princess Casamassima," The *Liberal Imagination*, p. 61. Or, as Ronald Rosbottom succinctly summarizes the plot of Marivaux's novel: "It is the story of how a young girl, with neither money nor family, yet convinced of her superiority, rises to the social rank of countess solely by means of her beauty and intelligence. Everything else is a function of this basic theme." *Marivaux's Novels*, p. 108. I refer the reader to this excellent introduction to (and rehabilitation of) Marivaux's novels (for an American public); Rosbottom also provides a complete bibliography of Marivaux scholarship.

4. I follow the Garnier edition (Paris, 1963); p. 13.

5. Rosbottom comments: "This short paragraph is a resumé of the action of the entire novel. Marianne is unwilling to remain with the crowd because of her attributes, both natural and acquired, which she feels entitle her to a higher station in life." *Marivaux's Novels*, p. 137.

6. Frédéric Deloffre, editor of the Garnier edition, signals in a note on this passage the similarities between this analysis of love and others where Marivaux "notes the fear that is immediately mingled with the pleasure of loving" (p. 66). He cites, as do most Marivaudians, Georges Poulet's now classic reference in *Etudes sur le temps humain*, vol. 2, pp. 10–15. What is less noticed, however, is the *feminization* of the experience in its very coding.

7. It is not surprising that a slight accident should stimulate so much anguished activity. Since the positive heroine is fragile, this sort of fall serves as a proof of vulnerable, hence ideal, femininity: "According to the rules, women in the novel can scarcely walk without risking a twisted ankle, even if they are in perfect health." Pierre Fauchery, *La Destinée féminine*, p. 192. Moreover, the mere mention of a foot, as is the case in *Pamela*, causes embarrassment for the virtuous heroine because it is an erotically coded focus in the period—particularly in Rococo painting.

8. Stopping over this moment, Rosbottom points out the vicissitudes of *amour-propre* but elides the matter of "reputation": Marianne "does not care if Valville knows that she is an orphan, or poor, but to be known as an assistant in a linen shop would do irreparable injury to her pride" (p. 156). It is perhaps in the politics of pride that the differences between Marianne and Pamela emerge most clearly. Unlike Pamela, who although briefly and giddily tempted by the trappings of aristocratic life, accepts and even takes pride in the class to which she belongs because it contains, in her eyes, a *founding* virtue, Marianne, doomed to mediocrity by the status quo, would be above or below it all.

9. Although, as the title of her text announces, Marianne is earmarked for success, the narrative structures of ascent generically are dependent upon obstacles. Marianne's rise, then, is intermittent: for every advance there is a setback; complacency is converted to despair; pathos follows pride. Or in narratological terms: "Two processes of amelioration can only follow each

other if the amelioration brought about by the first process leaves something to be desired. . . .
The narrator therefore must introduce into his narrative the equivalent of a phase of degradation. The still relatively deficient state which results serves as the point of departure for the new
phase of amelioration." Claude Bremond, "La logique des possibles narratifs," p. 63. See also
my chapter 1, fn. 14, p. 161.

10. I should mentioned here, belatedly accounting for the title of this chapter, that *The Virtuous Orphan* was the title of the eighteenth-century English translation of Marivaux's novel.
Although Brooks feels that the "overtones of bourgeois self-righteousness" generated by that de-
nomination sound "the wrong note: never do we as readers question the nobility of Marianne's
birth" (p. 97), the logic of the narrative *is* dependent upon her orphan-ness (doubled by the
Tervire story), and, however equivocal, upon her virtue. The English title is perhaps not so far
"off" intertextually in that it points to the appeal of a *type*; and we might note a 1765 edition of
the novel: *Marianne, ou la Nouvelle Paméla.*

11. Marianne—in her capacity as narrator—takes up the matter of Valville's fickleness:
"Vous avez oublié que c'était ma vie que je vous racontais. . . . Un héros de roman infidèle!
on n'aurait jamais rien vu de pareil" (375). This breach of conduct, however, is precisely *not*
about life but the needs of a certain fiction: a fiction about the impossible consolidation of a
social self, an interminable process of self-realization (interminable because based on unerasa-
ble class difference) excluded from the containment—narrative and ideological—of passion
(and/or in the English model, marriage).

12. "Both women," English Showalter writes, "know by intuition that their only protection
is to have complete control of their own appearance while seeing through the defensive poses of
others." *The Evolution of the French Novel*, p. 343–44.

13. On the role of Tervire as double, see Sylvère Lotringer's "Le roman impossible," pp.
297–321, and p. 315 ff.

14. In the Garnier *Marianne*, p. 605, fn. 2.

15. "Madame Riccoboni's reading of Marivaux's novel was not at variance with the rest of
his public, and her creation is also a young girl who wishes to protect her amour-propre at all
costs, even that of happiness, and does so through the use of all the tricks—or *coquetterie*—at
her disposal." Rosbottom, *Marivaux's Novels*, p. 159.

16. In his introduction to *La Religieuse*, p. xiv.

17. "Actually, in these matters it is often like watching a tightrope act ["équilibrisme"]: a fine
line, a golden line, separates the chaste Marianne from an adventuress, or Pamela from a
'tease.' " Fauchery, *La Destinée féminine*, p. 231.

18. "If Marianne were to appear in Laclos's society, she too would probably be destroyed;
her virtue, which makes such a strong impression on Marivaux's characters, would pass unno-
ticed by Laclos's." Showalter, *The Evolution of the French Novel*, p. 343. Showalter goes on to
note some interesting parallels between the style and language of the two heroines.

3: *The Rewards of Virtue*

Epigraph: I owe the Addison "rewriting" to the fine eye of Ellen Pollak; "Perspectives on a
Myth: Women in the Verse of Swift and Pope," Diss. Columbia University 1979.

1. Harry Levin, in his foreword to *Les Liaisons dangereuses*, alludes to Huysmans's comment (p. x), which in fact appears in the preface to *A Rebours* (Paris: Fasquelle, 1903); and

remarks that in Laclos's novel, "that is all a foregone conclusion." That is not a foregone conclusion in 1740, the date of what some say is the first English psychological novel.

2. The term courtship, minus the inverted commas, is Ian Watt's. As a retroactive reading of the novel, Watt's label is quite correct. And I have argued for such readings in these pages. Still, to call the relationship between Mr. B. and Pamela *as it unfolds* a courtship, is to empty the text of its implicit violence. *The Rise of the Novel*, p. 135. The doubling of difference—sex and class—would seem to be a grammatical feature of the eighteenth-century feminocentric novel of ascent, and *Pamela* lays the syntax bare. The difference of conditions, however, intersects with sexual difference in all the novels under consideration here—with the singular exception of the war between those two aristocrats: the Marquise de Merteuil and the Vicomte de Valmont. On the role of social difference in the structuration of the eighteenth-century novel in France, see Sylvére Lotringer's "Le roman impossible," pp. 297–321.

3. This inner nobility, of course, would not mean much without the deeper underpinnings of chastity. The most important common denominator in the characterizations of Pamela and Marianne is their gift for negotiating their desirability while remaining intact. They could be seen as stand-ins for Steele's Prude and Coquette as they are described in *Tatler* no. 126: "The Prude and Coquette, as different as they appear in their behaviour, are in reality the same kind of women. . . . The distant behaviour of the Prude tends to have the same purpose as the advances of the Coquette; and you have as little reason to fall into despair from the severity of the one, as to conceive hopes from the familiarity of the other. What leads you into a clear sense of their character is, that you may observe each of them has the distinction of sex in all her thoughts, words and actions."

4. Watt writes: "The appearance of *Pamela* marks a very notable epiphany in the history of our culture: the emergence of a new, fully developed and immensely influential stereotype of the feminine role." *The Rise of the Novel*, p. 161. Describing the type further, Watt cites the findings of R. P. Utter and G. B. Needham in their excellent study *Pamela's Daughters*: "They show how the model heroine must be very young, very inexperienced, and so delicate in physical and mental constitution that she faints at any sexual advance; essentially passive, she is devoid of any feelings towards her admirer until the marriage knot is tied—such is Pamela and such are most of the heroines of fiction until the end of the Victorian period" (p. 161). That Pamela is "devoid of any feelings" before the tying of the knot is the ideology Richardson both promotes and undercuts at the same time.

5. I follow the Norton Library Edition (New York, 1958); here, p. 3.

6. Utter and Needham comment that while to a twentieth-century reader Pamela "seems grovelingly submissive . . . [she] has spirit and energy; it is only because she holds herself to a strictly defensive position that we call her submissive." *Pamela's Daughters*, p. 9.

7. Watt, *The Rise of the Novel*, p. 165.

8. The story (2 Samuel 13) makes Pamela's unconscious fears and desires clear: "Then Amnon hated her exceedingly; so that the hatred wherewith he hated her *was* greater than the love wherewith he had loved her. And Amnon said unto her, Arise, be gone. And she said unto him, *There is* no cause: this evil in sending me away *is* greater than the other that thou didst unto me." But Pamela does not yet know that she loves, nor would she leave, the man she cannot hate (224).

9. The escape, successful or abortive, and whatever its modalities, is a recurrent configura-

tion in novels where persecution is a structuring theme. (Its recurrence is so predictable that it assumes the status of narrative cliché.) An escape scene necessarily involves exposure to danger and physical harm to the escapee, for its function is to create pathos and to demonstrate authenticity of motive. A *feminine* protagonist, however, emerges from this exceptional endeavor not merely affirmed as courageous, but *virtuous*, and hence worthy of her role as positive heroine. She must literally *flee* sexuality: Clarissa, Sade's Justine, Diderot's Suzanne Simonin, *et al.*

10. Stuart Wilson comes to similar conclusions: "The single most important consequence of the ordeal by the pondside is Pamela's recognition of her growing affection for her master, in spite of the moral and social difference between them." "Richardson's *Pamela*," p. 87. Toying with the possibility of *reform*, moreover, is a further mark of slippage. Playing the prude to Mr. B.'s rake, Pamela, like Mme de Tourvel and, of course, Clarissa, provides herself with an alibi for an otherwise guilty exchange. In her case, however, it works. Mr. B. does eventually reform. Unlike Valmont and Lovelace, he changes in time to reap the benefits of virtue and "true" love.

11. Watt reads Pamela's fainting as proof of her *inherent* upward mobility: "Pamela's humble birth hardly entitles her to this trait; but in fact her full possession of it only shows that her total being has been so deeply shaped by ideas above her station that even her body exhibits—to invoke the assistance of a neologism . . . a not uncommon form of what can only be called sociosomatic snobbery." *The Rise of the Novel*, p. 161–62. But Wilson, more concerned with the *psycho*sexual dynamics of Pamela's characterization, sees this swoon in particular as an example of the novel's "psychological accuracy": "When her anxiety becomes so great that her mind cannot tolerate it, she reacts like the typical hysteric—she loses consciousness. . . . Unlike so many later heroines of the sentimental novel, Pamela does not faint at will; there is more than adequate motivation for her 'dying' at the climax of a severe traumatic experience, an experience whose scars must be completely effaced before she can gain the release into tranquillity that an uninhibited love will provide." "Richardson's *Pamela*" p. 88. As a positive heroine Pamela can *only* faint in the face of sexual demands: to be "otherwise," as she casts it, would mean—literally—the death of her text. Pamela's swoon, however, like Julie's after the first kiss, also points to a masculine notion about the power of repressed female sexuality.

12. Watt states that "the new ideology granted [Pamela and her sisters] a total immunity from sexual feelings, and if they married it was not because they had any need of *medicina libidinis*, but because the pieties of marriage and the family were safe only in their hands." *The Rise of the Novel* p. 160. True, but the countertext coexists, as I have tried to suggest.

13. "Pamela undergoes a prolonged, intense, and disruptive emotional experience, one that severely affects her psychic balance, and the marriage is only the first step toward a final resolution of the tensions set up in the first half of the novel. . . . For Pamela, the reward of virtue is not primarily her marriage to a rich patrician but the reconciliation of a character severely tested." Wilson, "Richardson's *Pamela*," pp. 79, 91.

14. Again, Richardson's French "translator" would seem to be Rousseau. Saint-Preux, transformed by Julie's virtue, exclaims: "Non, non; les feux dont j'ai brûlé m'ont purifié; je n'ai plus rien d'un homme ordinaire." And he too seeks to exist on *feminine* terms.

15. The metaphor of the ship of life as fragile vessel on life's ocean is capable of supporting a variety of meanings according to the context in which it occurs (although the oppositional

structure is a constant). Thus Clarissa's will, her sense of direction, are disoriented by the "foam-ing billows" of parental authority which keep her from the desired port; in *Les Liaisons dangereuses*, Mme de Tourvel prefers the safety of her life on shore to the sea of stormy pas-sions. Here, curiously, it is marriage that is encoded as danger, and the component of fragility is actualized in the *self*-concept, negatively scored: "inconsiderate will" posed—anaphorically—as synonym to "conduct" by Pamela's person ("my own").

16. Wilson, again taking a psychological stance, observes: "The comparison of past anxieties with present composure leads to a realization that the scenes no longer function as symbols of the time when she was tortured by ambivalent emotions; they are now seen as elements in a divine plan by which Pamela's integrity would be tested." "Richardson's *Pamela*," p. 90.

17. However, and as Mark Kinkead-Weekes points out in his *Samuel Richardson*, the trans-formation, and the magic, lie in the eye of the beholder. Griselda, Pamela's textual predecessor in long-suffering female virtue, "is always the same, really; Cinderella always as beautiful as a princess beneath her rags, though nobody will see it until she is gowned at the ball" (p. 11).

4: *A Harlot's Progress: II*

1. For an account of the publication (dates, titles, etc.) of Cleland's novel, see David Foxon's *Libertine Literature in England*; especially his appendix, pp. 52–63.

2. I follow the Signet edition (New York, 1965); here, p. 15.

3. Thus Fanny's memoirs, like Marianne's "life," are essentially truncated autobiography: narratives whose point of arrival is delimited by the end of adolescence.

4. Leo Braudy notes the apparent literary allusion to *Pamela* in his "rehabilitation" of *Fanny Hill*, "Fanny Hill and Materialism," p. 29. In *Pamela-Shamela*, Bernard Kreissman suggests that the names Fanny and Pamela become interchangeable after 1740. He cites *Fanni, ou la Nouvelle Paméla* of Baculard d'Arnaud (1767) (p. 39), and John Piper's 1760 novel, *The Life of Miss Fanny Brown; or, Pamela the Second (A Clergyman's Daughter)* (p. 6). Curiously, how-ever, he does not cite *Fanny Hill*.

5. This relationship is both obvious and problematic. As Braudy points out, the novel "has too broad a sense of social milieu and literary tradition for the writer interested in describing the 'pure' elements of pornography as a literary genre, and . . . too much erotic content for the literary historian to treat it with much seriousness." "*Fanny Hill* and Materialism," p. 21. Braudy's case is based largely on the novel's ideological relations to materialism and sentimen-talism. I argue for an eighteenth-century *literariness* based on intertextuality and what Michael Riffaterre calls the renewal of cliché: "These . . . substitutions share a common feature: they force the reader to become aware of both the renewing element and the renewed element. This phenomenon of a double reading is therefore not different (except for the transformation) from what happens when the reader decodes a cliché: the cliché is simultaneously seen [for the first time] and already seen ["déjà vu"], perceived in the text and in the recollected metatext." *Essais de Stylistique structurale*, p. 170.

6. In Pamela's "mirror" scene, however, and necessarily because she is writing "to the moment," specular pleasure is mitigated only by the possibility of a return to the old and "ordi-nary." At the time, the new self is perceived as entirely satisfactory: "And when I was equipped, I took my straw hat in my hand, with its two blue strings, and looked about me in the glass, as proud as anything—To say truth, I never liked myself so well in my life." The *topos*, in other

words, is not so much about "then/now" as the vicissitudes of class, femininity . . . and representation.

7. Braudy, *"Fanny Hill* and Materialism," p. 37.

8. To read an episode of female sexualization as locus of violence in *Fanny Hill* with *Justine* requires a certain "violence" to Sade's text: a comparable scene not only involves several participants and more than one mode of penetration, but manifestations of sexual behavior characterized by the heroine as cruel and unnatural. For the sake of clarity I do not include them here. Nevertheless, since Justine rates the episode cited below as marking the destruction of her virtue—she was unconscious the very first time—the juxtaposition seems pertinent.

9. To bring out the purely lexical relations between the two texts, I have cited Sade in translation (New York: Grove Press, 1966), pp. 569–72. The corresponding pages in French are pp. 134–36 (Paris: 10/18, 1969).

10. The formulation is Peter Quennell's, quoted by J. H. Plumb in his introduction to the novel, pp. xiii–xiv. We might just as well speak of the longitudinal *phallacy*. Thus, for example, when Fanny decides to have an affair with Will, the messenger boy, she overcomes her initial fear in the face of his "oversized machine" (95), "a maypole of so enormous a standard . . . it must have belonged to a young giant" (94). Always an egalitarian, Fanny appreciates Will for "his outward form, and especially in that *superb piece of furniture* [nature] had so liberally enriched him with" (107; italics mine). Positive metaphor for Fanny, however, is negative metonymy for Justine. She fears perforation by a literal, concrete substitute: "one of those *articles of furniture* usually found in nunneries, which decency forbids me from naming and which was of an *exorbitant thickness*" (p. 619; italics mine; in the French, p. 187). Fanny becomes enamored of size, Justine persists in fearing it. In both cases, whatever the modalities of reception, it is the (fantasmatic) phallus that is prized.

11. Similarly, in *Manon Lescaut*, Des Grieux's father intervenes, though less successfully, to put an end to a *ménage* that disrupts the family order. In this sense, we are in the presence of a predictable sequence: when illicit love is grounded in a disparity of social condition, a member of the "wronged" family intercedes, in the name of higher and hierarchical values, to disunite the couple. Thus, Valville's relatives in *La Vie de Marianne*, Mr. B.'s sister in *Pamela*, Julie's father in *la Nouvelle Héloïse*, all perform in the same sequence. Rousseau "renews" the cliché by assigning inferiority to the male.

12. Braudy, *"Fanny Hill* and Materialism," p. 31.

13. The cries of admiration on the part of the spectators belong to the paradigm of preliminaries in the Sadian orgy. But where Fanny derives pleasure from her status as attractive commodity, Justine is appalled. (Again one might note that every act marked with a positive sign for Fanny is negativized for Justine.)

14. This performance parodies the social and literary overvaluation of virginity as founding innocence and reinscribes the cliché: "The frank negation of the taboo occurs especially in the licentious novel, which takes pleasure in denouncing the fiduciary nature of this essence. The novice heroines are promptly lectured by their often eloquent 'protectresses' . . . Mrs. B., for example, who sells Fanny Hill's young beauty to a lord." Pierre Fauchery, *La Destinée féminine*, p. 312.

15. Interestingly, it was Fanny's ability to manage money, which she attributes to Mrs. Cole's tutelage, that inspired her benefactor's confidence. In this respect, at least, her past paid

off—as does, ultimately, Moll's. In both cases, however, financial success brings neither contentment, nor, more to the point, closure.

16. The chance encounter between prospective lovers (Marianne and Valville outside the church, Manon and Des Grieux at the coach) or separated lovers (Moll and Jemmy at Newgate) functions as a literary checkpoint, a sign and reminder to the reader that "destiny" is at work and romance in the works. Surprise is furthermore the occasion for proof of unprepared hence authentic emotion. Here, Fanny swoons at her discovery of Charles. All of this as opposed, for example, to the resolutely unsentimental calculations of the *Liaisons*.

17. Or, as Balzac writes of Eugénie's response to her Charles's misfortune: "Depuis la veille, elle s'attachait à Charles par tous les liens de bonheur qui unissent les âmes; désormais la souffrance allait donc le corroborer. N'est-il pas dans la noble destinée de la femme *d'être plus touchée des pompes de la misère* que des splendeurs de la fortune?" *Eugénie Grandet*, p. 69; italics mine. What price nobility?

18. J. H. Plumb, in his introduction, p. xiii. He goes on to say: "In quality of writing, in delineation of character, these *Memoirs* can hold their own with the general run of eighteenth-century literature. But these are not, of course, the reasons for its long and continuing success" (p. xiv). Plumb's tact is remarkable throughout.

5: *Love for a Harlot*

1. I refer of course to Freud's essay "A Special Type of Choice of Object made by Men," in "Three Contributions to the Psychology of Love." It offers a suggestive frame and focus against which to read Prévost's novel:

[T]he person in question never chooses as an object of love a woman who is unattached . . . but only one in regard to whom another man has some right of possession. . . . [T]his attraction is exercised only by one who is more or less sexually discredited, whose fidelity and loyalty admit of some doubt . . . from . . . a married woman . . . to the openly polygamous way of life of a prostitute, or of a *grande amoureuse*. . . . By a rough characterization this condition could be called that of "love for a harlot."

I cite the essay as collected in *On Creativity and the Unconscious*, pp. 163–64.

2. "Le sourire du sphinx, p. 185.
3. I follow the Garnier edition of the novel (Paris, 1965); pp. 11–12.
4. Freud writes of the "impulse to 'rescue' the beloved" in this scenario: "Her propensity to fickleness and infidelity brings the loved woman into dangerous situations, so it is natural that the lover should do all he can to protect her by watching over her virtue and opposing her evil ways." "A Special Type of Choice of Object," p. 170. The rescue pattern thus structures Des Grieux's trajectory from the beginning.
5. See above, chapter 1, p. 7.
6. Except for (hence confirming the rule) the added but prefiguring episode of the Italian prince, and the final sequence of the novel. As "the" amante incomparable," Manon is true—at last—to her word, and the betrayal comes from *without* the couple.
7. Georges Matoré, for example, in the introduction to his critical edition of the novel.
8. That is, in conformity with eighteenth-century attitudes toward lower-class women. If we are to believe the Goncourt brothers: "From childhood, these daughters of the common people

grow up to seduce. . . . . The idea of duty, of female virtue is only acquired by the censure of the neighbors." *La Femme au dix-huitième siècle*, vol. 2, p. 11. For a less hysterical vision, see Vera Lee's *The Reign of Women*, pp. 27–44.

9. *Seduction and Betrayal*, p. 192.

10. *The Second Sex*, p. 174.

11. In this sense, Manon is *linguistically* consistent: "The stereotype contains . . . a binary group made up of a microcontext and an element contrasting with this context. . . . This contrast of two opposite but inseparable poles is fixed: its effect is therefore, on hold, as it were." Riffaterre, *Essais de Stylistique structurale*, pp. 162–63.

12. Rather, she is predictably unpredictable. On Manon's "irreducibility," see Sylvère Lotringer's analysis of this episode. "Manon L'Echo," p. 105.

13. Thus, Saint-Preux writes to Julie: "Viens, ô mon âme! dans les bras de ton ami réunir les deux moitiés de notre être. . . . Soyons heureux et pauvres, ah! quel trésor nous aurons acquis! Mais ne faisons point cet affront à l'humanité, de croire qu'il ne restera pas sur la terre entière un asile à deux amants infortunés." But perhaps the most dramatic instance of this fantasy is to be found in *Clarissa*. For what is Lovelace's dream if not to contain Clarissa away from the world and its paternal strictures? He would have her accept him as her world.

14. Marshall Berman, *The Politics of Authenticity*, p. 234.

15. That something must always be missing in this tale of desire is, of course, the ideological matrix of the novel. See Lotringer's analysis, in "Manon L'Echo," pp. 109–10.

16. *The Evolution of the French Novel*, pp. 303–04.

17. Marriage in *Manon Lescaut* would have required the death of the father *and* the social opposition he incarnated (like the death of M. de Climal in Marianne). But it is clear that Prévost's novel is about impossibility, and the father's death, like Des Grieux's eleventh-hour desire for legitimacy, comes too late.

6: The Misfortunes of Virtue: I

1. "On *Clarissa Harlowe*," in *The English Novel*, p. 60.

2. H. R. Hays, *The Dangerous Sex*, p. 180.

3. *The English Novel*, p. 60.

4. *Clarissa: or, The History of a Young Lady*. I follow the Everyman edition (New York, 1962), in 4 volumes; reference here, vol. 1, p. 345.

5. *The English Novel*, p. 60.

6. Although I have some reservations about aspects of the analysis, I send the reader to Judith Wilt's brilliant piece on the rape, "He Could Go No Farther," pp. 19–32.

7. "*Clarissa*," Leo Braudy writes, "explores and helps define the cultural moment when the self-willed isolation of the individual that insures a security against the world becomes first an opposition between self and society and finally a *mutually exclusive definition of the images of male and female*." "Penetration and Impenetrability," p. 189; italics mine.

8. In Leslie Fiedler's view, this agon in fact marks the birth of the genre: "The novel proper could not be launched until some author imagined a prose narrative in which the Seducer and the Pure Maiden were brought face to face in ritual combat destined to end in marriage or death; the form and its mythology were born together, in the works of Samuel Richardson." *Love and Death in the American Novel*, p. 62.

9. Van Ghent, *The English Novel*, p. 78.

10. At odds with her natural family, Clarissa contemplates the *orphan's* solution: domestic work. A daughter of the middle classes, however, she does not intend to become a servant, merely to "pass" in order to benefit from the protection brought by temporary *déclassement*. Indeed, the disguise—though not here—ultimately ensures her escape from Lovelace's clutches later in the novel. She thinks she would have preferred a nunnery, but in literature that retreat usually proves no retreat at all. The point is, of course, that there is no exit but death for the heroine whose expectations are at variance with the sociolect.

11. As Elizabeth Hardwick puts it, parenthetically: "Clarissa's prudence is sexual; otherwise she makes every mistake possible to a clever, bossy, morally vain . . . girl." *Seduction and Betrayal*, p. 197.

12. Watt, *The Rise of the Novel*, p. 209.

13. Ibid., p. 231.

14. Patricia Meyer Spacks, commenting on Lovelace's "obsessive relation with female purity," observes: "As an angel [Clarissa] is of course a focus of fear; and equally of course an object of what passes for love in Lovelace. Her angelic nature declares her superiority, her power actual and potential. . . . His fear of her, both before and after his betrayal of her, feels intolerable; he is driven to ever more outrageous devices to exorcise this fear by degrading its object." "Early Fiction and the Frightened Male," p. 9. Lovelace's approach/avoidance "pathology" can be read also as an acting out of a more archaic male ambivalence in the face of virginity. Simone de Beauvoir remarks: "The virgin would seem to represent the most consummate form of the feminine mystery; she is therefore its most disturbing and at the same time its most fascinating aspect." *The Second Sex*, p. 141.

15. Clarissa's metaphors bear the weight of a long literary tradition. For an analysis and history of the verbal oppositions rose vs. worm, the reader should consult Michael Riffaterre's essay on Blake's "The Sick Rose," "The Self-sufficient Text" (pp. 39–45). In every case, two descriptive systems are posed in opposition but signify only by that polarized relation: purity is inseparable from its destruction. For Mark Kinkead-Weekes, however, such an intertextual reading "would be both superficial and significantly mistaken. For what it leaves out of account is just the most striking feature: that from the first image onwards, the emphasis is not on violation or desecration of purity, but on the destruction of potential fertility, growth, warmth, and colour. . . . This is not sex seen as desecration . . . but *rape as seen as a desecration of true sex*, and the difference is crucial." *Samuel Richardson*, p. 237. He goes on to argue that two conceptions of sex are opposed, Clarissa's "growth, fertility, harvest, warmth, richness," and Lovelace's "ego-endorsement . . . poisonous, corrupt, and diseased" (p. 238). I have cited his argument at some length because this is indeed a vexed issue, but cannot accept Clarissa's text as a message of disappointment and frustrated fulfillment, particularly in the context of the rape. On this passage, see also Wilt's "He Could Go No Farther," p. 26.

16. Again Lovelace has misread his text. Shortly before the rape he had declared: "The haughty beauty will not refuse me, when her pride of being corporally inviolate is brought down" (III, 190). As usual, the two are at cross-purposes, because after the same thing at bottom: like Lovelace, Clarissa's "deepest and most morally questionable desire . . . is not sex at all, but power. . . . Clarissa, famous for chastity, cannot acquiesce to Lovelace, who wants her acknowledgement that he is the only man in the world who can *change her mind*;

Lovelace, famous as a sexual conqueror, cannot be reformed by Clarissa, who would assert her power by changing the man dedicated to destroying it." Rachel Mayer Brownstein, " 'An Exemplar to Her Sex,' " p. 39; italics mine.

17. "Clarissa knows the truth of her frailty: *weakness comes from within*. . . . The mind is its own place—and the body as well. Against Lovelace she defines her will as a totally mental and spiritual entity, not only separate from desire but opposed to it as well." Braudy, "Penetration and Impenetrability," p. 195.

18. Clarissa's *best* self is an innocence that cannot be recaptured. Hence her desperate nostalgia for what Wilt describes as a "self that is presexual, naively (but wonderfully) pure person, existing essentially in the way one perceives oneself." "He Could Go No farther," p. 30. On this notion, see too my "Novels of Innocence," pp. 325–39.

19. Lovelace hopes, while the Harlowe family assumes, that Clarissa is pregnant: "It would be the pride of my life to prove, in this charming frost-piece, the triumph of nature over principle, and to have a young Lovelace by such an angel; and then, for its sake, I am confident she will live and will legitimate it" (IV, 38). Such a fantasmatic solution implies the recognition on Clarissa's part of an internalized *conflict* between nature (flesh) and principle (spirit). But Clarissa (unlike Julie, who for a time admits to the coexistence of the two terms) rejects the flesh as not part of her. In her self-concept she is angel indeed, and not woman. Moreover, if one follows Elizabeth Hardwick's argument, Clarissa could not be both a tragic heroine and pregnant: "Those who suffer from a mere consequence of love, pregnancy, are implicated in their own fall. The consequence is mechanical, universal, repetitive; it will not . . . make a tragic heroine or a heroine of any kind." *Seduction and Betrayal*, p. 187.

20. The (broken) lily is the flower Lovelace evoked in describing Clarissa's imminent defloration; the rose is the flower through which Clarissa metaphorized the rape. It would seem, then, that in her "postmortem" Clarissa acknowledges her vulnerability—the rose as the flower of feminine corporality and sexuality—but that in her final analysis, ending the "silent war of lilies and roses," she selects as definition the flower of purity; returning, at last, to the immaculate.

21. As Julie writes to Saint-Preux: "Après tant de sacrifices, je compte pour peu celui qui me reste à faire: ce n'est que mourir une fois de plus."

22. In this anxiety about temptation, however, Clarissa does prefigure Julie, who in her dying words, confesses to the dangers of her project: "Un jour de plus peut-être, et j'étais coupable! qu'était-ce de la vie entière passée avec vous?" And Wilt, suspicious of Richardson's own faith in Clarissa, observes: "Clarissa, poignantly, *does not trust herself, while in the body*, to stay free of error, even egregious error, damnation" "He Could Go No Farther," p. 31; italics mine.

23. Braudy, "Penetration and Impenetrability," p. 199.

7: *The Misfortunes of Virtue: II*

1. I follow the Garnier edition of the novel (Paris, 1960); p. 12.
2. Christie McDonald Vance, *The Extravagant Shepherd*, p. 77.
3. *The Second Sex*, p. 611.
4. Ibid., p. 620.
5. Tony Tanner comments on the psychoanalytic implications of Julie's script in his ex-

cellent essay, "Julie and 'La Maison Paternelle,' " p. 27: "A . . . careful reading reveals that the summons amounts to an emasculation. [Saint-Preux] is to bring *no* weapons—not even his sword. . . . It is clear that Julie's imagination is fixed much more on the 'sword' of the father than of her lover. Her fantasies center on seeing her father stab the unarmed lover . . . then, it becomes clear, the root fantasy is of being herself stabbed by her father. That is the dreaded/desired penetration. Saint-Preux is invited into her bed, not so much to satisfy her love for him as to indulge her imagination of the aroused and irresistible father."

6. Tanner again zeroes in on the role of the father: "It is as though such is his power and his anger that he can reach into the latent future and eradicate a life that has already been engendered. . . . In this way such physicality as [Julie and Saint-Preux's] relationship enjoyed is rendered effectively nonexistent. . . . The father can also reach into the past and eliminate a sexuality concerning his family which had neither his sanction nor his license. Such a father is indeed close to the awesome figure dominating the primal horde in Freud's vision of the powers of the primitive father," "Julie and 'La Maison Paternelle,' " p. 31.

7. For an interesting, Deleuzian analysis of the structure of these repetitions, see Godelieve Mercken-Spaas's "*La Nouvelle Héloïse*: La Répétition à la Deuxième Puissance," pp. 203–13.

8. This structure of contained opposites characterizes Julie's representation throughout. In her dying moments she whispers to her husband: " 'On m'a fait boire jusqu'à la lie la coupe amère et douce de la sensibilité.' " Oxymoron, like all the others in the novel, which only death can unyoke.

9. In "Aspects of Motif," David Anderson analyzes the function of the Héloïse and Abelard text in the structure of the novel. On this point he observes: "Julie, like Héloïse, while cognizant of the impossibility of sexual love, takes the next best alternative, that of a ritualistic association in which carnal appetites are taken into account while maintaining an illusion of innocence in an established moral order. Saint-Preux, on the other hand, will have nothing to do with a surrogate love that is anything less than Julie, herself, and he is confident in his ability to resist temptation by means of a religious projection, or eternization of his love." (45).

10. "Juliet et 'La Maison Paternelle,' " p. 40.

11. This formula concludes Naomi Schor's reading of the riddle of female sexuality in Zola and the nineteenth-century text: "Le sourire du sphinx," p. 193.

12. Tanner concludes his analysis—of the fall of the House of Clarens—with particular attention to Claire; I owe him that crucial refocusing. Parts of this chapter were published under the title, "Female Sexuality and Narrative Structure in *La Nouvelle Héloïse* and *Les Liaisons dangereuses*."

8: *The Misfortunes of Virtue: III*

Epigraph: as cited by Peter Brooks in *The Novel of Worldliness* (Princeton: Princeton University Press, 1969), p. 40, who comments: "The statement captures perfectly the sense of the libertine's quest to uncover, find out, define—then to fix, dismiss, and move on. If it indicates the male need to know in order to conquer, and to conquer in order to know, it also establishes the necessity of the woman's effort to attach and fix, to break the chain of seduction and infidelity in order to overthrow a system of violation and subjugation." The chain remains unbroken in these novels.

1. I follow the Pléiade edition of the novel (Paris: Gallimard, 1959); p. 8.

2. Laclos's novel has probably received more sophisticated critical attention than any single other French eighteenth-century novel. My debts should be obvious although they are not always explicit. On another level of partiality, I should explain the absence of Cécile in this study. Although this hapless maiden is crucial to the plot as a pawn in the maneuvers between the victimizers, and, on the face of things, an exemplary eighteenth-century heroine—young, pretty, innocent, inexperienced, vulnerable, etc.—I have not included her here. For although she is, as James describes her type, "like a sheet of blank paper—the ideal *jeune fille* of foreign fiction," she is not an interesting heroine, except in the sense that Sade's Justine is "cette intéressante fille." Cécile's story, essentially, is a plot *summary*; a deliberately trivialized linearity.

3. Elizabeth Hardwick, *Seduction and Betrayal*, p. 208.

4. Unlike the adulterous configuration in the nineteenth-century novel where the husband—Charles Bovary, M. de Mortsauf et al.—is more than a signifier and a very present referentiality.

5. Mme de Tourvel is a member of the *haute bourgeoisie*. Although she is quite literally at home with her aristocratic friends—as the houseguest of Valmont's aunt—her values reflect the bourgeois ideals espoused by Julie, a member of the aristocracy by birth.

6. This renewal of the Lucretian *locus classicus* overdetermines not only the explicit metaphor of the shipwreck, but the implicit pleasure of vicarious fear which lurks at the heart of Mme de Tourvel's countertext.

7. The hostility underlying male/female relations expressed here is a linguistic and cultural phenomenon hardly restricted to eighteenth-century letters: " 'Indeed, when referring to their love relations, the most civilized speak of conquest, attack, assault, siege, and of defense, defeat, surrender, clearly shaping the idea of love upon that of war. The act, involving the pollution of one person by another, confers a certain pride upon the polluter, and some humiliation upon the polluted, even when she consents.' " Julien Benda, cited by Simone de Beauvoir in her chapter on sexual initiation, in *The Second Sex*, p. 351.

8. *Seduction and Betrayal*, p. 208.

9. In her "Early Fiction and the Frightened Male," Patricia Meyer Spacks reads the anxiety otherwise: "*Clarissa* depicts a man afraid of woman's fantasized *a*sexuality. Through Lovelace's repeated seductions he attempts to dominate women specifically by reducing them to the sexual, then despising them for it" (9).

10. Paul Hoffmann, "Aspects de la condition féminine," p. 48.

11. Ibid., p. 48; italics mine.

12. Parts of this chapter were published as "Female Sexuality and Narrative Structure in *La Nouvelle Héloïse* and *Les Liaisons dangereuses*."

9: *The Negative Heroine*

1. I follow the Pléiade edition (Paris: Gallimard, 1951); here, p. 177.

2. I take up Merteuil's crime in the context of Laclos criticism in my "Exquisite Cadavers."

3. Henri Duranton makes the point in "*Les Liaisons dangereuses* ou le miroir ennemi," p. 125.

4. That statement, Aram Vartanian points out in his reading of our heroine, "Mistaken Identity" (p. 178), "is totally lacking in social substance. It exists precariously in her own con-

sciousness and in the eyes of Valmont alone—a fact which makes her still more dependent . . . on her accomplice."

5. "The double-standard *continues to apply to her despite her private emancipation,* and her fate depends more than she likes to believe possible on the standards of those women in the novel who fall victim to her." "Mistaken Identity," p. 179; italics mine.

6. I refer the reader to Judith Wilt's analysis of woman as enemy to woman in "He Could Go No Farther," p. 29.

7. Todorov comments: "If Valmont had not transgressed the laws of his own morality (and those of the structure of the novel), we would not have seen the publication of his correspondence, nor that of Merteuil: this publication of their letters is a consequence of their rupture and more generally of the infraction of the law." *Littérature et signification,* p. 75. However, Valmont's transgression is perhaps the truest sign of ideological *conformity* to the laws of feminocentric fiction. Fiction which is always and finally about the greater solidarity of men and the law.

8. On this threat to difference, Julia Kristeva writes: "To tamper with the taboos of grammar . . . is to tamper with the tacit mandate of sexual identity." *Polylogue,* p. 88. She refers to another revolution in language, but the stakes of linguistic rebellion here are no less bound to sexual and social logics.

9. Danceny's words echo faithfully the editor's "moral" stance: "Il me semble au moins que c'est *rendre un service aux moeurs,* que de *dévoiler* les moyens qu'emploient ceux qui en ont de mauvaises pour corrompre ceux qui en ont de bonnes" (p. 8; italics mine). He thus narrows the focus from "ceux" to "une femme," inflecting the femininity implicit in "*dévoiler.*"

10. In this, the novel reveals its mythic dimensions: "Individual freedom has alienation as its corollary; the reintegration of values must be accompanied by the [re]establishment of order, which is to say, by the renunciation of individual freedom." A. J. Greimas (rewriting Lévi-Strauss) in *Sémantique structurale,* p. 210. It is important to note, however, that the reintegration of values is selective here: reinstating Valmont via same-sex identification with Prévan, and banishing the Marquis. Valmont, by going public—via Danceny—gives up libertine freedom in the name of the social continuum.

11. "Mistaken Identity," p. 176.

12. Ibid., p. 180.

Epilogue

1. I am obviously not arguing that women did not actually read these novels, rather that the feminocentric novel and its corollary fiction of the "lectrice" ultimately served—as literary history has shown—the establishment of a predominantly male tradition by masculine *recognition.*

2. *Toward a Recognition of Androgyny,* p. 56.

3. I paraphrase, while obviously taking my distance from, Lévi-Strauss's well-known argument based on the homology between the circulation of signs and the circulation of women. Lévi-Strauss, *Structural Anthropology,* p. 60.

4. Without, however, going along with Spitzer's oft-cited claim that the subject of the novel is "not so much the narrative of the life of an intrepid young woman, but the glorification of

the *feminine principle in human thought* as it reveals itself in life and literature." "A propos de *la Vie de Marianne*," p. 122; his italics.

5. I am indebted to Peggy Brawer, a graduate student in the Department of English and Comparative Literature at Columbia University, who has coined this useful expression to account for the male appropriation of the first-person feminine in the novel; and for other things as well.

6. I have done so myself in an earlier incarnation: "*Juliette* and the Posterity of Prosperity and "*Justine*, Or, the Vicious Circle."

7. *La Destinée féminine*, p. 93.

8. I am essentially borrowing here from John Richetti's lexicon and argument in *Popular Fiction before Richardson*. He is particularly good on the fiction of Mrs. Manley and Mrs. Haywood.

9. The point is made by Patricia Meyer Spacks: "Female novelists, upholding the established system, find images and actions to express profound ambivalence. They convey the energy of impulse as well as of repression; asserting that women are to be valued for their goodness, they wistfully hint a yearning for other grounds of value." *Imagining a Self*, p. 63.

10. I am grateful to Karen Newman for her analysis of power and limits in Austen in her, "Can This Marriage Be Saved."

11. One might also wonder in these speculations about the heroine's text *before* the eighteenth century, in particular the legacy of Mme de Lafayette. I have tried to do so recently in an essay on women's writing, "Emphasis added," where I argue essentially for the presence of what could be called a "synchronic" woman's plot.

Works Cited

Anderson, David L. "Aspects of Motif in *La Nouvelle Héloïse.*" *Studies on Voltaire and the Eighteenth Century* (1972), 44:25–72.

Balzac, Honoré de. *Eugénie Grandet.* Paris: Garnier-Flammarion, 1964.

Beauvoir, Simone de. *The Second Sex.* H. M. Parshley, trans. New York: Bantam Books, 1970.

Berman, Marshall. *The Politics of Authenticity: Radical Individualism and the Emergence of Modern Society.* New York: Atheneum, 1970.

Braudy, Leo. "*Fanny Hill* and Materialism." *Eighteenth-Century Studies* (Fall 1970), 4:21–40.

—— "Daniel Defoe and the Anxieties of Autobiography." *Genre* (March 1973), 6(1):76–97.

—— "Penetration and Impenetrability in *Clarissa.*" *New Approaches to Eighteenth-Century Literature,* pp. 177–206. New York: Columbia University Press, 1974.

Bremond, Claude. "La logique des possibles narratifs." *Communications* (1966), no. 8, pp. 60–76.

Brooks, Peter. *The Novel of Worldliness: Crébillon, Marivaux, Laclos, Stendhal.* Princeton: Princeton University Press, 1969.

Brownstein, Rachel Mayer. " 'An Exemplar to Her Sex': Richardson's Clarissa." *The Yale Review* (Autumn 1977), pp. 30–47.

Cleland, John. *Memoirs of Fanny Hill.* Introduction by J. H. Plumb. New York: Signet, 1965.

Defoe, Daniel. *Moll Flanders.* Introduction by Mark Schorer. New York: Random House, 1950.

—— *The Fortunes and Misfortunes of the Famous Moll Flanders.* Edited and with an introduction by G. A. Starr. London, New York, Toronto: Oxford University Press, 1971.

Diderot, Denis. *La Religieuse.* Introduction by Robert Mauzi. Paris: Armand Colin, 1961.

Duranton, Henri. "*Les Liaisons dangereuses* ou le miroir ennemi." *Revue des sciences humaines* (1974), no. 153, pp. 125–43.

Fauchery, Pierre. *La Destinée féminine dans le roman européen du dix-huitième siècle: 1713–1807. Essai de gynécomythie romanesque.* Paris: Armand Colin, 1972.

Fiedler, Leslie. *Love and Death in the American Novel.* New York: Stein and Day, 1966.

Foxon, David. *Libertine Literature in England, 1660–1745.* New Hyde Park: University Books, 1965.

Freud, Sigmund. "A Special Type of Choice of Object made by Men," in "Three Contributions to the Psychology of Love." *On Creativity and the Unconscious: Papers on the Psychology of Art, Literature, Love, Religion.* New York: Harper, 1958.

Goncourt, Edmond and Jules de. *La Femme au dix-huitième siècle.* Paris: Charpentier, 1887.

Greimas, A. J. *Sémantique structurale.* Paris: Larousse, 1966.

Hamon, Philippe. "Pour un statut sémiologique du personnage." In *Poétique du récit.* Paris: Seuil, Points, 1977.

Hardwick, Elizabeth. *Seduction and Betrayal: Women and Literature.* New York: Random House, 1970.

Hays, H. R. *The Dangerous Sex: The Myth of Feminine Evil.* New York: Pocket Books, 1964.

Heilbrun, Carolyn. *Toward a Recognition of Androgyny.* New York: Harper Colophon, 1974.

Hoffmann, Paul. "Aspects de la condition féminine dans *Les Liaisons dangereuses.*" *L'Information littéraire (mars-avril* 1963), pp. 47–53.

Jenny, Laurent. "Structure et fonctions du cliché." *Poétique* (1972), no. 12, pp. 495–517.

Kinkead-Weekes, Mark. *Samuel Richardson: Dramatic Novelist.* Ithaca, N.Y.: Cornell University Press, 1973.

Kreissman, Bernard. *Pamela-Shamela.* Lincoln: University of Nebraska Press, 1960.

Kristeva, Julia. "Le sujet en procès." In *Polylogue.* Paris: Seuil, 1977.

Laclos, Choderlos de. *Oeuvres complètes.* Paris: Gallimard, 1951.

Lee, Vera. *The Reign of Women in Eighteenth-Century France.* Cambridge: Schenkman, 1975.

Lerenbaum, Miriam. "Moll Flanders: 'A Woman on her own Account.' " In Arlyn Diamond and Lee R. Edwards, eds., *The Authority of Experience: Essays in Feminist Criticism,* pp. 101–17. Amherst: University of Massachusetts Press, 1977.

Levin, Harry. Foreword to *Les Liaisons Dangereuses.* New York: Signet, 1962.

Lévi-Strauss, Claude. *Structural Anthropology.* Claire Jacobson and Brooke Grundfest Schoepf, trans. New York: Anchor Books, 1967.

Lotringer, Sylvère. "Le roman impossible." *Poétique* (1970), no. 3, pp. 297–321.

—— "Manon L'Echo." *Romanic Review* (April 1972), 63:92–110.

Marivaux, Pierre Carlet de Chamblain de. *La Vie de Marianne.* Introduction by Frédéric Deloffre. Paris: Garnier, 1963.

May, Georges. *Le Dilemme du roman au XVIIIe siècle: Etudes sur les rapports du roman et de la critique (1715–1761).* New Haven and Paris: Yale University Press and P.U.F., 1963.

Mercken-Spaas, Godelieve. "*La Nouvelle Héloïse:* La Répétition à la Deuxième Puissance." *Studies in Eighteenth-Century Culture* (1976), 5:203–13.

Miller, Nancy K. "The Exquisite Cadavers: Women in Eighteenth-Century Fiction." *Diacritics* (Winter 1975), 5(4):37–43.

—— "*Juliette* and the Posterity of Prosperity." *L'Esprit Créateur* (Winter 1975), 15(4):413–24.

—— "*Justine,* Or, the Vicious Circle." *Studies in Eighteenth-Century Culture* (1976), 5:215–28.

—— "Female Sexuality and Narrative Structure in *La Nouvelle Héloïse* and *Les Liaisons dangereuses.*" *Signs: Journal of Women in Culture and Society* (Spring 1976), 1(3/1):609–38.

—— "Novels of Innocence: Fictions of Loss." *Eighteenth-Century Studies* (Spring 1978), 11(3):325–39.

—— "Emphasis added: Plots and Plausibilities in Women's Fiction," *PMLA* (forthcoming, 1980–81).

Moers, Ellen. *Literary Women: The Great Writers.* New York: Doubleday, 1976.

Newman, Karen. "Can This Marriage Be Saved: In Defense of The Happy Ending," MS.

Pollak, Ellen. *Perspectives on a Myth: Women in the Verse of Swift and Pope.* Diss. Columbia University, 1979.

Poulet, Georges. *Etudes sur le Temps humain. Vol. 2, La Distance intérieure.* Paris: Plon, 1953.

Prévost, Antoine-François. *Histoire du Chevalier des Grieux et de Manon Lescaut.* Introduction by Georges Matoré. Geneva: Droz, 1953.

—— *Histoire du Chevalier des Grieux et de Manon Lescaut.* Introduction by Frédéric Deloffre and Raymond Picard. Paris: Garnier, 1965.

Richardson, Samuel. *Pamela: or Virtue Rewarded.* New York: Norton, 1958.

—— *Clarissa: or the History of a Young Lady.* New York: Dutton, 1962.

Richetti, John J. *Popular Fiction before Richardson: Narrative Patterns, 1700–1739.* Oxford: Clarendon, 1969.

—— *Defoe's Narratives: Situations and Structures.* Oxford: Clarendon, 1975.

Riffaterre, Michael. *Essais de Stylistique structurale.* Paris: Flammarion, 1971.

—— "Système d'un genre descriptif." *Poétique* (1972), no. 9, pp. 15–30.

—— "The Self-sufficient Text." *Diacritics* (Fall 1973), pp. 39–45.

—— "On Deciphering Mallarmé." *The Georgia Review,* (Spring 1975), 29(1):75–91.

Rosbottom, Ronald. *Marivaux's Novels: Theme and Function in Early Eighteenth-Century Narrative.* Rutherford, Madison, Teaneck, N.J.: Fairleigh Dickinson University Press, 1974.

Rousseau, Jean-Jacques. *Julie ou La Nouvelle Héloïse.* Paris: Garnier, 1960.

Sade, D. A. F. *The Marquis de Sade: Three Complete Novels: Justine, Philosophy in the Bedroom, Eugénie de Franval, and other writings.* New York: Grove Press, 1965.

—— *Justine ou les malheurs de la vertu.* Paris: 10/18, 1969.

Schor, Naomi. "Le sourire du sphinx: Zola et l'enigme de la féminité. *Romantisme* (1976), no. 13–14, pp. 183–95.

Showalter, English, Jr. *The Evolution of the French Novel, 1641–1782.* Princeton: Princeton University Press, 1972.

Spacks, Patricia Meyer. "Early Fiction and the Frightened Male." *Novel* (Fall 1974), 8(1):5–15.

—— *Imagining a Self: Autobiography and Novel in Eighteenth-Century, England.* Cambridge: Harvard University Press, 1976.

Spitzer, Leo. "A propos de *La Vie de Marianne.*" *Romanic Review* (1953), 44:102–26.

Starr, George A. *Defoe and Casuistry.* Princeton: Princeton University Press, 1971.

Stewart, Philip. "The Child Comes of Age." *Yale French Studies* (1966), no. 40, pp. 134–41.

Tanner, Tony. "Julie and 'La Maison Paternelle:' Another Look at Rousseau's *La Nouvelle Héloïse.*" *Daedalus* (Spring 1976), pp. 23–45.

Todorov, Tzvetan. *Littérature et Signification.* Paris: Larousse, 1967.

Trilling, Diana. "The Liberated Heroine." *Partisan Review* (1978), 45(4):501–22.

Trilling, Lionel. *The Liberal Imagination.* Rpt. New York: Scribner's, 1976.

Utter, R. P., and Needham, G. B. *Pamela's Daughters.* New York: Macmillan, 1937.

Vance, Christie McDonald. *The Extravagant Shepherd: A study of the pastoral in Rousseau's Nouvelle Héloïse. Studies in Voltaire and the Eighteenth Century.* Vol. 105. Banbury, Oxfordshire: The Voltaire Foundation, 1973.

Van Ghent, Dorothy. *The English Novel: Form and Function.* New York: Harper & Row, 1953.

Vartanian, Aram. "The Marquise de Merteuil: A Case of Mistaken Identity." *L'Esprit Créateur* (Winter 1963), 3(4):172–80.

Watt, Ian. *The Rise of the Novel.* Rpt. Berkeley and Los Angeles: University of California Press, 1971.

Wilson, Stuart. "Richardson's *Pamela*: An Interpretation." *PMLA* (January 1973), 88:79–91.

Wilt, Judith. "He Could Go No Farther: A Modest Proposal about Lovelace and Clarissa." *PMLA* (January 1977), 92:19–32.